D1737182

AVA GARDNER

Ava as Kitty Collins in the 1946 film *The Killers*.

AVA GARDNER

A Bio-Bibliography

Karin J. Fowler

Bio-Bibliographies in the Performing Arts, Number 14
James Robert Parish, Series Adviser

Greenwood Press
New York • Westport, Connecticut • London

Library of Congress Cataloging-in-Publication Data

Fowler, Karin J.
   Ava Gardner: a bio-bibliography / Karin J. Fowler.
     p. cm.—(Bio-bibliographies in the performing arts, ISSN
0892-5550 ; no. 14)
   Includes bibliographical references.
   ISBN 0-313-26776-6 (lib. bdg. : alk. paper)
   1. Gardner, Ava, 1922- . 2. Gardner, Ava, 1922- —
Bibliography. 3. Motion picture actors and actresses—United
States—Biography. I. Title. II. Series.
PN2287.G37F68 1990
791.43 '028 '092—dc20
  [B]   90-3317

British Library Cataloguing in Publication Data is available.

Library of Congress Catalog Card Number: 90-3317
ISBN: 0-313-26776-6
ISSN: 0892-5550

First published in 1990

Greenwood Press, 88 Post Road West, Westport, CT 06881
An imprint of Greenwood Publishing Group, Inc.

Printed in the United States of America

The paper used in this book complies with the
Permanent Paper Standard issued by the National
Information Standards Organization (Z39.48-1984).

10 9 8 7 6 5 4 3 2 1

Copyright Acknowledgments

All photos are reprinted with permission of the Don Eckhart Collection.

This book is dedicated to my sister, Mary Fowler.

"Every man's life is a fairy-tale
written by God's fingers."

Hans Christian Andersen
1805–1875

CONTENTS

Photo essay follows p. 22

PREFACE

Ava Gardner's screen career has spanned five decades, and her biography is as dramatic and compelling as many of her films' screenplays. From her country roots to her world travels, Ava has constantly been a favorite of the media. Her personal strengths and weaknesses have served to keep the public ever-interested in this beautiful screen legend.

This book is divided into six main sections:

1. A biography of Ava Gardner's life and career.

2. Chronological listing of her life achievements.

3. Listings of her productions: movies are preceded by the mnemonic "F"; television appearances are preceded by the mnemonic "T"; radio guest spots are preceded by mnemonic "R"; and musical recordings are preceded by the mnemonic "S". Cross-references are provided.

4. A bibliography of writings about Ava Gardner: annotated books are preceded by the mnemonic "AB" while unannotated books are preceded by "UB"; annotated sources in periodicals are preceded by the mnemonic "AP" with unannotated sources preceded by "UP"; "AN" denotes newspaper annotations. Cross-references are provided.

5. Archival sources (denoted by mnemonic "A").

6. An index of personal names and titles (access is to entry codes).

ACKNOWLEDGMENTS

My thanks go to those who have assisted or
contributed to the completion of this book:

Marilyn Brownstein, Humanities Editor, Greenwood Press, for
        her invitation to do the book and take a chance on a
        newcomer.

James Robert Parish, whose friendly inspiration was much
        welcomed and appreciated.

Helen Gadberry, who helped me begin my odyssey at the
        start of my research and provided friendship that is
        prized.

Those who have provided resource material and other help:
        Don Eckhart, Margie Schultz, Michael Pitts,
        Edwin M. Matthias, and Irene Schubert.

My friends and family, especially Chris Darula, for their
        camaraderie and thoughtfulness.

AVA GARDNER

BIOGRAPHY

In the 1940s, the movie industry was prospering even though the rest of the world was still recovering from the effects of the 1930s' Depression. Movies helped the average person escape the worries of World War II. Women took over the workforce in America while the male population defended the country overseas. In the throng of beautiful blondes that bombarded the films, one raven-haired young woman captivated the world of make-believe. Her name was Ava Gardner.

Humble Beginnings

Ava Lavinnia Gardner was born on December 24, 1922, the last of seven children to tobacco farmer Jonas Gardner and his wife, Mary Elizabeth (Molly) Baker. Between Raleigh-Durham and Wilson, North Carolina is situated the tiny berg known as Brogden, where Ava first saw the light of day. Brogden is so small it isn't even detailed on a map. In biographies of actress Ava Gardner, the town of Smithfield is most often listed as her birthplace.

Ava's siblings were, in order of birth, Beatrice (nicknamed Bappie), Elsie Mae, Inez, Raymond (died at age two), Melvin (called Jack--he later was elected North Carolina Representative to the State Legislature), and Myra.

The Gardners were church-going Baptists who were poor but relatively well off compared to neighbors in the area. Ava inherited her dark hair, oval face, green eyes, and dimpled chin from her tall, lanky father. Her short, dark-haired mother was strict and rigid but was the source of strength in the family. Despite the 18-year difference in their ages, Ava was closest to Bappie, who essentially became her second mother.

The Great Depression had a profound impact on the once-happy family. Jonas sold the farm for a paltry sum, which so angered Molly that she took her two youngest daughters (Myra and Ava) to a "teacherage" in Smithfield. The boarding house for teachers is where Ava whiled away her hours playing like any other ten-year-old tomboy. She wasn't interested in education at that point. One favorite past-time was reading movie magazines. She loved to go to the movies. One of her favorites was <u>Red Dust</u>, with Clark Gable, Jean Harlow, and Mary Astor.

In 1934, Molly and the girls moved to Newport News, Virginia. While her mother ran a boarding house for two years, Ava attended Newport News High School. Two years later they returned to Smithfield, where Ava completed her high school education at Smithfield High School.

Ava was sixteen when her sixty-one-year-old father died mysteriously from an unknown virus. Molly became sullen, withdrawn, and distrustful of others, and there-after instilled a deep-seated fear of men in her youngest child. Ava loved her mother dearly, but tension was high. Ava thought of using secretarial skills acquired at Atlantic Christian College in Wilson, North Carolina as a means of striking out on her own. However, her southern drawl caused her to be so self-conscious that she eventually dropped out and gave up on the idea of being a secretary.

Ava was a dazzling beauty by the age of 17, although she lacked social amenities. She worshipped her sister, Bappie, who had married photographer Larry Tarr and moved to New York. Their apartment near Broadway provided a haven for Ava in the early summer of 1941. That summer would be the turning point in her life.

Biggest Movie Star in the World

Ava posed as a model for her brother-in-law. Without her knowledge, he placed copies of her photos in his shop window at 607 Fifth Avenue. Barney Duhan, a clerk at the New York M-G-M Studio office, spotted the pictures and brought them to the attention of studio executive Marvin Schenck and publicity chief Howard Dietz.

Initially, Ava was outraged at Tarr's lack of consent. But, out of curiousity, Ava had Bappie accompany her to a script reading that had been set up. According to <u>Saturday Evening Post</u> journalist Pete Martin, she introduced herself as "Aa-vuh-Gahdnah," and "dropped her g's like magnolia blossoms."

Shortly thereafter, Ava had a screen test. Director Al Altman told her to "sit down in a chair and emote." She was considered hopeless. But when the test was run, they were in for a collective surprise. The silent test proved they had found a real treasure. She was one of the most photogenic, sensual women ever photographed.

Relieved to have the experience behind her, Ava nonetheless was preparing for a potential trip to Hollywood. She mentioned that, if she made it to Hollywood, "I'll marry the biggest movie star in the world." Within days, Bappie Tarr chaperoned her 18-year-old sister to California. Ava was completely taken aback by the lack of glamour and splendor. To her, southern California was dreary, her apartment so tiny, and everything so different from what she had envisioned in her daydreams.

Ava was slated for a second film test to be on a sound stage and screened by none other than Louis B. Mayer, head of Metro-Goldwyn-Mayer Studio. After seeing her on the screen, he mandated that she was to be instructed by dramatic coach Lillian Burns and voice coach Gertrude Vogeler. They were to give Ava a year's worth of training, after which she was to be re-tested. Mayer also insisted that the studio augment her biography. At his insistence, they gave out her name as Ava Gardner, nee Lucy Johnson.

Ava became an M-G-M family member, earning $75 a week through her seven-year contract. She attended acting classes and abided the strict rules of deportment ascribed to all starlets. Her natural beauty was enhanced by studio hair stylists and make-up artists. She became even more ravishing and alluring. She posed for the most prominent photographic artists in the industry: Clarence Bull, Eric Carpenter, and Edward Hurrell. She took dancing lessons, changed her voice patterns, and adopted a sense of sophistication to hide her basic shyness. She knew she wasn't a real actress, but she was determined to become a recognizable asset to the Hollywood elite.

During a tour of the studio, Ava met the most powerful young star on the lot. Mickey Rooney was working in the Andy Hardy movie series and was busy filming Babes on Broadway. Dressed in four-inch wedge shoes and garbed for a Carmen Miranda impersonation, Mickey was love-struck at the sight of Ava Gardner. He decided she was to be his. His boyish charm and ebullient personality were over- whelming. Ava was surprised to know that he was the biggest movie star in the world. At first, she was standoffish to the young actor, but he was used to getting what he wanted. Because of his clout and popularity at the studio and with the public, Mickey's requests of movie executives were largely obeyed. Besides being madly in love with her, he took Ava under his wing and coached her as much as Lillian Burns. In fact, Mickey was probably the most responsible for her initial rise to stardom.

Six months after arriving in Hollywood, Ava married the biggest movie star in the world. She and Mickey exchanged vows on January 10, 1942, in Ballard, California, before Reverend Glenn. She wore a blue suit and looked radiant. Mickey was ecstatic. He was 21, she 19.

Ava began to get walk-on roles in several motion pictures in 1942. She played a fashion model in the Joan Crawford film Reunion in France. She appeared as a Czech resistance fighter in M-G-M's Hitler's Madman. Her first speaking role was as a waitress in a drive-in diner in Kid Glove Killer, with Van Heflin, Lee Bowman, and Marsha Hunt. In Two Girls and a Sailor, Ava was a canteen hostess who falls asleep as she dances. She was loaned to Monogram Studio for a part in Ghosts on the Loose, featuring the Dead end Kids, where she showed a flair for comedy that was well-received.

Nineteen forty-three gave rise to bigger and better roles for Ava, but her marriage was unraveling. The vast differences in their personalities, lifestyles, and expectancies for the future proved to be their marital doom. On May 2, 1943, Ava filed for divorce from her husband of more than a year. May 21, 1943 was a double heartbreaker for Ava: her final divorce decree from Mickey was received along with the news that her mother had died of breast cancer following a long battle with the illness. Ava flew home to Brogden to find scores of fans eager to see her.

Upon her return to California, Three Men in White gave Ava enough work to keep her mind off her troubles. Her part was more substantial in this film which was one of the Dr. Gillespie series so popular since the 1930s, starring Lionel Barrymore. Ava played a girl who is hired by Gillespie to seduce a young intern applicant (Van Johnson) in order to prove his strength of character. Ava proved to be very popular on the screen and garnered a 62% war-time audience of women alone.

Next came Maisee Goes to Reno, another one of the popular World War II movie series starring Ann Sothern as a young woman who can take care of herself without a man. Ava's role was that of a millionaire's wife, little more than a walk-on. She had hoped for better things to come for her career.

The Bashful Billionaire and The Swing King

The year 1944 proved to be very busy for Ava onscreen and off. After divorcing Rooney, she became a party-goer. She made friends at the studio--both cast and crew. Lana Turner became a confident. The two beauties were often spotted at nightspots with other co-stars and studio-arranged dates. Both of the young women caught the eye of billionaire Howard Hughes, who had a penchant for young, nubile actresses. Initially, Hughes dated Lana Turner, but he quickly became enamored of the luscious Ava Gardner.

Hughes leased a small house for Ava and Bappie. From the onset, their relationship was stormy. Hughes expected that she be at his beck and call, as had his previous loves. The end of their romantic liaison followed a party Ava had attended with another date and friends from the studio. She had invited them back to the house for a nightcap. Hughes unexpectedly showed up to find the party going full swing and everyone imbibing. Enraged (he was a teetotaler), he ordered everyone out and slapped Ava across the face. In an angry reaction, she hurled a heavy vase at his head and knocked him out. They eventually parted company. However, Hughes remained friends with her thereafter.

Ava continued her love of nightlife. Luckily, she was able to handle drinking and eating anything she desired. She remained beautiful and energetic, even though she considered herself "basically lazy." She still hoped to achieve the second step to stardom that eluded her. Yet, she hungered for a normal life as well. Soon she met the man who would play another important role in her life.

Artie Shaw had been one of the leading swing bandleaders. At the height of his success, he was stricken with agranulocytopenia, a rare blood disease. Beating the odds, he survived the disease that had struck him in 1939, just before he went into the Navy. He returned from World War II a broken man, physically, emotionally, and financially. However, he hadn't lost his charm. He had been briefly married to Lana Turner; their union filled the scandal columns regularly during their time together. Artie Shaw was a man rarely without a woman in his life.

Ava's beauty captivated him. A self-made intellectual, Artie insisted that Ava improve her mind. She took courses at U.C.L.A. in English Literature and Economics. She wanted to please his insatiable need to force her up to his intellectual level. He even insisted that she go into psychoanalysis, as he had. He played on Ava's insecurities. She was very maternal in her feelings toward men and soon found herself succumbing to his advances. After several upsetting spats, they suddenly married. Again dressed in a dark blue, tailored suit adorned with an orchid corsage, Ava married Artie at his home at 1112 South Peck Drive in Beverly Hills on October 17, 1945. Frances Heflin, wife of actor Van Heflin, was her maid of honor. Hy Croft was best man. Shortly thereafter, Ava and Artie moved to a house on Bedford Drive.

It was no secret that Ava began drinking to hide the pain of her disastrous second marriage. No matter what she did, she never quite measured up to Artie Shaw's expectations of a marital partner. Ava filed for divorce on August 16, 1946, after just ten months of marriage. It was finalized on October 25, 1946. After the split, Ava lived for a time with agent Minna Wallis, sister of producer Hal B. Wallis.

Ironically, during the early stages of their relationship, one of their major spats occurred when Shaw found Ava reading the novel Forever Amber, written by Kathleen Winsor. He considered the book trash and forbade her to read such works in the future. Within months of his divorce from Ava, Artie Shaw married author Kathleen Winsor.

More Than a Pretty Face

Within a year of her split from Shaw, Ava's career finally took a turn for the better. Meatier parts were offered that would enhance her screen persona and popularity even more.

John Huston and Anthony Veiller were working on a screenplay for The Killers, based on an Ernest Hemingway short story. Huston gave full credit to Veiller, since he was serving in the United States Army and didn't want Uncle Sam to know he "was not devoting all my time to the job." The film was to co-star another newcomer, Burt Lancaster.

Ava was cast as Kitty Collins, a gangster moll. Lancaster was a boxer (Swede) who becomes mixed up in racketeering under a powerful gangster (Albert Dekker). Edmond O'Brien was Riordan, an insurance detective who sets out to solve the crimes committed by Lancaster and Dekker. Swede's involvement with the beautiful and cunning Kitty makes his life a mess. The killers (Charles McGraw and William Conrad) are sent to a dingy room above a diner where Swede is hiding. In a voice-over by Riordan, the audience learns why Swede meets his particular kind of death.

Ava literally smoldered on film in The Killers. For her role, she won Look magazine's Most Promising Newcomer Award in 1947.

Next Ava appeared briefly in She Went to the Races, a comedy about professors applying science to betting, starring James Craig and Frances Gifford.

She was kept quite busy and was next teamed with Clark Gable, Deborah Kerr, and Sydney Greenstreet in The Hucksters.

Ava played a nightclub singer who is in love with
Gable, a war veteran, who finds his ideals and virtues
compromised in his post-war job. He falls in love with a
prim and proper widow (Kerr) for whom he eventually decides
to give up the corrupt rat race that had threatened their
relationship. Ava's part was much too short. She adored
working with Gable, who liked her personally although not
romantically. Gable knew this was Ava's chance to show
she could be more than window-dressing, so he sometimes
flubbed his own lines purposely when he noticed she was
struggling. His helpfulness showed in her performance.

Shortly after filming The Hucksters, Ava was loaned
to Universal. Her final movie in 1947 was Singapore, with
Fred MacMurray. In another post-war film, Ava portrayed
an amnesia victim who survives bomb raids in Singapore.
She picks up her life upon reestablishing her love affair
with special agent MacMurray. Singapore was considered
banal and was not a box office hit for Universal.

In 1947, Ava endorsed products for Max Factor and Lux
Toilet Soap. She was crowned queen at the 1947 Convention
of the Coiffeurs Guild of Los Angeles. She was the main
attraction at the Harvest Moon Festival for the Purple
Heart Fund of Chicago. She also found time to appear as
a guest on such radio shows as Hollywood U.S.A., Bob Hope,
Louella Parsons, Command Performance, Hollywood Calling,
and The Prudential Summer Show.

While on a trip to New York to promote The Killers,
Ava met brash young actor Howard Duff. Throughout 1947
and 1948, they dated. It was rumored that during their
love affair, Ava became pregnant and had an abortion (after
which she was unable to carry a fetus to delivery).

Universal Studios again borrowed Ava for One Touch of
Venus, co-starring Robert Walker. She showed comedic
timing and, despite bad reviews, the movie displayed her
sensuality with wit and tenderness. Robert Walker played
the department store window decorator who kisses the
Anatolian statue of Venus and makes her come to life. Ava
posed for the statue done by Italian sculptor Joseph
Nicolosi. She also briefly dated Walker during this time,
while he was estranged from wife Jennifer Jones.

Ava's next film for M-G-M was The Bribe, with Robert
Taylor, Charles Laughton, John Hodiak, and Vincent Price.
Taylor was cast as a federal agent who tracks racketeers.
Price is ringleader in war surplus parts smuggling in the
Caribbean. Ava is a cafe singer married to former U.S.
flier (Hodiak), who had aided and abetted Price. Laughton
is Price's accomplice, who smuggles engines for high profits.
Taylor falls for Ava and she eventually leaves her husband
for him. Ava's work in The Bribe was considered lacking.
Although she was still partying heavily, it didn't seem to
phase her photogenic qualities. But critics felt she had

yet to come into her own in developing character authority and poise. The Bribe is considered by many to be her worst film.

The Great Sinner was Ava's next screen project. Her co-star was Gregory Peck as Fedja, a Russian compulsive gambler. Ava was cast as his love Polina, who was also a heavy gambler. The story is based on the autobiographical novel by Dostoevski, originally titled The Gambler, set in a Wiesbaden casino in the 1880s. While working on this M-G-M film, Ava gained the respect of the cast and crew for her informality and sense of humor.

During this time, Ava bought her first home. She revisited Smithfield and was presented the keys to the city by the mayor. Photoplay magazine did a layout with Ava sitting on the porch of her childhood home in Brogden. Thereafter in interviews Ava began to refer to her home town as Grabtown. Upon her return to her new home in Hollywood, Ava was scheduled to appear in East Side, West Side.

East Side, West Side was the tenth novel to be filmed by M-G-M in 1949. The story was about the nouveau riche of New York post-World War II. Ava portrayed Isobel Lorrison, a not very popular figure in the coterie. The film did not do very well at the box office that year, even though it had such heavy-weight stars as Barbara Stanwyck, James Mason, and Van Heflin in the title roles.

The Sinatra Connection

Ava met many famous entertainers at the various parties and galas she attended during the latter part of the 1940s. One skinny, short Italian singer who had been the singing rage of bobbysoxers just a few short years previously was Frank Sinatra. His career was declining when he met the beautiful Ava. He fell for Ava as quickly as had her two ex-husbands. Fans were outraged at Sinatra's "desertion" of his wife, Nancy, and their three children (Nancy, Jr., Frank, Jr., and Tina). But Sinatra was determined to be with the woman of his dreams. At the outset, Ava had finally found someone who was compatible with her--they both liked the nightlife, music, and the heady physical attraction.

Her career really began to blossom. She was next slated to appear with James Mason in Pandora and The Flying Dutchman. Ava portrayed Pandora Reynolds, a beautiful woman who encounters mysterious Hendrick Van Der Zee (Mason). Bullfighter Mario Cabre was Ava's love interest in this fantasy romance. While on location in Barcelona, Spain, Ava casually dated Cabre. Sinatra was livid with jealousy. Pandora and The Flying Dutchman

was exquisitely photographed. Perfectly suited for the role,
Ava exuded sensuality and believability. This movie is
considered one of the "forgotten films to be remembered."

Show Boat was the major M-G-M movie in 1951. Although
not initially considered for the role, Ava was eventually
cast as the poignant, half-caste Julie. Among those competing
for the part were Dinah Shore and Lena Horne. Ava's southern
accent served her well. She loved making the movie and
enjoyed working with her co-stars and crew. Her singing was
dubbed by Lena Horne for the screen test and performed by
Annette Warren for the film. However, Ava's angry insistence
on doing her own vocalizing was rewarded and her voice was
used on the soundtrack recording. Show Boat made Ava M-G-M
Studio's number one female star.

With little time between films, Ava was next to work
on My Forbidden Past, an 81-minute film set in Antebellum
New Orleans. Ava never looked more beautiful. She played
the young woman who had a family skeleton to hide. Robert
Mitchum co-starred as her love interest. He ends up
marrying another and is accused of her murder. Ava gets
revenge at his trial and confesses the family's secrets.
The film was originally titled Carriage Entrance. Mitchum
took the part in this minor film in order to pay the $1,000
bail for his marijuana drug bust that caused a scandalous
sensation weeks before. He ended up paying a fine of $500
after spending a few days in jail. My Forbidden Past ranks
as truly forgettable for both of them.

Frank Sinatra was still married to wife Nancy, although
Ava and he had moved to another home. Their quarrels were
evident on many occasions. Hollywood reporters Louella
Parsons and Hedda Hopper often reported their spats and
wondered if the two would ever really get married. Nancy
Sinatra, Sr., was getting all the sympathy in the world.
Sinatra's career was skidding lower, and Ava became known
as a home-wrecker.

Clark Gable was scheduled to co-star with Ava again in
the M-G-M movie Lone Star. Ava was cast as a newspaper
journalist, something in real life she had grown to dislike
intensely. Neither Gable nor Ava liked the script for this
western set during the days of the State of Texas fight for
independence from Mexico. On location, the work was long,
tedious, and hot. It was suspected that Gable's health was
deteriorating due to the onset of Parkinson's Disease. All
in all, Lone Star became another forgettable film.

Several days subsequent to Sinatra's final decree
of divorce from Nancy, Sr., Ava married him on November 7,
1951. She wore a mauve cocktail-length dress designed by
Howard Greer. The ceremony, officiated by Judge Sloan,
was filmed by conductor Axel Stordahl, who attended with

his wife, June, Sinatra's parents, friend Ben Barton,
arranger Dick Jones, and Bappie. Ava's honeymoon outfit
was designed by Christian Dior.

Ava and Frank flew to Cuba for their honeymoon.
Upon their return, they found they had been burglarized
during their absence. Ava's favorite gift from Sinatra,
a diamond and emerald necklace, and other jewelry amounting
to $68,000 were taken. It was an ominous beginning to their
marriage.

Contrary to what the public might have thought, Ava
got along with Frank's three children. Nancy was in awe
of the new wife but came to like her. Ava liked children
and knew what it took to make them comfortable. Nancy
received her first lipstick from Ava.

Early in 1952, Ava was signed to star in another
Ernest Hemingway story titled The Snows of Kiliminjaro.
The 20th Century-Fox production also featured Gregory
Peck and Susan Hayward. Ava (replacing Anne Francis in
the role of Cynthia) is the dark-haired young woman who
is the first love of famous novelist/big game hunter
(Peck). She leaves him after following him to Africa,
meeting with his cold indifference, and losing their
child. Later, during the Spanish Civil War, they meet
again and she dies in his arms after being injured in
an ambulance accident. He meets a rich widow (Hayward)
who he thinks looks like Cynthia. They marry and she tries
her utmost to make him care for her. While recovering
from a life-threatening fever, he finally realizes he
does love Helen and he recognizes that she has sacrificed
so much to prove her love for him. The film was set in
Africa but was filmed entirely on the Hollywood studio lot.
It won two Academy Award nominations: for Art and Set
Decoration and Cinematograpy.

The Snows of Kiliminjaro launched Ava as an
international movie star. Critics agreed that she was
surprisingly good in the role.

On May 22, 1952, Ava planted her hands and feet in
the forecourt of Hollywood's Grauman's Chinese Theater.

Next, Ride, Vaquero teamed Ava with Robert Taylor
in a western filmed in the sweltering little town of
Kanab, Utah. The long days on the set were torturous.
Ava intensely disliked director John Farrow (husband of
actress Maureen O'Sullivan, father of Mia Farrow),
because of his sadistic treatment of horses during filming
and his rather perverse personal habits on and off the
set. No one really cared for the script, and the film
made no great statement for the industry.

Shortly after wrapping up Ride, Vaquero, Ava was to begin work on Mogambo, the remake of the 1939 movie Red Dust, which had starred Clark Gable, Jean Harlow, and Mary Astor. Red Dust had been one of Ava's favorite movies as a child. Little did she know then that thirty years later she'd be co-starring with Clark Gable in this remake! Ava reprised the role originally played by Jean Harlow; Grace Kelly took the role performed by Mary Astor.

Mogambo was shot in Nairobi and Thika, in Kenya, Tanganyika, and the Belgian Congo. The cast and crew dealt with heat, wild animals, and even the threat of attack from Mau Mau terrorists. Ava took most of this in stride. She was accepted as "a good guy" and roared with laughter when she was accused of parading in the buff (which she reportedly did upon hearing the gossip!).

Meanwhile back at the home front, Frank and Ava's marital problems continued. The continental separation did nothing to help matters. Frank visited the African set for their first wedding anniversary and their tenuous relationship continued.

Frank's career was on the skids. He was hoping to land the role of Maggio in From Here to Eternity, scheduled to begin shooting in Hollywood. It was intimated that Ava begged Columbia Pictures boss Harry Cohn to consider Frank for the part in the James Joyce best-selling story.

Frank returned to Hollywood for a screen test. The test proved he was right for the part and he was awarded the role of Maggio. During this time, Ava reportedly suffered a miscarriage. Conflicting rumors from others painted a different picture: Ava was ready to break up their marriage, so she flew to London for an abortion.

While Frank was in Hollywood filming From Here to Eternity, Ava traveled to Rome. She and Grace Kelly had become fast friends, and they decided to visit several European sites on their time off. It was hinted that Gable and Kelly were romantically involved during shooting of Mogambo. The cast members lived up to Mogambo which, in Swahili, means "passion."

Ava's reviews were well-received and even she agreed that she had done "a pretty good job." She received an Oscar nomination for her role, which finally proved to the industry that she could act. Ironically, she lost and Frank Sinatra won as Best Supporting Actor. Ava was happy for her husband, but their marriage was still on very shaky ground.

Ava left for London to film interior shots for Mogambo and to begin work on Knights of The Round Table. This

costume period piece was filmed at the English castle that
had previously been used in the film Ivanhoe. Knights of
The Round Table co-starred Robert Taylor (who also starred
in Ivanhoe) as Lancelot to Ava's Guinevere. The vile
weather, continuing fights with visiting husband Frank, and
her wooden performance did nothing for Ava's profession.
The only consolation for Ava was a hefty increase in salary
and the possibility of being loaned to other studios
without the usual legal entanglements which had taken place
in the past.

United Artists wanted Ava for the starring role in
The Barefoot Contessa, co-starring Humphrey Bogart. Her
character, Maria Vargas, was supposedly based on the life
of Rita Hayworth during her tempestuous years with Aly
Khan. Shot in Rome, it became a signature role for Ava,
as a young girl who leaves the slums of Madrid to become one
of the most popular actresses in the world. She marries
an impotent aristocrat (Rossano Brazzi) who thinks she
is having an affair with another so he kills her. Maria's
life is related in flashbacks, narrated by Humphrey Bogart.
Edmond O'Brien appeared as her agent, for which he won an
Academy Award for Best Supporting Actor.

Ava threw herself wholeheartedly into her performance
as Maria Vargas. One of the most memorable scenes had her
involved in a ferocious flamenco dance which won her
accolades from the crew for her tireless, painfilled takes.
Ava truly relished making Barefoot Contessa. However, for
some reason, Humphrey Bogart didn't appreciate her and
tried to unsettle her in many key scenes. She gave the
performance of her career. This period also marked the
end of her marriage to Frank Sinatra.

Latin Love

While filming The Barefoot Contessa, Ava met rich,
handsome Spanish bullfighter Luis Miguel Dominguin. The
language barrier did little to falter their romance.
Dominguin introduced Ava to his close friend Ernest
Hemingway while she was hospitalized for gallstone surgery.
Hemingway considered The Killers the best of his filmed
stories, and he was eager to meet Ava. She and Papa
Hemingway became fast, platonic friends. His wife, Mary,
grew to care for Ava, too, since Ava was one of the few
women to not have an affair with the popular author. He
called Ava "daughter," and even collected one of her
gallstones as a souvenier. In subsequent years, Ava
frequently visited with the Hemingways. She was
devastated when Hemingway committed suicide in 1960.

By the beginning of 1955, Ava's affair with Dominguin
had begun to cool somewhat. He eventually met and fell in
love with Italian actress Lucia Bose when Ava went off to
shoot Bhowani Junction. Ava gave them her blessing.

Bhowani Junction was a controversial film, involving Anglo-Indian politics. Because of the tense situation in India at the time, the movie was shot in Lahore, Pakistan. According to Ava, the conditions were even worse than those at the Utah setting of Ride, Vaquero. Everything was miserable, from the oppressive heat to the barely palatable food to the lack of electricity to the illness that plagued almost everyone, except Ava.

Ava's strength and professionalism again endeared her to the cast and crew. She won rave reviews as the half-caste young woman who falls in love with an English officer (Stewart Granger) during World War II. Bill Travers was featured. Although the film was heavily edited before release, the critics loved her performance. Ava's looks had begun to change, but her ranking in stardom continued on course.

Upon completion of Bhowani Junction, Ava bought a home in Spain and moved there on December 22, 1955. Later that year, Frank Sinatra journeyed to Spain with starlet Peggy Connolly to begin shooting the Stanley Kramer film The Pride and The Passion. Although they had been separated for some time, Ava and Frank were still legally married. At first, Ava was livid with the situation. But soon she began dating the "Italian Danny Kaye," actor Walter Chiari. Her affair with Chiari was reminiscent of her earlier liaison with Howard Duff - they shared fun, great times, and had frequent spats, but no true commitment on Ava's part.

Chiari appeared in Ava's next film, The Little Hut, a lame comedy set on a desert island where Ava was the only woman among three admiring men. It was another regrettably forgettable addition to her filmography.

Twentieth Century-Fox borrowed Ava for The Sun Also Rises, based on another Hemingway novel. Ava portrayed Lady Brett. She was director Henry King's only choice for the part. He hired Peter Viertel to do the final screenplay. Viertel, son of screenwriter Salka Viertel, was also a close friend of the publicity-shy, very private Greta Garbo. Garbo was a fan of Ava's and considered Ava the most beautiful woman on celluloid. In an unusual change of heart, Greta Garbo invited Ava as a guest to her home.

Co-starring with Ava in The Sun Also Rises were Errol Flynn, Tyrone Power, and Mel Ferrer. The cast got along famously, often partying nightly. Yet they all managed to be on the set ready for work each day. King was pleased that he was working with a happy company in the Mexican locations of Morelia and Mexico City. The only drawback during filming was young actor Robert Evans, who had been cast as a bullfighter that Lady Brett falls in love with. Off-screen their relationship was extremely cool, because Ava had hoped to have Walter Chiari in the role.

After wrap-up of The Sun Also Rises, Ava flew to Havana, Cuba to visit the Hemingways. She then proceeded to her home in Madrid, Spain. While luxuriating in a much-needed rest, Ava was intrigued by a script she received based on the life of famous lady bullfighter Conchita Cintron. Her personal interest in the sport of bullfighting would alter the tenor of Ava's life.

That Face

Angel Peralta was a renowned trainer of bulls for the corrida. At his ranch in nearby Seville, Spain, Peralta arranged for Ava to perform a demonstration of "toreo a caballo" (bullfighting on horseback). Within minutes of mounting the steed, the bull attacked. The horse reared and Ava was thrown to the ground. She was unable to stop the charging toro. The bull's horn struck her left cheek, tossing her into the air.

Ava was immediately flown to a London surgeon. There wasn't much he could do, however, since the hematoma would have to heal on its own. Ava was terrified that her stock-in-trade beauty would be damaged, her career ruined. The trauma of the incident would thereafter cause her a neurotic fear of photographers and publicity. She began to rethink the strategy of her livelihood: save money and stay out of the public eye.

Toward the end of 1957, Ava agreed to take the role of the Duchess of Alba in the film based on the life of Spanish painter Francisco Goya. She desperately hoped to be able to film The Naked Maja in Spain. However, the Franco government refused to let filming take place in Spain, due to complaints from Goya's descendents.

In May, 1958, Ava left for Rome to make the movie, co-starring Anthony Franciosa. It was not a happy experience because of Shelley Winters, wife of Franciosa. Winters' erratic behavior was triggered by her insistence that Ava and Tony were having an affair. The Naked Maja was disastrous at the box office. Ava's name and beautiful, though heavily-made up face, did nothing to save it.

Soon thereafter, Ava finally picked up her Mexican divorce papers from Frank Sinatra. The only high point of her life at that time was her good notices for The Sun Also Rises.

Ava was not the happiest of women, but there was a light at the end of the tunnel. It came in the form of the script based on a novel by Nevil Shute titled On The Beach. Stanley Kramer produced the film shot in Australia, also the setting of the story, about a group of people who survive a nuclear holocaust.

Long-time Friend, Another Beginning

John Huston was preparing to direct <u>Night of The Iguana</u>.
He wanted Ava for the role of Maxine Faulk, hotel-keeper of
a rundown resort in Mexico. He knew that, at this stage in
Ava's life, she fit the role perfectly. He believed Ava was
a very fine actress and insisted that she take the part.

Ava was flown to Puerto Vallarta on October 28, 1963.
Her co-stars in the Tennessee Williams story were Richard
Burton (as the defrocked minister), Deborah Kerr (as the
penniless daughter of a poet), and Sue Lyon (as a fetching
young teenager). Peter Viertel, who had been a frequent
escort of Ava's years before, was now married to Deborah
Kerr and accompanied her to the location shooting.

Elizabeth Taylor joined husband Burton. Evelyn Keyes
was a member of the party, being the wife of Huston (and
former wife of Artie Shaw). The scandal sheets were busy
cranking out stories of suspected affairs, rivalries, and
feuds. They all proved to be untrue.

Huston's faith in Ava carried over into her performance.
She was earthy, sexy, and totally believable. Again, her
southern drawl served her well. She truly earned her good
reviews and accolades.

One year later, Huston hired Ava for the role as Sarah
in his new movie, <u>The Bible</u>. Huston played Noah and
provided the voice of God in relating stories from the Old
Testament. George C. Scott was cast as Abraham, Sarah's
husband. Scott fell madly in love with Ava and they became
passionately involved during location shooting in Rome.
He left his wife, actress Colleen Dewhurst, truly believing
Ava would marry him. He was so enraptured of her, he could
not bear it when she decided to end their liaison. Totally
despondent over their breakup, Scott suffered an emotional
breakdown. He soon went back to Colleen Dewhurst (they
eventually divorced and he later married actress Trish
Van Devere.

Huston coaxed a fine performance from Ava in the 1966-
released <u>The Bible</u>. He believed Ava was one of the
century's great women. In Ava's opinion, John Huston was
the only great director for whom she worked.

Last Stages

At age 45, Ava appeared as the 60-year-old Empress of
Austria in the 1966 remake of the 1936 film <u>Mayerling</u>. The
tragic love affair of Crown Prince of Austria and his young
teenage commoner girlfriend, Maria Vetsera, was recognized
by all to be a pleasure to the eye but dreadfully lacking
in substance. Ava was teamed with James Mason (as Emperor
Franz Joseph), with whom she enjoyed being reunited.

Because of the lack of public response to <u>Mayerling</u>, Ava decided to take a departure from performing and public life.

However, a year later she was convinced by long-time friend Roddy McDowall to appear in a gothic movie he was directing titled <u>Tam-Lin</u> (eventually retitled <u>Toys</u> and released as the <u>Devil's Widow</u>). The movie was a ludicrous, preposterous story of a rich widow (Ava) who has a lover among a group of much younger people. When she is dumped by her amour, she plans revenge. Her role as the wicked fanatic was the only worthwhile performance in the film. Very few people saw the released version. Ava was ready to give up acting forever.

In the late 1960s, Ava began experiencing health problems. She was hospitalized following surgery (a possible hysterectomy). This was a very traumatic time for Ava, for she had feared the possibility she had cancer. Several months later, she was stronger. Aging and illness had not faded her basic beauty.

Ava loved living in London. The weather suited her moods and need for privacy. She took pride in her pet Corgi dogs. She had pleasant visits from her aging sister Bappie and a small group of friends.

Finances were something Ava had come to respect. Not too proud to acknowledge her need to work, Ava reported to Los Angeles to co-star in another epic, <u>Earthquake</u>. Disaster films were popular in the 1970s, and <u>Earthquake</u> was no exception. With a large, star-studded cast headed by Charlton Heston, Ava faced real-life peril while filming. In one sequence, Heston and Ava are trapped beneath rubble of a collapsed multi-level parking lot. The terror on their faces was real for six tons of debris fell all around them.

Co-star George Kennedy reported that the best part of working on <u>Earthquake</u> was getting to meet and work with Ava. In his opinion, she was the most beautiful woman in films. Although <u>Earthquake</u> did little to elevate any of the stars' acting plaudits, the movie was a huge success. Released in Sensurround in 1972, it was one of Universal Studio's all-time moneymakers.

Ava's next film was <u>Permission to Kill</u>, released in 1976, co-starring Dirk Bogarde. Neither she nor the ticket-buying public thought much of the film, and it suffered a quick demise at the box office.

Soon thereafter, Ava flew to Russia with a cast that included Elizabeth Taylor, Jane Fonda, Cicely Tyson, and Robert Morley for <u>The Blue Bird</u>, a musical remake of the 1936 film originally starring Shirley Temple.

The troup spent weeks sharing the studio and housing with their Soviet co-workers. In fact, Ava and Elizabeth Taylor shared a room plus bathroom facilities.

The Blue Bird was a lovely story about two children seeking the Blue Bird of Happiness. The sets and scenery were gorgeous and excellent child actors were featured. However, musicals were passe and not well-received. Even the star-studded cast could not save the film from the obscurity into which it rapidly descended.

Ava's final film in 1976 was The Cassandra Crossing, featuring Sophia Loren, Richard Harris, Burt Lancaster, and Martin Sheen. Another disaster movie, the story takes place on a European train that has been contaminated by a deadly virus which strikes everyone on board.

During filming of The Cassandra Crossing, Ava, Sophia Loren, and Richard Harris were accused of stealing priceless art works and money. After a harrowing run-in with the law, they were all exonerated. Neither the film's contrived plot nor the much-publicized legal entanglements served the picture or stars well.

The horror story The Sentinel was Ava's only venture on film in 1977. She was cast as a real estate agent who rents an apartment to a young girl in a building that is the gateway to hell. Ava looked classy and gave a surprisingly bright performance in this heavy, occult theme.

Two years elapsed and Ava again found herself appearing in another disaster film titled City on Fire. The title was self-explanatory. Critics liked Ava in the film but largely ignored the movie. Released briefly to theaters in August, 1979, it fared better on television.

Another year passed before Ava was again seen at the movies. The Kidnapping of The President featured Hal Holbrook, William Shatner, and Van Johnson in a story of terrorism. Because of the political uprisings worldwide at the time and the possibility of reality mirroring the film, The Kidnapping of The President became another quickly released and forgotten movie. Ava's role was very similar to her role in Seven Days in May. She brought a humanism to the role that showed she could still act with the best of them. Cast as the wife of the Vice President of the United States (Johnson) who must take over after Third World terrorists kidnap the President (Holbrook), Ava brought great pathos to her character.

Priest of Love would be Ava's final theater-released work. The 1981 movie co-starred Ian McKellen and Janet Suzman as author D. H. Lawrence and his wife Frieda, respectively. Ava played their friend, Mabel Dodge Luhan, who visits the Lawrences at the time he wrote Lady

Chatterly's Lover. This slow-paced drama was an intelligent
film that was limited in general public interest.

Ava returned to her home in London. She savored her
friendships. She corresponded and visited with Grace Kelly
during their long and enduring acquaintanceship. Ava had
been a guest at Grace Kelly's wedding to Prince Rainier III
of the tiny principality of Monaco in 1956. She was also
a guest at the wedding of Grace's daughter Princess Caroline
when she married Philip Junot. In September, 1982, Ava
Gardner attended the funeral of Princess Grace of Monaco
following her death from injuries sustained in an
automobile accident.

One by one, Ava's old co-stars were passing away.
She was, by now, one of the few old-timers of the M-G-M
Studio stock players to still have that star quality.

Three years later, Ava again decided to grace the
screen--the small screen. She made her television debut
as Agrippina in the 12-hour epic mini-series A.D.,
broadcast March 31-April 4, 1985. At age 63, Ava could
still hold her own. Her co-stars included James Mason,
John Houseman, Richard Kiley, Ian McShane, Colleen Dewhurst,
and Anthony Edwards, in this long tale of religious
clashes during the Roman Empire.

That same year, Ava lent her talents to another
television mini-series in the remake of the 1958 feature
film The Long Hot Summer. Ava's laid-back southern
personality fit the ambience of this highly-rated showing,
which featured the immensely popular Don Johnson in the
Paul Newman role of Ben Quick, a drifter who comes into
the lives of a gentile southern family. Ava's role as
Minnie Littlejohn was considered a highlight.

Ava was offered a recurring role in the CBS TV series
Knots Landing. She made her television series debut in
the role of Ruth Galveston on February 28, 1984, in the
episode titled "The Deluge," followed by: "A Piece of The
Pie" on March 7, 1985; "Four No Trump" on April 11, 1985;
"A Price to Pay" on May 2, 1985; "One Day in a Row" on
May 9, 1985; and "Vulnerable" on May 16, 1985. The
still-voluptuous, sexy Ava brought a smoldering, tongue-
in-cheek touch of class and mystery to her role. She was
a welcome breath of freshness on the night-time soap
opera. She won praise and a new generation of fans.

On February 9-10, 1986, a forgettable, four-hour
television mini-series featured Ava as a harem grand dame,
in Harem. She was teamed again with Omar Sharif, her
co-star in Mayerling. They picked up their friendly
comraderie, since Sharif had greatly admired Ava. However,
this mini-series was so vacuous it did poorly in the
ratings.

Finale

Not long after filming <u>Harem</u>, Ava was reported to have
suffered a slight stroke which necessitated another stay in
a Los Angeles hospital. Rumors of heart trouble also
persisted. Many feared her long-time alcohol consumption
had finally caught up with her.

Ava maintained a pleasant relationship, albeit
long-distance, with ex-husbands Mickey Rooney and Frank
Sinatra. She supported Mickey, both in friendship and
finances, at a low point in his career. Likewise, Frank
had done the same for Ava, making sure she had been cared
for during her hospitalizations and recuperation periods.

Ava eluded publicity hounds for almost two decades
but did find time to pay tribute to her fellow actors,
most notably that of her friend Robert Mitchum.

Fans the world over were saddened to learn that on
January 25, 1990, Ava died in her sleep from the effects
of pneumonia that had plagued her sporadically since 1986.
Only one month and one day previously she had turned age 67.

Ava Gardner, often labeled lazy, cantankerous, lovable,
warm, sultry, cool, reserved, friendly, and down-to-earth,
was one of the great beauties of the film world. Her career
spanned 45 years. She left a legacy of wonderful movies
that will never grow old. With the new video technology,
her films will be with us for new generations to enjoy.

Newlyweds Ava Gardner and Mickey Rooney, 1942.

Ava in *Life* magazine article on celebrities in film bath scenes, 1948.

Ava as Kitty Collins in the 1946 film *The Killers*.

Ava Gardner as Venus in the 1948 movie *One Touch of Venus.*

Ava Gardner and Fred MacMurray in the film *Singapore* (1947).

Ava in movie still from the 1947 film *Singapore*.

Ava Gardner in Hollywood studio portrait.

Ava Gardner and Bill Travers from the 1957 film *Bhowani Junction*.

Ava Gardner circa 1960.

CHRONOLOGY

1922   Ava Lavinnia Gardner is born in Brogden, North
        Carolina (near Smithfield), on Christmas Eve.

1938   Ava's father dies at age 61.

1941   Ava visits her sister and brother-in-law in New York
        where her photographs were displayed and noticed by
        a clerk from M-G-M's New York office. Ava had her
        first Hollywood screen test.

1942   Ava marries Mickey Rooney in California after a
        six-month romance. She was 19, he 21. Ava appears
        in walk-on parts in We Were Dancing, Joe Smith,
        American. She has her first bit speaking part in
        Kid Glove Killer.

1943   Ava files for divorce from Mickey Rooney. Her mother
        dies from breast cancer. Ava plays nonspeaking model
        role in Reunion in France. She also appears in bit
        parts in Young Ideas, Lost Angel, Du Barry was a Lady,
        Pilot #5, and Hitler's Madman. Her only speaking role
        was in Ghosts on The Loose.

1944   Ava has nonspeaking parts in Swing Fever, Blonde
        Fever, Music for Millions, and Two Girls and a Sailor.
        She appears as a young seductress in Three Men in
        White and a sophisticated rich lady in Maisee Goes to
        Reno.

1945   Ava meets and marries Artie Shaw.

1946   Ava divorces Artie Shaw after a ten-month marriage.
        She has small role in She Went to the Races then
        an admirable audience for her role as Kitty Collins
        in The Killers. Her first major role is in Whistle
        Stop.

1947   Ava is voted Most Promising Newcomer Award by Look
        magazine. She has nonspeaking role in This Time for
        Keeps. Her next important film role was as Jean
        Ogilvie in The Hucksters. She is Linda in her next
        film Singapore.

1948   Ava appears as the statue that comes to life in One
        Touch of Venus.

1949   Ava plays Elizabeth Hintten in The Bribe. Her next
        role was as Pauline Ostrovski in The Great Sinner.

1950   Ava co-stars in East Side, West Side, as Isobel
        Lorrison.

1951   Ava marries Frank Sinatra in Pennsylvania. They are
        robbed of $68,000 in jewelry while on their honeymoon.
        Ava is hospitalized with viral infection. She stars
        as Pandora Reynolds in Pandora and The Flying Dutchman.
        Her next role is in My Forbidden Past, as Barbara
        Beaurevel. She wins accolades for her role as Julie
        LaVerne in Show Boat.

1952   Ava plays Martha Ronda in the western Lone Star. That
        year she plants her handprints at Grauman's Chinese
        Theatre in Hollywood.

1953   Ava separates from Frank Sinatra. She is busy this
        year appearing as Cynthia in The Snows of Kiliminjaro,
        Cordelia Cameron in Ride, Vaquero, and herself in a
        cameo for The Band Wagon. She is nominated for Oscar
        as Best Actress for her role in Mogambo.

1954   Ava loses Oscar to Audrey Hepburn. Her estranged
        husband, Frank Sinatra, wins Best Supporting Actor for
        his role in From Here to Eternity. Ava begins affair
        with Spanish bullfighter Luis Miguel Dominguin. Ava
        meets Ernest Hemingway. She stars as Guinevere in Knights
        of The Round Table. Her international star status is
        enhanced with her role as Maria Vargas in The Barefoot
        Contessa.

1955   Ava buys a home at La Moraleja, a few miles outside of
        Madrid, Spain. Her nearby neighbor is Ernest
        Hemingway.

1956   Ava attends Grace Kelly's wedding to Prince Rainier
        of Monaco. She is gored by a bull after being thrown
        from a horse during a toreo a caballo at the ranch of
        Angel Peralta, which thereafter causes her a neurotic
        paranoia of the press. She has cameo role in Around
        The World in 80 Days. Her next major role was as
        Victoria Jones in Bhowani Junction.

1957   Ava receives a Mexican divorce decree from Frank
        Sinatra after a four-year separation. She stars as
        Lady Brett Ashley in The Sun Also Rises. Her next
        film is The Little Hut, in which she plays Lady
        Susan Ashlow.

1959   Ava stars as Moira Davidson in On The Beach. She later
        appears as the Duchess of Alba in The Naked Maja.

1960   Ava is Soledad in The Angel Wore Red, her only movie
        released this year.

1962   After a two-year absence from film, Ava appears as
        Baroness Natalie Ivanoff in 55 Days at Peking.

1964   Due to financial difficulties, Ava agrees to appear
        on the screen again, although she still suffers from
        a lack of confidence because of her previous facial
        trauma. She has small role in Seven Days in May. John
        Huston convinces her to take the pivotal, important
        role of Maxine Faulk in Night of The Iguana.

1966   John Huston again convinces the under-rated Ava to
        star as Sarah in his epic The Bible.

1968   Ava moves to a flat above Park Lane in London, England.

1970   Ava stars as Elizabeth in Mayerling.

1972   Ava has bit role as Lily Langtry in The Life and Times
        of Judge Roy Bean, also directed by friend John Huston.
        Director pal Roddy McDowall gets Ava to star as
        Michaela in the poorly-received The Devil's Widow.

1974   Ava has principal role as Remy Graff in Earthquake,
        the first film produced in Sensurround.

1975   Ava's only film this year was Permission to Kill, as
        Katina Peterson.

1976   Ava is Luxury in The Blue Bird. Ava plays Nicole in
        The Cassandra Crossing.

1977   Ava has small part in The Sentinel, as Miss Logan.

1978   Ava appears as Maggie in City on Fire.

1980   Ava appears as Betty Richards in The Kidnapping of The
       President.

1981   Ava co-stars as Mabel Dodge Luhan in Priest of Love.

1982   Ava attends the funeral of long-time friend Grace
       Kelly in Monaco.

1985   Ava returns to the screen (television) as Agrippina in
       A.D., as Minnie Littlejohn in The Long Hot Summer, and
       in recurring role as Ruth Galveston in Knots Landing.

1986   Ava has small part in television mini-series Harem.
       She returns to California after suffering health
       problems.

1990   Ava Gardner succumbs of pneumonia in her London flat
       on January 25, 1990, at age 67.

PRODUCTIONS

FILM

Ava Gardner's film credits are listed in chronological order by year of release and include her earliest-known bit parts. Beginning with Ava's larger speaking roles, cast and roles are given. Synopses of the films are included.

F1 WE WERE DANCING

M-G-M, released 1942, 94 minutes

Director: Robert Z. Leonard
Producer: O. O. Dull
Screenplay: Claudine West, George Froeschel, and Hans Rameau

From the Nöel Coward play <u>Tonight at 8:00</u>

Starring: Norma Shearer, Melvyn Douglas, Gail Patrick, Marjorie Main, Reginald Owen, Connie Gilchrist, Heather Thatcher, Sig Ruman, and Florence Bates

Story: Romantic comedy about a princess who runs off with another man who attends her engagement party. This movie marked Ava's debut in films in a walk-on part.

Reviews: <u>Time</u>, Volume 39, page 75, March 23, 1942
                <u>Musician</u>, Volume 47, page 75, May, 1942
                <u>New York Times</u>, page 23, May 1, 1942
                <u>New York Times</u>, Section VIII, page 3, May 3, 1942

See: AB101

F2   JOE SMITH, AMERICAN

M-G-M, released April 1, 1942, 63 minutes
Available on video cassette (M-G-M/United)

Director: Richard Thorpe
Screenplay: Allen Rivkin

From the novel The Big Operator by Paul Gallico

Starring: Robert Young, Marsha Hunt, Harvey Stephens,
             Darryl Hickman, William Forrest, Jonathan
             Hale, Russell Hicks, Mark Daniels, and
             William Tannen

Story: World War II yarn about a kidnapped
             munitions worker who refuses to let Nazis
             intimidate him into giving them secrets.
             Ava had walk-on.

Reviews: Scholastic, Volume 40, page 34,
                 February 9, 1942
             Newsweek, Volume 19, page 72, February 16,
                 1942
             Time, Volume 39, page 86, February 16, 1942
             Commonweal, Volume 35, page 536, March 20,
                 1942
             New York Times, page 27, April 2, 1942
             Musician, Volume 27, page 75, May, 1942

F3   REUNION IN FRANCE

M-G-M, released April 4, 1943, 104 minutes

Director: Jules Dassin
Producer: Joseph L. Mankiewicz
Screenplay: Jan Lustig, Marvin Borowsky, and
                   Marc Connelly

Based on an original story by Ladislas Bus-Fekete

Starring: Joan Crawford, John Wayne, Philip Dorn,
             Reginald Owen, Albert Baserman, John
             Carradine, Ann Ayars, Harry Daniell,
             Howard da Silva, Moroni Olsen, Charles
             Arnt, Morris Ankrum, Edith Evanson,
             Ernest Dorian, Edward Bromberg, Margaret
             Laurence, Odette Myrtil, and Peter Whitney

Story: World War II propaganda film with Crawford
             and Wayne in love as they try to leave
             Nazi-occupied France. Ava played a model
             in a nonspeaking role.

Reviews: <u>Film Daily</u>, page 6, December 2, 1942
             <u>Hollywood Reporter</u>, page 3, December 2,
                 1942
             <u>Variety</u>, page 8, December 2, 1942
             <u>Motion Picture Herald Prod. Digest</u>,
                 page 1041, December 5, 1942
             <u>Time</u>, Volume 41, page 86, January 4, 1943
             <u>Commonweal</u>, Volume 37, page 350,
                 January 22, 1943
             <u>New Yorker</u>, Volume 18, page 52,
                 February 6, 1943
             <u>New York Times</u>, page 20, March 5, 1943

See: AB30, AB49

F4   KID GLOVE KILLER

M-G-M, released 1942, 74 minutes

Director: Fred Zinneman
Producer: Jack Chertok
Screenplay: John Higgins and Allen Rivkin

Starring: Marsha Hunt, Van Heflin, Eddie Quillan,
                Lee Bowman, James Flavin, Cliff Clark,
                Samuel S. Hinds, John Litel, and Nella
                Walker

Story: Ava's first speaking role as a waitress in
                a drive-in diner in this solid film about
                a police chemist who uncovers the killing
                of a mayor.

Reviews: <u>New York Times</u>, page 21, April 17, 1942
                <u>Commonweal</u>, Volume 36, page 39, May 1, 1942

See: AB176

F5   YOUNG IDEAS

M-G-M, released 1943, 77 minutes

Director: Jules Dassin
Producer: Robert Sisk
Screenplay: Ian McL. Hunter

Starring: Susan Peters, Herbert Marshall, Mary Astor,
                Elliott Reid, Richard Carlson, and Allyn
                Joslyn

Story: Romantic comedy about a young writer who
                is not well-liked by his wife's family.
                Another walk-on bit part for Ava.

Reviews: <u>Commonweal</u>, Volume 38, page 443,
                    August 20, 1943

F6   LOST ANGEL

M-G-M, released 1943, 91 minutes
Available on video cassette (M-G-M/United)

Director: Roy Rowland
Producer: Robert Sisk
Screenplay: Isobel Lennart

From a story idea by Angna Enters

Starring: Margaret O'Brien, James Craig, Marsha Hunt,
               Philip Merivale, Henry O'Neill, Donald Meek,
               Keenan Wynn, Alan Napier, Sara Haden,
               Kathleen Lockhart, Elizabeth Risdon, Howard
               Freeman, and Bobby Blake

Story: Tale of a precocious child who learns about
               the simple things in life after moving in
               with a reporter (Craig). Ava had small
               walk-on.

Reviews: Photoplay, Volume 24, page 6, January, 1944
               Newsweek, Volume 23, page 52, January 3,
                    1944
               Nation, Volume 158, page 81, January 15,
                    1944
               Time, Volume 43, page 154, February 7, 1944
               New York Times, page 14, April 10, 1944

F7   DU BARRY WAS A LADY

M-G-M, released 1943, 101 minutes
Available on video cassette (M-G-M/United)

Director: Roy Del Ruth
Producer: Arthur Freed
Screenplay: Irving Brecher
Photography: Karl Freund

Starring: Lucille Ball, Red Skelton, Gene Kelly,
               Virginia O'Brien, Rags Ragland, Zero Mostel,
               Donald Meek, Douglass Dumbrille, George
               Givot, Louise Beavers, Tommy Dorsey and his
               orchestra, Jo Stafford, Dick Haymes, and
               Buddy Rich

Story: Lushly-photographed version of Broadway's
               1939 smash hit about a young man who's
               slipped a mickey and dreams he's in King
               Louis XIV's court. Ava was part of the
               scenery.

Reviews: Life, Volume 13, page 304, November 16, 1942
Good Housekeeping, Volume 116, page 2,
    March, 1943
Woman's Home Companion, Volume 70, page 2,
    March, 1943
American Mercury, Volume 135, page 2, April,
    1943
Cosmopolitan, Volume 114, page 2, April,
    1943
Theatre Arts, Volume 27, page 220, April,
    1943
Variety, page 8, May 5, 1943
Motion Picture Herald Prod. Digest, page 1301,
    May 8, 1943
Time, Volume 41, page 94, May 31, 1943
Cosmopolitan, Volume 114, page 66, June,
    1943
Newsweek, Volume 21, page 108, June 28,
    1943
Photoplay, Volume 23, page 24, July, 1943
New York Times, page 13, August 20, 1943
New Yorker, Volume 19, page 58, August 21,
    1943

F8   PILOT #5

M-G-M, released June 24, 1943, 70 minutes

Director: George Sidney
Producer: B. P. Fineman
Screenplay: David Hertz

Starring: Franchot Tone, Marsha Hunt, Gene Kelly, Van
Johnson, Alan Baxter, Dick Simmons, Frank
Puglia, William Tannen, and Steve Geray

Story: Tone is on a World War II suicide mission.
Those who knew him recall his life in
flashbacks. Ava had nonspeaking role.

Reviews: Commonweal, Volume 38, page 252, June 25,
    1943
New York Times, page 13, June 25, 1943
New Yorker, Volume 19, page 38, July 3,
    1943
Time, Volume 42, page 96, July 12, 1943

F9   HITLER'S MADMAN

M-G-M, released August 27, 1943, 84 minutes
Available on video cassette (M-G-M/United)

Director: Douglas Sirk
Producer: Seymour Nebenzal
Screenplay: Peretz Hirschbein, Melvin Levy, and
                   Doris Malloy

From an original story by Emil Ludwig and Albrecht
Joseph

Starring: Patricia Morison, John Carradine, Alan
                   Curtis, Ralph Morgan, Ludwig Stossel,
                   Howard Freeman, Edgar Kennedy, Al Shean,
                   Elizabeth Russell, Jimmy Conlin, Blanche
                   Yurka, Jorja Rollins, Victor Killian,
                   Johanna Hofer, Wolfgang Zilzer, and Tully
                   Marshall

Story: World War II film about the razing of a
                   Czech town whose citizens were suspected
                   of harboring a Nazi assassin. Ava's
                   nonspeaking part was as a Czech resistance
                   fighter.

Reviews: Film Daily, page 8, June 10, 1943
                   New York Times, page 15, August 28, 1943
                   BFI Monthly Film Bulletin, Volume 45,
                        page 185-6, September 28, 1943
                   Hollywood Reporter, page 4, December 3,
                        1943
                   Motion Picture Herald Prod. Digest,
                        page 1361, December 12, 1943

See: AB40, AB49

F10   GHOSTS ON THE LOOSE
      (also titled THE EAST SIDE KIDS MEET BELA LUGOSI)

Monogram Pictures, released June, 1943, 65 minutes
Available on video cassette (Budget Films)

Director: William Beaudine
Producer: Sam Katzman
Screenplay: Kenneth Higgins

Starring: Leo Gorcey, Huntz Hall, Bobby Jordan, Bela
                   Lugosi, Rick Vallin, Minerva Urecal, and
                   Ava Gardner

Story: This typical Dead End Kid movie featured
                   Ava as a newlywed. On loan from M-G-M,
                   she showed a flair for comedy.

Reviews: Mojarski, Richard, The Films of Bela
                        Lugosi, Citadel Press, New Jersey,
                        1980, page 199

See: AB136, AB193

F11   SWING FEVER

M-G-M, released 1944, 80 minutes

Director: Tim Whelan
Producer: Irving Starr
Screenplay: Nat Perrin and Warren Wilson

Starring: Kay Kyser, Marilyn Maxwell, William
                   Gargan, Lena Horne, Maxie Rosenbloom,
                   Curt Bois, and Nat Pendleton

Story: Kyser stars in this lame musical that
                   mixed boxing with romance. Ava had
                   another nonspeaking bit.

Reviews: New York Times, page 14, January 28, 1944

F12   BLONDE FEVER

M-G-M, released 1944, 69 minutes
Available on video cassette (M-G-M/United)

Director: Richard Whorf
Producer: William H. Wright
Screenplay: Patricia Coleman

From the novel Delilah by Ferenc Molnar

Starring: Philip Dorn, Mary Astor, Felix Bressart,
                   Gloria Grahame, and Marshall Thompson

Story: Romance triangle of a widow traveling in
                   Europe. Ava had a nonspeaking role.

Reviews: Canadian Forum, Volume 25, page 189,
                       November, 1945

F13   MUSIC FOR MILLIONS

M-G-M, released 1944, 120 minutes
Available on video cassette (M-G-M/United)

Director: Henry Koster
Producer: Joseph Pasternak
Screenplay: Myles Connolly

Starring: Margaret O'Brien, Jimmy Durante, June
                   Allyson, Marsha Hunt, Hugh Herbert, Jose
                   Iturbi, Connie Gilchrist, Harry Davenport,
                   Marie Wilson, Larry Adler, Ethel Griffies

Story: Musical about a family of sisters who join
              Jose Iturbi's orchestra. Margaret O'Brien
              won a special Oscar in 1944 for Outstanding
              Juvenile Acting. Ava had a very short bit.

Reviews: New York Times, page 12, December 22, 1944
              New Yorker, Volume 20, page 49, December 23,
                  1944
              Newsweek, Volume 25, page 95, January 15,
                  1945
              Time, Volume 45, page 96, January 15, 1945
              Cosmopolitan, Volume 118, page 90, March,
                  1945
              Nation, Volume 160, page 602, May 26, 1945

F14   TWO GIRLS AND A SAILOR

M-G-M, released 1944, 124 minutes
Available on video cassette (M-G-M/United)

Director: Richard Thorpe
Producer: Joseph Pasternak
Screenplay: Richard Connell and Gladys Lehman

Starring: June Allyson, Gloria de Haven, Van Johnson,
              Tom Drake, Jimmy Durante, Henry Stephenson,
              Henry O'Neill, Frank Jenks, Donald Meek,
              Frank Sully, Jose Iturbi and his orchestra,
              Amparo Iturbi, Lena Horne, Virginia O'Brien,
              Lyn Wilde, Lee Wilde, Ben Blue, Carlos
              Ramirez, Gracie Allen, Harry James and his
              orchestra

Story: Ava was cast as a canteen hostess who falls
              asleep while dancing in this romantic
              comedy where Allyson and de Haven are
              rivals for Johnson.

Reviews: New York Times, page 16, June 15, 1944
              Time, Volume 43, page 94, June 19, 1944
              Commonweal, Volume 40, page 231, June 23,
                  1944
              New Yorker, Volume 20, page 59, June 24,
                  1944
              Newsweek, Volume 23, page 99, June 26, 1944
              Nation, Volume 159, page 24, July 1, 1944
              New Republic, Volume III, page 16, July 3,
                  1944
              Life, Volume 17, page 63-4, July 17, 1944
              Musician, Volume 49, page 150, August, 1944
              Photoplay, Volume 25, page 24, August, 1944
              Woman's Home Companion, Volume 71, page 10,
                  August, 1944

F15   THREE MEN IN WHITE

Paramount, released 1944, 85 minutes

Director: Willis Goldbeck
Producer: Willis Goldbeck
Screenplay: Martin Berkeley and Harry Ruskin
Photography: Ray June
Music: Nathaniel Shilkret

Based on characters by Max Brand

Starring: Marilyn Maxwell, Lionel Barrymore, Van
              Johnson, Ava Gardner, Keye Luke, Rags
              Ragland, Alma Kruger, Walter Kingsford,
              Nell Craig, and George Reed

Story: Ava is hired by Dr. Gillespie (Barrymore)
              to seduce young dictor (Johnson), who must
              prove himself as a new resident. Ava
              played her role with relish and was
              well-received in her comedic part.

Reviews: New York Times, page 23, May 26, 1944

See: AB154, AB176, AN8

F16   MAISIE GOES TO RENO

M-G-M, released 1944, 90 minutes

Director: Harry Beaumont
Producer: George Haight
Screenplay: Mary McCall, Jr.
Photography: Robert Planck
Music: David Snell

Starring: Ann Sothern, Harry Ruby, James O'Hanlon,
              John Hodiak, Tom Drake, Paul Cavanagh,
              Marta Linden, Ava Gardner, Bernard Nedell,
              Chick Chandler, and Donald Meek

Story: This World War II movie was one of the
              popular series starring Sothern as a
              brassy showgirl who finds herself in
              situations where she proves that a woman
              can take care of herself. Ava played the
              sophisticated wife of a very rich man.

Reviews: New York Times, Section II, page 3,
                  April 16, 1944
              New York Times, page 18, September 29, 1944
              Commonweal, Volume 40, page 615,
                  October 13, 1944

F17   THE KILLERS

Universal, released January 13, 1946, 105 minutes
Available on video cassette (Universal)

Director: Robert Siodmak
Producer: Mark Hellinger
Screenplay: Anthony Veiller and John Huston
Photography: Woody Bredell and D. S. Horsley
Music Score: Miklos Rozsa

Based on a story by Ernest Hemingway

Starring: Burt Lancaster (Swede), Ava Gardner (Kitty
             Collins), Edmond O'Brien (Riordan), Albert
             Dekker (Colfax), Sam Levene (Lt. Lubinsky),
             Jack Lambert (Dum Dum), Jeff Corey (Blinky),
             Donald McBride (Kenyon), Vince Barnett
             (Charleston), Charles D. Brown (Packy),
             Virginia Christine (Lilly), Phil Brown
             (Nick Adams), John Miljan (Jake), Charles
             McGraw (Killer), and William Conrad (Killer)

Story: Swede is a boxer who becomes mixed up in
             racketeering under a powerful gangster
             (Dekker). O'Brien is an insurance detective
             who sets out to solve crimes done by them,
             and he explains how and why Swede meets his
             particular kind of death. A smoldering Ava
             plays a beautiful and cunning girl who
             causes Swede's life to be a mess. Edmond
             O'Brien won an Oscar for Best Supporting
             Actor for his role as Riordan.

Reviews: Hollywood Reporter, page 3, August 7, 1946
             Variety, page 15, August 7, 1946
             Film Daily, page 6, August 12, 1946
             Motion Picture Herald Prod. Digest,
                   page 3150, August 17, 1946
             New York Times, Section II, page 3,
                   August 25, 1946
             New York Times, page 24, August 29, 1946
             New York Times, Section II, page 1,
                   September 1, 1946
             Life, Volume 21, pages 59-61, September 2,
                   1946
             New Yorker, Volume 22, page 49,
                   September 7, 1946
             Newsweek, Volume 28, page 106, September 9,
                   1946
             Time, Volume 48, page 100, September 9, 1946
             Nation, Volume 163, page 305, September 14,
                   1946

Rob Wagner's Script, Volume 32, page 13,
    September 28, 1946
New Republic, Volume 115, page 415,
    September 30, 1946
Cosmopolitan, Volume 121, page 73,
    October, 1946
Theatre Arts, Volume 30, page 603, October,
    1946
Scholastic, Volume 49, page 37, October 14,
    1946
Photoplay, Volume 29, page 4, November, 1946
Life, Volume 22, page 86, March 10, 1947
Take One, Volume 4, pages 17-19, November,
    1974
BFI Monthly Film Bulletin, Volume 48,
    page 208, October, 1981

See: AB5, AB10, AB78, AB100, AB137, AB144, AB148, AB172,
AB176, AB195, AB197, AB200, AB202, AB226, AB230,
AN11-12, AP2, AP5

F18   SHE WENT TO THE RACES

M-G-M, released January 21, 1946, 86 minutes

Director: Willis Goldbeck
Producer: Federick Stephani
Screenplay: Lawrence Hazard
Photography: Charles Salerno
Music: Nathaniel Shilkret

From a story by Alan Friedman and DeVallon Scott

Starring: Edmund Gwenn, James Craig, Frances Gifford,
                   Sig Ruman, Reginald Owen, M. J. Kerrigan,
                   Charles Halton, and Ava Gardner

Story: Comedy about a young woman who develops a
                   scientific method for placing bets and
                   falls in love with her horse trainer. Ava
                   had a minor speaking role.

Reviews: New York Times, page 29, February 1, 1946

F19   WHISTLE STOP

United Artists, released May 6, 1946, 85 minutes
Available on video cassette (United Artists)

Director: Leonid Moguy
Producer: Philip Yordan
Screenplay: Philip Yordan
Photography: Russell Metty
Music: Nathaniel Shilkret
Art Direction: Rudy Feld

Starring: George Raft (gangster), Ava Gardner (Mary),
             Victor McLaglen (hood bartender), Tom Conway,
             Jorja Curtright, Florence Bates, and Charles
             Drake

Story: Ava is a nice girl who tries to change the
             life of hard-drinking playboy love (Raft),
             who gets mixed up with evil nightclub
             owner (McLaglen). This was Ava's first
             starring role.

Reviews: Commonweal, Volume 43, page 383,
                  January 25, 1946
             Newsweek, Volume 27, page 86, March 4, 1946
             New York Times, Section II, page 3,
                  March 17, 1946
             New York Times, page 24, March 18, 1946

See: AN9

F20   THIS TIME FOR KEEPS

M-G-M, released 1947, 105 minutes
Available on video cassette (M-G-M/United)

Director: Richard Thorpe
Producer: Joseph Pasternak and Lauritz Melchior
Screenplay: Gladys Lehman

Starring: Esther Williams, Jimmy Durante, and Johnny
             Johnston

Story: Average musical with little plot. Ava had
             little more than a walk-on part.

Reviews: New York Times, Section II, page 3,
                  July 28, 1947
             Variety, page 8, October 8, 1947
             Film Daily, page 10, October 17, 1947
             Motion Picture Herald Prod. Digest,
                  page 3873, November 11, 1947
             New York Times, Section I, page 5,
                  November 30, 1947
             New York Times, page 33, December 5, 1947
             New Republic, Volume 117, page 33,
                  December 22, 1947
             Newsweek, Volume 30, page 81,
                  December 22, 1947
             Time, Volume 50, page 82, December 22, 1947
             Commonweal, Volume 47, page 304,
                  January 2, 1948

F21   THE HUCKSTERS

M-G-M, released August 4, 1947, 115 minutes
Available on video cassette (M-G-M/United)

Director: Jack Conway
Producer: Arthur Hornblow, Jr.
Screenplay: Luther Davis
Photography: Harold Rosson
Art Direction: Cedric Gibbons and Urie McCleary
Musical Score: Lennie Hayton
Editor: Frank Sullivan

Based on a novel by Frederic Wakeman, adapted by
Edward Chodorov and George Wells

Starring: Clark Gable (Vic Norman), Deborah Kerr
             (Mrs. Dorrence), Ava Gardner (Jean Ogilvie),
             Adolphe Menjou (Mr. Kimberly), Sydney
             Greenstreet (Llewellyn Evans), and Keenan
             Wynn (Buddy Hare), with: Edward Arnold,
             Aubrey Mather, Richard Gaines, Frank
             Albertson, Douglas Fowley, Clinton Sundberg,
             Gloria Holden, Connie Gilchrist, Kathryn
             Card, Lillian Bronson, Vera Marshe, Ralph
             Bunker, Virginia Dale, and Jimmy Conlin

Story: Gable is a World War II veteran who returns
             to his old stomping grounds to find his
             values compromised. Ava plays a young
             singer who secretly loves him, but his
             heart belongs to prim Kerr. Kerr means
             so much to him that he leaves the advertising
             rat-race to pursue a life with her.

Reviews: New York Times, page 37, January 1, 1947
             New York Times, Section II, page 5,
                  January 19, 1947
             New York Times, Section II, page 5,
                  March 9, 1947
             Life, Volume 22, pages 51-52, March 31, 1947
             Film Daily, page 10, June 27, 1947
             Hollywood Reporter, page 3, June 27, 1947
             Motion Picture Herald Prod. Digest,
                  page 3701, June 28, 1947
             Variety, page 13, July 2, 1947
             New York Times, Section II, page 3,
                  July 13, 1947
             New York Times, page 21, July 18, 1947
             New Yorker, Volume 23, page 46, July 19,
                  1947
             New York Times, Section II, page 1,
                  July 20, 1947
             Newsweek, Volume 30, page 76, July 21, 1947
             Time, Volume 50, page 91, July 21, 1947

Life, Volume 23, pages 103-104, July 28, 1947
Commonweal, Volume 46, page 386, August 1,
        1947
Nation, Volume 165, page 130, August 2, 1947
New Republic, Volume 117, page 34,
        August 11, 1947
Cosmopolitan, Volume 123, page 58,
        September, 1947
Photoplay, Volume 31, page 4, September,
        1947
Woman's Home Companion, Volume 74, pages 10-
        11, October, 1947

See: AB27, AB77-78, AB96, AB124, AB178, AB197, AB222,
     AN14-15, AP3-8

F22 SINGAPORE

Universal-International Pictures, released September,
1947, 79 minutes
Available on video cassette (Swank Motion)

Director: John Braham
Producer: Jerry Bresler
Screenplay: Seton I. Miller and Robert Thoern
Photography: Maury Gertsman
Music: Daniel Amfitheatrof

Starring: Fred MacMurray (Matt Gordon), Ava Gardner
                   (Linda), Roland Culver (Michael Van Leyden),
                   Richard Haydn (Inspector Hewitt), Spring
                   Byington (Mrs. Bellows), Porter Hall
                   (Mr. Bellows), Thomas Gomez (Mr. Mauribus),
                   Maylia (Ming Ling), George Lloyd (Sascha
                   Barda), Holmes Herbert (Rev. Barnes), Edith
                   Evanson (Miss Barnes), Frederick Worlock
                   (Cadum), Lal Chand Mehra (Mr. Hussein), and
                   Curt Conway (Pepe)

Story: Ava is an amnesia victim who meets her old
                   lover (MacMurray), who has returned to
                   Singapore to recover pearls he deserted
                   when the Japanese invaded the city.

Reviews: Hollywood Reporter, page 3, August 6, 1947
                   Variety, page 12, August 6, 1947
                   Film Daily, page 8, August 13, 1947
                   Motion Picture Herald Prod. Digest,
                        page 3782, August 16, 1947
                   New York Times, page 31, September 17,
                        1947
                   Newsweek, Volume 30, page 94, September 29,
                        1947
                   Time, Volume 50, pages 101-102, October 6,
                        1947

See: AB100, AN17, AP10-11

F23   ONE TOUCH OF VENUS

Universal-International, released 1948, 82 minutes
Available on video cassette (Budget Films)

Director: William A. Seiter
Producer: Lester Cowan
Screenplay: Harry Kurnitz and Frank Tashlin
Photography: Franz Planer
Music: Kurt Weill and Ogden Nash
Dance Routines: Billy Daniels
Vocal Dubbing: Eileen Wilson

From the stage musical by S. J. Perelman, Ogden Nash,
and Kurt Weill

Starring: Ava Gardner (Statue of Venus/Venus Jones),
            Robert Walker (Eddie Hatch), Dick Haymes
            (Joe), Eve Arden (Molly Grant), Olga San
            Juan (Gloria), Tom Conway (Whitfield
            Savorny), with James Flavin and Sara Allgood

Story: Ava starred in the role originally created
            for Mary Martin on stage, as a statue of
            Venus who springs to life for one day after
            being kissed by a window dresser (Walker)
            in a department store.

Reviews: Vogue, Volume 103, page 76, February 15,
                 1948
            New York Times, Section II, page 5,
                 March 14, 1948
            Film Daily, page 6, August 23, 1948
            Variety, page 8, August 25, 1948
            Motion Picture Herald Prod. Digest,
                 page 4275, August 28, 1948
            Newsweek, Volume 32, page 102,
                 September 20, 1948
            Time, Volume 52, page 96, September 27, 1948
            Theatre Arts, Volume 32, page 53, October,
                 1948
            New York Times, page 29, October 29, 1948

      See: AB50, AB139, AB158, AB170, AB172, AB197, AB199,
           AN18-19, AP13-16

F24   THE BRIBE

M-G-M, released February 3, 1949, 98 minutes
Available on video cassette (M-G-M/United)

Director: Robert Z. Leonard
Producer: Pandro S. Berman
Screenplay: Marguerite Roberts
Photography: Joseph Ruttenberg
Music: Miklos Rozsa
Editor: Gene Ruggiero
Song: Nacio Herb Brown and William Katz

Based on a short story by Frederick Nebel

Starring: Robert Taylor (Rigby), Ava Gardner
             (Elizabeth Hintten), Charles Laughton
             (J. J. Bealler), Vincent Price (Carwood),
             John Hodiak (Tug Hintten), Samuel S. Hinds
             (Dr. Warren), John Hoyt (Gibbs), Tito
             Renaldo (Emilio Gomez), and Martin
             Garralaga (Pablo Gomez)

Story: Ava is a cafe singer married to former U.S.
             flier (Hodiak), who has gotten himself
             involved in smuggling war-surplus parts in
             the Caribbean. Taylor is a federal agent
             who tracks the racketeers and falls for Ava
             in the process, luring her away from her
             husband.

Reviews: New York Times, page 31, February 4, 1949
             Time, Volume 53, page 84, February 7, 1949
             New Yorker, Volume 24, page 70,
                   February 12, 1949
             Newsweek, Volume 33, page 78,
                   February 14, 1949
             New Republic, Volume 120, page 31,
                   February 21, 1949
             Rotarian, Volume 74, page 34, June, 1949

See: AB62, AB75, AB133, AN21, AP19-23, AP271

F25   THE GREAT SINNER

M-G-M, released December 12, 1949, 110 minutes
Available on video cassette (M-G-M/United)

Director: Robert Siodmak
Producer: Gottfried Reinhardt
Screenplay: Christopher Isherwood
Photography: George Folsey
Music: Bronislau Kaper

Starring: Gregory Peck (Fyodor Dostoevsky), Ava
             Gardner (Pauline Ostrovski), Melvyn Douglas
             (Armand D. Glasse), Walter Huston (General
             Ostrovski), Ethel Barrymore (Granny),
             Frank Morgan (Aristide Pitard), and Agnes
             Moorehead (Emma Getzel)

Story: This story is loosely based on the life of
             Dostoevsky, at a time when the evil of
             gambling overtook him. Ava played a young
             woman who also gambles and they fall in love.

Reviews: New York Times, Section II, page 5,
               January 9, 1949
             Variety, page 14, June 29, 1949
             Hollywood Reporter, page 3, June 30, 1949
             New York Times, page 19, June 30, 1949
             Motion Picture Herald Prod. Digest,
               page 4665, July 2, 1949
             New Yorker, Volume 25, page 38, July 9,
               1949
             New York Times, Section II, page 1,
               July 10, 1949
             Newsweek, Volume 34, page 68, July 11, 1949
             Commonweal, Volume 50, page 342, July 15,
               1949
             Time, Volume 54, page 76, July 18, 1949
             Photoplay, Volume 36, page 22, September,
               1949
             Rotarian, Volume 75, page 38, October, 1949

See: AB74, AB140, AB150, AB191, AB205, AN20, AN22,
     AP24-27

F26   EAST SIDE, WEST SIDE

M-G-M, released June 19, 1950, 108 minutes
Available on video cassette (Films, Inc.)

Director: Mervyn Leroy
Producer: Voldemar Vetluguin
Screenplay: Isobel Lennart
Photography: Charles Rosher
Editor: Harold T. Kress
Music: Miklos Rozsa
Costumes: Helen Rose

From the novel by Marcia Davenport

Starring: Barbara Stanwyck (Jessie Bourne), James
                 Mason (Brandon Bourne), Van Heflin (Mark
                 Dwyer), Ava Gardner (Isobel Lorrison),
                 Cyd Charisse (Rose Senta), Nancy Davis
                 (Helen Lee), Gale Sondergaard (Nora
                 Kernan), William Conrad (Lt. Jacobi),
                 Raymond Greenleaf (Horace Howland),
                 Douglas Kennedy (Alec Dawning), Beverly
                 Michaels (Felice Backett), William
                 Frawley (Bill), Lisa Golm (Josephine),
                 and Tom Powers (Owen Lee).

Story: Lives and loves of unhappy, rich New York
                 socialites. Heflin, just back from the
                 war, falls for married Stanwyck. Ava is
                 in love with Stanwyck's husband (Mason).
                 In this stylish soap opera, Ava's role is
                 very much the same as that in The
                 Hucksters.

Reviews: New York Times, page 17, December 23, 1949
            Newsweek, Volume 34, page 57, December 26,
                1949
            Commonweal, Volume 51, page 415,
                January 20, 1950
            Time, Volume 55, page 86, January 30, 1950
            Library Journal, Volume 75, page 180,
                February 1, 1950
            Nation, Volume 170, page 162, February 18,
                1950
            Christian Century, Volume 67, page 319,
                March 8, 1950

See: AN23, AP28-29, AP31

F27 PANDORA AND THE FLYING DUTCHMAN

M-G-M/British Lion-Romulus, released March 5, 1951
123 minutes

Director: Albert Lewin
Producer: Albert Lewin and Joseph Kaufman
Screenplay: Albert Lewin
Photography: Jack Cardiff
Music: Alan Rawstherne

From the story by Albert Lewin, suggested by The Legend
of The Flying Dutchman

Starring: James Mason (Hendrick van Der Zee), Ava
            Gardner (Pandora Reynolds), Nigel Patrick
            (Stephen Cameron), Harold Warrender
            (Geoffrey Fielding), Sheila Sim (Janet),
            Mario Cabre (Juan Montalvo), Marius Goring
            (Reggie Demarest), John Laurie (Angus),
            Pamela Kellino (Jenny), and Margarita
            D'Alvarez (Mrs. Montalvo), with: La Pillina,
            Abraham Sofaer, Francisco Igual, Guillermo
            Beltran, Lila Molnar, Phoebe Hodgson,
            Gabriel Carmona, and Antonio Martin

Story: Ava plays a young romantic girl who falls
            in love with Mason, a man with no past or
            future.

Reviews: London Times, page 12, January 30, 1951
            Hollywood Reporter, page 3, February 2,
                1951
            Spectator, Volume 186, page 146,
                February 2, 1951
            New Statesman and Nation, Volume 51,
                page 1057, February 10, 1951
            London Times, page 8, February 30, 1951
            BFI Monthly Film Bulletin, Volume 18,
                page 229, March, 1951
            Library Journal, Volume 76, page 883,
                May 15, 1951

Time, Volume 57, paes 105-106, May 28, 1951
Motion Picture Herald Prod. Digest,
          page 1057, October 13, 1951
Variety, page 6, October 10, 1951
Film Daily, page 6, October 15, 1951
New York Times, page 35, December 7, 1951
New York Times, Section II, page 5,
          December 9, 1951
Commonweal, Volume 55, page 254, December 14,
          1951
New Yorker, Volume 27, page 148, December 15,
          1951
Newsweek, Volume 38, page 98, December 17,
          1951
Holiday, Volume 11, page 19, March, 1952
Christian Century, Volume 69, page 351,
          March 19, 1952
BFI Monthly Film Bulletin, Volume 52,
          pages 261-262, August, 1985

See: AB48, AB50, AB98, AB102, AB130, AB172, AB176, AB223,
     AN39-41, AP38, AP42-3, AP265, AP57-58, AP64

F28   MY FORBIDDEN PAST

RKO, released July 9, 1951, 81 minutes
Available on video cassette

Director: Robert Stevenson
Producer: Robert Sparks and Polan Banks
Screenplay: Marion Parsonnet
Adaptation: Leopold Atlas
Photography: Harry J. Wild
Editor: George Shrader
Music: Frederick Hollander
Music Director: C. Kakaleinikoff
Art Direction: Albert S. D'Agostino and Alfred Herman

Based on the novel Carriage Entrance by Polan Banks

Starring: Robert Mitchum (Dr. Mark Lucas), Ava Gardner
              (Barbara Beaurevel), Melvyn Douglas (Paul
              Beaurevel), Lucile Watson (Aunt Eula), Janis
              Carter (Corinne), Gordon Oliver (Clay
              Duchesne), Basil Ruysdael (Dean Cazzley),
              Clarence Muse (Pompey), Walter Kingsford
              (Coroner), Jack Briggs (Cousin Phillippe),
              Will Wright (Luther Tuplady), Watson Downs
              (Hotel Clerk), Cliff Clark (Horse Vendor),
              and John B. Williams (Fishmonger)

Story: Ava plays a girl with a hidden past who gets
              convinced to marry another man whom she
              doesn't love in order to save the family's
              dwindling finances. Her true love (Mitchum)

marries another (Carter) and he is accused
of murdering her. At his trial, Ava
reveals the truth and exposes the family
secrets.

Reviews: Library Journal, Volume 76, page 418,
                 March 1, 1951
             Hollywood Reporter, page 3, March 21, 1951
             Film Daily, page 6, March 23, 1951
             Variety, page 6, March 28, 1951
             Motion Picture Herald Prod. Digest,
                 pages 786-787, March 31, 1951
             New York Times, page 34, April 26, 1951
             Newsweek, Volume 37, page 90, May 7, 1951
             Time, Volume 57, page 112, May 14, 1951
             Spectator, Volume 186, page 781, June 15,
                 1951
             BFI Monthly Film Bulletin, Volume 18,
                 page 298, July, 1951

See: AB42, AB74, AB119, AB171, AB211, AP38, AP42-43,
        AP265

F29   SHOW BOAT

M-G-M, released July 19, 1951, 107 minutes
Available on video cassette (M-G-M/United)

Director: George Sidney
Producer: Arthur Freed and Ben Feiner, Jr.
Screenplay: John Lee Mahin
Photography: Charles Rosher
Music Direction: Adolph Deutsch
Choreography: Robert Alton
Vocal Dubbing: Annette Warren

Based on the musical play by Jerome Kern and Oscar
Hammerstein II, from the novel by Edna Ferber

Starring: Kathryn Grayson (Magnolia Hawks), Ava
             Gardner (Julie LaVerne), Howard Keel
             (Gaylord Ravenal), Joe E. Brown (Capt.
             Andy Hawks), Marge Champion (Ellie May
             Shipley), Agnes Moorehead (Parthy Hawks),
             Gower Champion (Frank Schultz), Robert
             Sterling (Stephen Baker), Leif Erickson
             (Pete), Adele Jergens (Cameo McQueen),
             William Warfield (Joe), Frances Williams
             (Queenie), Owen McGiveney (Windy McClain),
             Regis Toomey (Sheriff Ike Vallon), and
             Sheila Clark (Kim Ravenal)

Story: Vividly-colorful version of the stage play
                about a show boat that travels the
                Mississippi to entertain the folks along
                the way.

Reviews: New York Times, Section II, page 5,
                    January 29, 1950
                New York Times, Section II, page 5,
                    July 8, 1950
                New York Times, Section II, page 5
                    November 5, 1950
                Film Daily, page 5, June 5, 1951
                Hollywood Reporter, page 3, June 5, 1951
                Variety, page 6, June 6, 1951
                Motion Picture Herald Prod. Digest,
                    page 877, June 9, 1951
                Saturday Review, Volume 34, page 265,
                    June 9, 1951
                Library Journal, Volume 76, page 1037,
                    June 15, 1951
                Commonweal, Volume 54, page 286,
                    June 29, 1951
                BFI Monthly Film Bulletin, Volume 18,
                    page 294, July, 1951
                Newsweek, Volume 38, page 78, July 2, 1951
                Time, Volume 58, page 94, July 2, 1951
                Cue, page 18, July 14, 1951
                New York Times, Section II, page 1, July 22,
                    July 22, 1951
                New Yorker, Volume 27, page 73, July 28,
                    1951
                Life, Volume 31, page 48, July 30, 1951
                Christian Century, Volume 68, page 903,
                    August 1, 1951
                Bright Lights, Volume 3, pages 21-24, ff9,
                    1980

See: AB66, AB68, AB106, AB124, AB131, AB144, AB158,
    AB162, AB172, AB174, AB197, AB202, AN25, AN27,
    AP44-46, AP48-51, AP53

F30   LONE STAR

M-G-M, released March 10, 1952, 94 minutes
Available on video cassette (M-G-M/United)

Director: Vincent Sherman
Producer: Z. Wayne Griffin
Screenplay: Borden Chase and Howard Estabrook
Photography: Harold Rosson
Music: David Buttolph
Art Direction: Cedric Gibbons and Hans Peters
Editor: Ferris Webster

From the magazine story by Borden Chase

Starring: Clark Gable (Devereaux Burke), Ava Gardner
                 (Martha Ronda), Broderick Crawford (Thomas
                 Craden), Lionel Barrymore (Andrew Jackson),
                 Beulah Bondi (Minniver Bryan), Ed Begley
                 (Claud Demmet), James Burke (Luther
                 Kilgore), William Farnum (Tom Crockett),
                 Lowell Gilmore (Capt. Elliot), Moroni Olsen
                 (Sam Houston), Russell Simpson (Maynard
                 Cole), Ralph Reed (Bud Yoakum), and Jonathan
                 Cott (Ben McCulloch), with: William Conrad,
                 Lucius Cook, Ric Roman, Victor Sutherland,
                 Charles Cane, Nacho Galindo, Trevor
                 Bardette, Harry Woods, Dudley Sadler, and
                 Emmett Lynn

Story: Loosely-based story on the annexation and
                 independence of Texas from the Mexicans.

Reviews: Hollywood Reporter, page 4, December 19, 1951
                 Variety, page 6, December 19, 1951
                 Motion Picture Herald Prod. Digest,
                     page 1161, December 22, 1951
                 London Times, page 2, January 5, 1952
                 Film Daily, page 6, January 7, 1952
                 Time, Volume 59, page 94, January 21, 1952
                 BFI Monthly Film Bulletin, Volume 19, page 6,
                     February, 1952
                 New York Times, page 11, February 2, 1952
                 New Yorker, Volume 27, page 105, February 9,
                     1952
                 Newsweek, Volume 39, page 89, February 11,
                     1952
                 Commonweal, Volume 55, page 544, March 7,
                     1952
                 Library Journal, Volume 77, page 522,
                     March 15, 1952
                 Christian Century, Volume 69, page 415,
                     April 2, 1952

     See: AB27, AB169, AB176, AB181, AB222, AN42, AP59,
          AP61-62, AP65, AP248

F31 THE BAND WAGON

     M-G-M, released 1953, 112 minutes
     Available on video cassette (M-G-M/United)

     Director: Vincente Minnelli
     Producer: Arthur Freed
     Screenplay: Adolph Green and Betty Comden
     Photography: Harry Jackson, Cedric Gibbons, and
                      Preston Ames
     Music: Howard Dietz and Arthur Schwartz

     Starring: Fred Astaire, Cyd Charisse, Oscar Levant,
                      Nanette Fabray, and Jack Buchanan

Story: Lavish musical featuring Astaire as a
                "washed up" actor who gets another chance
                to appear on Broadway. Ava had a cameo
                appearance.

Reviews: Hollywood Reporter, page 3, July 6, 1953
                Newsweek, Volume 42, pages 48-50, July 6,
                     1953
                Film Daily, page 6, July 7, 1953
                Variety, page 6, July 8, 1953
                New York Times, page 10, July 10, 1953
                Time, Volume 62, page 94, July 13, 1953
                America, Volume 89, page 405, July 18, 1953
                New Yorker, Volume 29, page 63, July 18, 1953
                New York Times, Section II, page 1,
                     July 19, 1953
                Saturday Review, Volume 36, page 28,
                     July 25, 1953
                Catholic World, Volume 177, page 384,
                     August, 1953
                Commonweal, Volume 58, page 423, July 31,
                     1953
                Films in Review, Volume 4, pages 360-361,
                     August-September, 1953
                Life, Volume 35, page 79, August 10, 1953
                Dance Magazine, Volume 27, pages 68-69,
                     September, 1953
                Farm Journal, Volume 77, page 118,
                     September, 1953
                McCall's, Volume 86, page 6, September, 1953
                National Parent-Teacher, Volume 48, page 38,
                     September, 1953
                Senior Scholastic, Volume 63, page 37,
                     September 16, 1953
                BFI Monthly Film Bulletin, Volume 20, n. 238,
                     page 170, November, 1953
                Holiday, Volume 15, page 17, January, 1954
                Sight and Sound, Volume 23, pages 142-143,
                     January-March, 1954

       See: AB149, AB158, AB161, AB202

F32   THE SNOWS OF KILIMINJARO

       20th Century-Fox, released February 2, 1953, 117 minutes
       Available on video cassette (Films Inc.)

       Director: Henry King
       Producer: Darryl F. Zanuck
       Screenplay: Casey Robinson
       Photography: Leon Shamroy
       Art Direction: Lyle Wheeler and John DeCuir
       Editor: Barbara McLean
       Sound: Bernard Fredericks and Roger Heman
       Set Decorations: Thomas Little and Paul S. Fox

Wardrobe: Charles LeMaire
Makeup: Ben Nye
Special Effects: Ray Kellogg
Music: Bernard Herrmann
Choreography: Antonio Triana

Based on a novel by Ernest Hemingway

Starring: Gregory Peck (Harry), Ava Gardner (Cynthia),
             Susan Hayward (Helen), Hildegarde Neff
             (Countess Liz), Leo G. Carroll (Uncle Bill),
             Torin Thatcher (Johnson), Ava Norring
             (Beatrice), Helen Staley (Connie), Marcel
             Dalio (Emile), Vincent Gomez (Spanish
             dancer), Richard Allan (Dr. Simmons), and
             Leonard Carey (Witch Doctor)

Story: Peck is a famous novelist/big game hunter
             who leaves Gardner after he becomes famous.
             She later meets him again and dies in his
             arms after an ambulance accident. He then
             meets Hayward, a rich widow, who finally
             gets his love after nursing him through a
             life-threatening fever. The film won Oscar
             nominations for Art and Set Decoration and
             Cinematography.

Reviews: Hollywood Reporter, page 3, September 9,
                  1952
             Film Daily, page 7, September 19, 1952
             New York Times, page 19, September 19, 1952
             Cue, page 16, September 20, 1952
             Motion Picture Herald Prod. Digest,
                  page 1533, September 20, 1952
             New Yorker, Volume 28, page 119,
                  September 20, 1952
             New York Times, Section II, page 1,
                  September 21, 1952
             Time, Volume 60, page 102, September 22,
                  1952
             Variety, page 6, September 24, 1952
             Newsweek, Volume 40, page 94, September 29,
                  1952
             Films in Review, Volume 3, pages 410-412,
                  October, 1952
             Library Journal, Volume 77, page 1605,
                  October 1, 1952
             Commonweal, Volume 56, page 630, October 3,
                  1952
             Life, Volume 33, page 147, October 6, 1952
             Saturday Review, Volume 35, page 31,
                  October 11, 1952
             New York Times, Section II, page 4,
                  October 12, 1952

BFI Monthly Film Bulletin, Volume 19,
    page 155, November, 1952
Catholic World, Volume 176, pages 142-
    1943, November, 1952
National Parent-Teacher, Volume 47, page
    38, November, 1952
Natural History, Volume 61, pages 424-425,
    November, 1952
Theatre Arts, Volume 36, page 77,
    November, 1952
Christian Century, Volume 69, page 1367,
    November 19, 1952
Spectator, Volume 189, page 670,
    November 21, 1952
New Statesman and Nation, Volume 44,
    page 636, November 29, 1952

See: AB72, AB120, AB148-149, AB173-174, AB191,
AN43-45, AP69-74

F33   RIDE, VAQUERO

M-G-M, released July 15, 1953, 90 minutes
Available on video cassette (M-G-M/United)

Director: John Farrow
Producer: Stephen Ames
Screenplay: Frank Fenton
Photography: Robert Surtees
Music: Bronislau Kaper
Editor: Harold F. Kress

Starring: Robert Taylor (Rio), Ava Gardner
(Cordelia Cameron), Howard Keel (King
Cameron), Anthony Quinn (Jose Esqueda),
Kurt Kasznar (Father Antonio), Ted
de Corsia (Sheriff Parker), Charlita
(Singer), Jack Elam (Barton), Walter
Baldwin (Adam Smith), Joe Dominguez
(Vincente), Frank McGrath (Pete),
Charles Stevens (Vaquero), Rex Lease
(Deputy), and Tom Greenway (Deputy)

Story: Western tale of a gang of outlaws who
terrorize a small Texas town. Ava is
married to Keel but has unrequited
romantic urges for Taylor.

Reviews: New York Times, page 17, July 16, 1953
Saturday Review, Volume 36, page 30,
    July 18, 1953
Newsweek, Volume 42, page 76, July 27,
    1953
Time, Volume 62, page 88, July 27, 1953
America, Volume 89, page 446, August 1,
    1953

> *Commonweal*, Volume 58, page 442, August 7,
> 1953
> *National Parent-Teacher*, Volume 48, page 39,
> October, 1953

See: AB24, AB75, AB133, AB169, AB181, AN46, AP81-83,
AP85-6, AP81-83, AP85-6

F34   MOGAMBO

M-G-M, released October 9, 1953, 115 minutes
Available on video cassette (M-G-M/United)

Director: John Ford
Producer: Sam Zimbalist
Screenplay: John Lee Mahin
Photography: Robert Surtees and Frederick A. Young
Art Direction: Alfred Junge
Costumes: Helen Rose
Editor: Frank Clarke

From the play *Red Dust*, by Wilson Collison

Starring: Clark Gable (Victor Marswell), Ava Gardner
              (Eloise Kelly), Grace Kelly (Linda Nordley),
              Donald Sinden (Donald Nordley), Philip
              Stainton (John Brown Pryce), Eric Pohlmann
              (Leon Boltchak), Laurence Naismith (Skipper),
              Dennis O'Dea (Father Joseph), Asa Etula
              (young native girl), and featured: the
              Wagenia Tribe of the Belgian Congo, the
              Bahaya Tribe of Tanganyika, and the
              M'Bety Tribe of French Equatorial Africa

Story: Remake of the 1932 Victor Fleming movie
              Red Dust, which also starred Clark Gable.
              Ava had the Jean Harlow role in this
              romantic triangle set on an African
              safari. Grace Kelly is Ava's rival for
              the affections of Gable. Ava's salty
              performance won her an Academy Award
              nomination for Best Actress.

Reviews: *New York Times*, Section I, page 5,
              January 4, 1953
              Life, Volume 34, page 80, January 26, 1953
              Film Daily, page 6, September 15, 1953
              Hollywood Reporter, page 3, September 15,
              1953
              Variety, page 6, September 16, 1953
              New York Times, page 18, October 2, 1953
              New Yorker, Volume 29, page 127,
              October 10, 1953
              Saturday Review, Volume 36, page 34,
              October 10, 1953

New York Times, Section I, page 1,
    October 11, 1953
Newsweek, Volume 42, pages 100-102,
    October 12, 1953
Time, Volume 62, page 114, October 12,
    1953
Library Journal, Volume 78, page 1840,
    October 15, 1953
Commonweal, Volume 59, page 39,
    October 16, 1953
Catholic World, Volume 90, page 82,
    October 17, 1953
Life, Volume 35, pages 6-8, October 19,
    1953
Films in Review, Volume 4, page 478,
    ff9, November, 1953
Natural History, Volume 62, page 429,
    November, 1953
Senior Scholastic, Volume 63, page 41,
    November 11, 1953
Nation, Volume 177, page 434,
    November 21, 1953
BFI Monthly Film Bulletin, Volume 20,
    page 173, December, 1953
National Parent-Teacher, Volume 48,
    page 39, December, 1953
Holiday, Volume 15, page 17, January, 1954

See: AB21, AB27, AB47, AB48, AB59, AB61, AB77, AB96,
    AB125, AB132, AB144, AB161, AB172, AB222, AB234,
    AN47-48, AP76, AP80, AP88-95, AP97, AP248

F35   KNIGHTS OF THE ROUND TABLE

M-G-M, released January 7, 1954, 115 minutes
Available on video cassette (M-G-M/United)

Director: Richard Thorpe
Producer: Pandro S. Berman
Screenplay: Talbot Jennings, Jan Lustig, and
                 Noel Langley

Based on Le Morte d'Arthur, by Sir Thomas Malory

Starring: Robert Taylor (Sir Lancelot), Ava Gardner
                 (Guinivere), Anne Crawford (Morgan Le
                 Fay), Stanley Baker (Sir Mordred),
                 Felix Aylmer (Merlin), Maureen Swanson
                 (Elaine), Gabriel Woolf (Percival),
                 Anthony Forwood (Gareth), Robert
                 Urquhart (Gawaine), Niall MacGinnis
                 (Green Knight), Ann Hanslip (Nan), Jill
                 Clifford (Bronwyn), and Stephen Vercal
                 (Agravaine)

Story: Costume piece filmed on location in England
                and Ireland which depicts the story of King
                Arthur, his court, his loves, his friends,
                and enemies through the time of his death,
                as taken from Books VI and XI of the epic
                poem of the 15th Century written by Sir
                Thomas Malory. Ava is Guinevere, who has
                passion and adultery on her mind.

Reviews: New York Times, Section II, page 5,
                     November 22, 1953
                Film Daily, page 6, December 23, 1953
                Variety, page 6, December 23, 1953
                Motion Picture Herald Prod. Digest,
                     page 2117, December 26, 1953
                Look, Volume 17, page 34, December 29, 1953
                New York Times, page 17, January 8, 1954
                New York Times, Section II, page 5,
                     January 10, 1954
                Library Journal, Volume 79, page 139,
                     January 15, 1954
                America, Volume 90, page 407, January 16,
                     1954
                New Yorker, Volume 29, pages 85-86,
                     January 16, 1954
                Saturday Review, Volume 37, page 32,
                     January 16, 1954
                Newsweek, Volume 43, page 88, January 18,
                     1954
                Life, Volume 36, pages 108-110, January 25,
                     1954
                Time, Volume 63, page 110, January 25, 1954
                Commonweal, Volume 59, page 427, January 29,
                     1954
                Films in Review, Volume 5, page 90, February,
                     1954
                Scholastic, Volume 64, page 27, Febraury 3,
                     1954
                Catholic World, Volume 178, page 460, March,
                     1954
                Farm Journal, Volume 78, page 94, March, 1954
                National Parent-Teacher, Volume 48, page 38,
                     March, 1954
                London Times, page 8, May 14, 1954
                Spectator, Volume 194, page 613, May 21, 1954
                New Statesman and Nation, Volume 47, page 661,
                     May 22, 1954
                Tatler, Volume 63, page 462, May 26, 1954
                Films and Filming, Volume 5, page 37,
                     June, 1963
                BFI Monthly Film Bulletin, Volume 21,
                     page 100, July, 1954

See: AB75, AB133, AB148, AB163, AN51-2, AP98-104

F36   THE BAREFOOT CONTESSA

United Artists, released September 29, 1954, 128 minutes
Available on video cassette (United Artists)

Director: Joseph L. Mankiewicz
Producer: Forrest Johnson
Screenplay: Joseph L. Mankiewicz
Music: Mario Nascimbene
Photography: Jack Cardiff

Starring: Humphrey Bogart (Harry Dawes), Ava Gardner
                 (Maria Vargas), Edmond O'Brien (Oscar
                 Muldoon), Marius Goring (Alberto Bravano),
                 Valentina Cortesa (Eleanora Torlato-
                 Favrini), Rossano Brazzi (Vincenzo Torlato-
                 Favrini), Warren Stevens (Kirk Edwards),
                 Elizabeth Sellars (Jerri), Franco
                 Interlenghi (Pedro), Mari Aldon (Myrna),
                 Maria Zanoli (Maria's mother), Renato
                 Chiantoni (Maria's father), Tonio Selwart
                 (the Pretender), and Margaret Anderson
                 (the Pretender's wife)

Story: In flashbacks told at her funeral, Maria's
                 life is given from her rise as a poor girl
                 from the Madrid slums to fame as an actress
                 to her marriage to rich aristocrat (Brazzi),
                 who kills her after thinking she has cheated
                 on him. Mankiewicz won an Oscar nomination
                 for his screenplay. O'Brien won an Academy
                 Award for Best Supporting Actor. Ava was
                 dubbed "The World's Most Exciting Animal."

Reviews: Film Daily, page 6, September 27, 1954
                 Hollywood Reporter, page 3, September 27,
                     1954
                 Variety, page 6, September 29, 1954
                 New York Times, page 37, September 30, 1954
                 Films in Review, Volume 5, page 430,
                     October, 1954
                 Motion Picture Herald Prod. Digest,
                     page 169, October 2, 1954
                 Newsweek, Volume 44, page 86, October 4, 1954
                 Commonweal, Volume 61, page 15, October 8,
                     1954
                 New Yorker, Volume 30, page 173, October 9,
                     1954
                 Saturday Review, Volume 37, page 31,
                     October 16, 1954
                 Time, Volume 64, page 102, October 18, 1954

Saturday Review, Volume 37, page 8,
    October 23, 1954
America, Volume 92, page 139, October 30,
    1954
Catholic World, Volume 180, page 138,
    November, 1954
Coronet, Volume 37, page 6, November, 1954
Farm Journal, Volume 78, page 73, November,
    1954
National Parent-Teacher, Volume 49, page 39,
    November, 1954
New York Times, Section II, page 1,
    November 3, 1954
London Times, page 10, November 8, 1954
The New Statesman and Nation, Volume 48,
    page 612, November 13, 1954
Illustrated London News, page 962,
    November 27, 1954
BFI Monthly Film Bulletin, Volume 21,
    page 170, December, 1954
Films and Filming, Volume 1, page 18,
    December, 1954
Films and Filming, Volume 1, page 21,
    January, 1955
Sight and Sound, Volume 24, page 146,
    January-March, 1955

See: AB1, AB8, AB10-12, AB14, AB43, AB55, AB65-66,
    AB71, AB77, AB105, AB131, AB135, AB148, AB159,
    AB172-3, AB176-77, AB179-80, AN53, AP109,
    AP111-120, AP173

F37   AROUND THE WORLD IN 80 DAYS

United Artists, released 1956, 167 minutes
Available on video cassette (United Artists)

Director: Michael Anderson
Producer: Michael Todd
Screenplay: S. J. Perelman

Based on the novel by Jules Verne

Starring: David Niven (Phineas Fogg), Cantinflas
                (Passepartout), Robert Newton (Mr. Fix),
                Shirley MacLaine (Princess Aouda), with:
                Robert Morley, Trevor Howard, Finlay
                Currie, Basil Sydney, Ronald Squires;
                cameos: Charles Boyer, Joe E Brown,
                Martine Carol, John Carradine, Charles
                Coburn, Ronald Colman, Melville Cooper,
                Nöel Coward, Reginald Denny, Andy Devine,
                Marlene Dietrich, Luis Miguel Dominguin,
                Fernandel, Sr. John Gielgud, Hermoine
                Ginghold, Jose Greco, Sir Cedric Hardwicke,
                Glynis Johns, Buster Keaton, Evelyn Keyes,
                Beatrice Lillie, Peter Lorre, Edmund
                Lowe, Victor McLaglen, as well as:

Tim McCoy, A. E. Matthews, Mike Mazurki,
John Mills, Alan Mowbray, Edward R.Murrow,
Jack Oakie, George Raft, Gilbert Roland,
Cesar Romero, Frank Sinatra, Red Skelton,
Harcourt Williams, and Ava Gardner

Reviews: Holiday, Volume 20, page 77, October, 1956
                Theatre Arts, Volume 40, page 18, October,
                        1956
                Film Daily, page 6, October 18, 1956
                Hollywood Reporter, page 3, October 18, 1956
                New York Times, Section II, page 1,
                        October 21, 1956
                Life, Volume 41, page 81, October 22, 1956
                Variety, page 6, October 24, 1956
                New Yorker, Volume 32, page 155, October 27,
                        1956
                New York Times, Section II, page 1,
                        October 28, 1956
                Newsweek, Volume 48, page 98, October 29,
                        1956
                Time, Volume 68, page 72, October 29, 1956
                Films In Review, Volume 7, page 457,
                        November, 1956
                Good Housekeeping, Volume 143, page 68,
                        November, 1956
                Travel, Volume 106, page 54, November, 1956
                America, Volume 96, page 140, November 3,
                        1956
                Saturday Review, Volume 39, page 28,
                        November 3, 1956
                Newsweek, Volume 48, page 114, November 5,
                        1956
                Commonweal, Volume 65, page 151, November 9,
                        1956
                Nation, Volume 183, page 417, November 10,
                        1956
                Library Journal, Volume 81, page 2676,
                        November 15, 1956
                National Parent-Teacher, Volume 51, page 38,
                        December, 1956
                Nation, Volume 183, page 470, December 1,
                        1956
                Scholastic, Volume 69, page 53, December 6,
                        1956
                Look, Volume 20, page 144, December 11, 1956
                Catholic World, Volume 184, page 301,
                January, 1957
                Reporter, Volume 16, page 36, January 24, 1957
                BFI Monthly Film Bulletin, Volume 24, page 94,
                        July, 1957
                Films and Filming, Volume 3, page 23,
                        August, 1957

> Christian Century, Volume 75, page 1239,
>   October 29, 1958
> Saturday Review, Volume 42, page 41,
>   March 14, 1959
> Classic Film Collector, Volume 65, page 20,
>   September, 1979
> Film News, Volume 36, page 38, November-
>   December, 1979
> New York Times, Section III, page 1,
>   January 20, 1984

See: AB99, AB145, AB146

F38   BHOWANI JUNCTION

M-G-M, U.S.-British, released October 29, 1956,
110 minutes
Available on video cassette (M-G-M/United)

Director:	George Cukor
Producer:	Pandro S. Berman
Screenplay:	Sonya Levien and Ivan Moffat
Music:	Miklos Rozsa
Photography:	F. A. Young
Costumes:	Elizabeth Haffenden

Based on the novel by John Masters

Starring: Ava Gardner (Victoria Jones), Stewart
             Granger (Col. Rodney Savage), Bill Travers
             (Patrick Taylor), Abraham Sofaer (Surabhai),
             Marne Maitland (Govindaswami), Peter Illing
             (Ghanshyam), Edward Chapman (Thomas Jones),
             Freda Jackson (The Sadani), Lionel Jeffries
             (Lt. Graham McDaniel), and Alan Tivern (Ted
             Dunphy)

Story: Ava plays a half-caste girl who falls for a
             young British colonel in India during the
             second World War.

Reviews: Hollywood Reporter, page 3, May 4, 1956
             Film Daily, page 10, May 7, 1956
             Variety, page 6, May 9, 1956
             New York Times, Section II, page 5, May 15,
                 1956
             Scholastic, Volume 68, page 35, May 17, 1956
             Life, Volume 40, pae 126, May 21, 1956
             New York Times, page 26, May 25, 1956
             Catholic World, Volume 183, page 223, June,
                 1956
             Films in Review, Volume 7, page 287, June-
                 July, 1956

National Parent-Teacher, Volume 50, page 37,
        June, 1956
Library Journal, Volume 81, page 1437,
        June 1, 1956
New Yorker, Volume 32, page 130, June 2,
        1956
Saturday Review, Volume 39, page 25,
        June 2, 1956
New York Times, Section II, page 1,
        June 3, 1956
Time, Volume 67, page 9, June 4, 1956
Commonweal, Volume 64, page 251, June 8,
        1956
America, Volume 95, page 272, June 9, 1956
Newsweek, Volume 47, page 118, June 11, 1956
Films and Filming, Volume 2, page 23,
        September, 1956
BFI Monthly Film Bulletin, Volume 23,
        Page 112, November, 1956

See: AB89, AB144, AB150, AB176, AB178, AN54-55, AP122-130

F39   THE SUN ALSO RISES

20th Century-Fox, released September, 1957, 129 minutes
Available on video cassette (Films Inc.)

Director:	Henry King
Producer:	Darryl F. Zanuck
Screenplay:	Peter Viertel
Photography:	Leo Tover
Music:	Hugo Friedhofer
Conductor:	Lionel Newman
Editor:	William Mace
Art Director:	Lyle R. Wheeler and Mark-Lee Kirk
Set Decorator:	Walter M. Scott, Paul S. Fox, and Jack Stubbs
Wardrobe:	Charles Le Maire and Fontana Sisters
Sound:	Bernard Fredricks and Frank Moran

From the novel by Ernest Hemingway

Starring: Tyrone Power (Jake Barnes), Ava Gardner
            (Lady Brett Ashley), Mel Ferrer (Robert
            Cohn), Errol Flynn (Mike Campbell), Eddie
            Albert (Bill Gorton), Gregory Ratoff
            (Count Mippipopolous), Juliette Greco
            (Georgette), Marcel Dalio (Zizi), Henry
            Daniell (Doctor), and Robert Evans (Pedro
            Romero)

Story: Story of four "lost generation" expatriates
            who are essentially running away from them-
            selves. Ava plays a woman engaged to Flynn
            yet loves an American newspaper correspondent
            (Power).

Reviews: <u>New York Times</u>, Section II, page 5, May 5,
                1957
            <u>New York Times</u>, Section V, page 66, May 26,
                1957
            <u>Film Daily</u>, Volume 112, page 5, August 23,
                1957
            <u>Hollywood Reporter</u>, page 3, August 23, 1957
            <u>New York Times</u>, page 12, August 24, 1957
            <u>Variety</u>, page 6, August 28, 1957
            <u>Motion Picture Herald Prod. Digest</u>,
                Volume 208, page 514, August 31, 1957
            <u>New Yorker</u>, Volume 33, page 54, August 31,
                1957
            <u>Time</u>, Volume 70, page 59, September 2, 1957
            <u>America</u>, Volume 97, page 604, September 7,
                1957
            <u>Saturday Review</u>, Volume 40, page 25,
                September 7, 1957
            <u>Newsweek</u>, Volume 59, page 110, September 9,
                1957
            <u>Commonweal</u>, Volume 66, page 588,
                September 13, 1957
            <u>Life</u>, Volume 43, page 61, September 16, 1957
            <u>New Republic</u>, Volume 137, page 22,
                September 30, 1957
            <u>Film Culture</u>, Volume 3, page 17, October,
                1957
            <u>Films in Review</u>, Volume 58, page 405,
                October, 1957
            <u>Library Journal</u>, Volume 82, page 2351,
                October 1, 1957
            <u>Nation</u>, Volume 185, page 251, October 12,
                1957
            <u>Catholic World</u>, Volume 186, page 143,
                November, 1957
            <u>National Parent-Teacher</u>, Volume 52, page 39,
                November, 1957
            <u>BFI Monthly Film Bulletin</u>, Volume 24,
                page 148, December, 1957
            <u>Films and Filming</u>, Volume 4, page 23,
                December, 1957

    See: AB26, AB108, AB115, AB123, AB126, AB141, AB144,
        AB150, AB161, AB194, AN61, AB95, AP141-48, AP150-152

F40   THE LITTLE HUT

M-G-M.-British, released November 18, 1957, 98 minutes
Available on video cassette (M-G-M/United)

Director: Mark Robson
Producer: F. Hugh Herbert and Mark Robson
Screenplay: F. Hugh Herbert
Photography: F. A. Young
Music: Robert Farnon
Song: Eric Maschwitz, Marcel Stellman, and
                Peggy Cochrane

Costumes: Christian Dior

Based on a play by Andre Roussin and English stage
adaptation by Nancy Mitford

Starring: Ava Gardner (Lady Susan Ashlow), Stewart
                   Granger (Sir Philip Ashlow), David Niven
                   (Henry Brittingham-Brett), Walter Chiari
                   (Mario), Finlay Currie (Rev. Brittingham-
                   Brett), Jean Cadell (Mrs. Brittingham-
                   Brett), Jack Lambert (Capt. MacWade),
                   Henry Oscar (Mr. Trollope), Viola Lyel
                   (Miss Edwards), and Jaron Yaltan
                   (Indian gentleman)

Story: Silly comedy about a beautiful woman (Ava)
                   stranded on a desert island with her
                   husband and her boyfriend.

Reviews: New York Times, Section II, page 7,
                       September 9, 1956
                   Catholic World, Volume 185, page 64,
                       April, 1957
                   Saturday Review, Volume 40, page 27,
                       April, 1957
                   Library Journal, Volume 82, page 1193,
                       May 1, 1957
                   Film Daily, Volume III, page 6, May 3, 1957
                   Hollywood Reporter, page 3, May 3, 1957
                   New York Times, page 25, May 4, 1957
                   Motion Picture Herald Prod. Digest,
                       Volume 207, page 369, May 11, 1957
                   New Yorker, Volume 33, page 152, May 11,
                       1957
                   Newsweek, Volume 49, page 116, May 13, 1957
                   Variety, page 6, May 15, 1957
                   Commonweal, Volume 66, page 183, May 17,
                       1957
                   BFI Monthly Film Bulletin, page 103,
                       August, 1957
                   Films and Filming, page 25, September, 1957
                   National Parent-Teacher, Volume 52,
                       page 33, September, 1957
                   Time, Volume 69, page 105, September, 1957

    See: AB74, AB89, AB176, AB204, AB212, AN56-57, AN82,
         AP133-135, AP138-140

F41   ON THE BEACH

      United Artists, released February 17, 1959, 135 minutes
      Available on video cassette (CBS/Fox Video)

      Director: Stanley Kramer
      Producer: Stanley Kramer
      Screenplay: John Paxton and James Lee Barrett
      Photography: Guisesppe Rotunno
      Music: Ernest Gold

Based on the novel by Nevil Shute

Starring: Gregory Peck (Dwight Towers), Ava Gardner
               (Moira Davidson), Fred Astaire (Julian
               Osborn), Anthony Perkins (Peter Holmes),
               Donna Anderson (Mary Holmes), John Tate
               (Admiral Birdie), Lola Brooks (Ltd. Hosgood),
               Guy Doleman (Ferrel), John Meillon (Swain),
               Harp McGuire (Sundstrom), Ken Wayne (Benson),
               Richard Meikle (Davis), Joe McCormick
               (Ackerman), and Lou Vernon (Davidson)

Story: The year is 1964 and a handful of people
               have survived the total nuclear destruction
               of the earth. From Australia, they take a
               submarine to San Diego and find that they
               are indeed the last ones to survive.

Reviews: Film Facts, Volume 2, page 299, January 6,
                    1959
               New York Times, Section II, page 7,
                    March 8, 1959
               Saturday Review, Volume 42, page 32,
                    October 24, 1959
               McCall's, Volume 87, page 6, November, 1959
               Life, Volume 47, page 93, November 30, 1959
               Coronet, Volume 47, page 18, December, 1959
               Film Daily, Volume 116, page 10, December 2,
                    1959
               Hollywood Reporter, page 3, December 2, 1959
               Variety, page 6, December 2, 1959
               Science News Letter, Volume 76, page 390,
                    December 5, 1959
               New Republic, Volume 141, page 21,
                    December 14, 1959
               New York Times, page 36, December 17, 1959
               New York Times, page 34, December 18, 1959
               Science, Volume 130, page 1679,
                    December 18, 1959
               America, Volume 102, page 381, December 19,
                    1959
               New York Times, Section II, page 3,
                    December 20, 1959
               Newsweek, Volume 54, page 95, December 21,
                    1959
               Commonweal, Volume 71, page 374,
                    December 25, 1959
               Time, Volume 74, page 44, December 28, 1959
               Nation, Volume 190, page 20, January 2, 1960
               New York Times, Section II, page 1,
                    January 17, 1960
               BFI Monthly Film Bulletin, Volume 27,
                    page 21, February, 1960

Films in Review, Volume 11, page 124,
    February, 1960
Science, Volume 133, page 1271, April 21,
    1960
Catholic World, Volume 190, pages 80-85,
    May, 1960
Commentary, Volume 29, page 522, June, 1960

See: AB10, AB44, AB76, AB83, AB121-122, AB131, AB140,
    AB144, AB148, AB172, AB183, AB191, AB202, AB210,
    AN62, AN64-66, AP160-161, AP163-173

F42   THE NAKED MAJA

United Artists-Titanus-M-G-M/American-Italian,
released November 29, 1959, 112 minutes
Available on video cassette (M-G-M/United)

Director: Henry Koster
Producer: Goffredo Lombardo
Screenplay: Giorgio Prosperi, Norman Corwin,
                   Albert Lewin, and Oscar Saul
Photography: Guiseppe Rotunno
Music: Francisco Lavagnino

Starring: Anthony Quinn (Francisco Goya), Ava
                   Gardner (Duchess of Alba), Lea Padovani
                   (Queen Maria Luisa), Gino Cervi (King
                   Charles IV), with: Massimo Serato, Carlo
                   Rizzo, Renzo Cesana, and Armedeo Nazzari

Story: Fictionalized version of the life of 18th
                   Century Spanish painter during the time
                   of the Spanish Inquisition. Goya paints
                   a portrait of the Duchess of Alba and falls
                   in love with her. He is arrested but
                   released upon the intercession of King
                   Charles. She is poisoned by an evil
                   aristocrat but forecasts a great future
                   for Goya before she dies.

Reviews: Time, Volume 73, page 90, April 6, 1959
                   Newsweek, Volume 53, page 115, April 20,
                       1959
                   Commonweal, Volume 70, page 102,
                       April 24, 1959
                   America, Volume 101, page 378, May 23, 1959
                   Catholic World, Volume 189, page 239,
                       June, 1959
                   New York Times, page 36, June 11, 1959
                   New Yorker, page 72, June 20, 1959
                   New York Times, page 15, July 2, 1959

See: AB152, AP154-159, AP274

F43   THE ANGEL WORE RED

M-G-M/American-Italian, released 1960, 105 minutes
Available on video cassette (M-G-M/United)

Director: Nunnally Johnson
Producer: Goffredo Lombardo
Screenplay: Nunnally Johnson
Photography: Guiseppe Rotunno
Music: Bronislau Kaper

Starring: Ava Gardner (Soledad), Joseph Cotten
             (Hawthorne), Dirk Bogarde (Father Arturo
             Carrera), and Vittorio de Sica (General
             Clave), with: Aldo Fabrizi, Arnoldo Foa,
             Finlay Currie, Rossana Rory, Enrico Maria
             Salerno, Robert Bright, and Nino
             Castelneuovo

Story: Grim drama of a scarlet woman who falls in
             love with a spoiled priest.

Reviews: Newsweek, Volume 56, page 102,
                  September 12, 1960
             Time, Volume 76, page 80, September 12, 1960
             Commonweal, Volume 73, page 17,
                  September 30, 1960
             America, Volume 104, page 26, October 1,
                  1960

See: AB151, AN68, AP174-177

F44   55 DAYS AT PEKING

Allied Artists, released 1962, 154 minutes
Available on video cassette (Budget Films)

Director: Nicholas Ray
Producer: Samuel Bronston
Screenplay: Philip Yordan and Bernard Gordon
Photography: Jack Hilyard
Music: Dimitri Tiomkin

Starring: Charlton Heston (Maj. Matt Lewis), David
             Niven (Sir Arthur Robertson), Ava Gardner
             (Baroness Natalie Ivanoff), Robert Helpmann
             (Prince Tuan), Flora Robson (Dowager
             Empress Tzu Hsi), Leo Genn (General Jung-Lu),
             Elizabeth Sellars (Lady Sarah Robertson),
             John Ireland (Sgt. Harry), Paul Lukas
             (Dr. Steinfeldt), Harry Andrews (Father
             de Bearn), Nicholas Ray (American
             Ambassador)

Kurt Kasznar (Baron Sergei Ivanoff) and
Alfred Lynch (Gerald)

Story: Fictionalized version of the Boxer
              Rebellion in China at the turn of the
              century. An American marine (Heston)
              tries to get foreigners out of China.
              Ava plays a Russian baroness who lives in
              a hotel. Her brother-in-law tries to
              steal her diamond necklace, so Heston gives
              her haven in his room.   During the
              uprising, she later becomes a nurse and
              eventually is shot and killed. Heston is
              the only survivor.

Reviews: New York Times, Section II, page 11,
                 December 9, 1962
              Film Daily, page 4, May 1, 1963
              Hollywood Reporter, page 3, May 1, 1963
              Variety, page 6, May 1, 1963
              International London News, Volume 242,
                 page 822, May 25, 1963
              New York Times, page 20, May 30, 1963
              Time, Volume 81, page 80, May 31, 1963
              BFI Monthly Film Bulletin, page 78,
                 June, 1963
              Films and Filming, page 28, June, 1963
              New Yorker, Volume 39, page 68,
                 June 1, 1963
              Newsweek, Volume 61, page 83, June 6,
                 1963
              Film Facts, page 101, June 6, 1963
              America, page 26, July 6, 1963
              Movie, page 46, July 8, 1963
              National Review, page 72, July 30, 1963

See: AB85, AB109, AB204, AB212, AN69-70, AP181-182

F45   SEVEN DAYS IN MAY

       Paramount/7 Arts/Joel production, released 1964,
       120 minutes
       Available on video cassette (Films Inc.)

       Director: John Frankenheimer
       Producer: Edward Lewis
       Screenplay: Rod Serling
       Photography: Ellsworth Fredericks
       Editor: Ferris Webster
       Art Director: Cary Odell
       Music: Jerry Goldsmith

       From the novel by Fletcher Knebel and Charles W.
       Bailey

Starring: Burt Lancaster (Gen. James M. Scott), Kirk
              Douglas (Col. Martin Casey), Fredric
              March (President Jordan Lyman), Ava Gardner
              (Eleanor Holbrook), Edmond O'Brien (Paul
              Girard), George Macready (Christopher Todd),
              Whit Bissell (Senator Prentice), Hugh
              Marlowe (Harold McPherson), Bart Burns
              (Arthur Corwin), Richard Anderson (Col.
              Murdock), Jack Mullaney (Lt. Hough),
              Andrew Duggan (Col. "Mutt" Henderson),
              John Larkin (Col. Broderick), Malcolm
              Atterbury (White House doctor), Helen Kleeb
              (Esther Townsend), John Houseman (Admiral
              Barnswell), and Collette Jackson (bar girl)

Story: Suspense film about a possible overthrow of
              the American government by the military.
              Ava is the former mistress of the Chief of
              Staff (Lancaster).

Reviews: Look, Volume 27, page 90, November 19, 1963
              Saturday Review, Volume 47, page 25,
                    February 1, 1964
              Film Daily, Volume 124, page 8,
                    February 2, 1964
              Hollywood Reporter, Volume 179, page 3,
                    February 2, 1964
              Motion Picture Herald Prod. Digest,
                    Volume 231, page 985, February 5, 1964
              Variety, page 6, February 5, 1964
              Vogue, Volume 143, page 20, February, 1964
              New York Times, page 22, February 20, 1964
              Time, Volume 83, page 94, February 21, 1964
              New Yorker, Volume 40, page 112,
                    February 22, 1964
              Newsweek, Volume 63, page 89, February 24,
                    1964
              Commonweal, Volume 79, page 632,
                    February 27, 1964
              Senior Scholastic, Volume 84, page 21,
                    February 28, 1964
              Films in Review, Volume 15, page 171,
                    March, 1964
              New York Times, Section II, page 1,
                    March 1, 1964
              America, Volume 110, page 323, March 7, 1964
              New Republic, Volume 150, page 35, March 7,
                    1964
              Nation, Volume 198, page 251, March 9, 1964
              BFI Monthly Film Bulletin, Volume 31,
                    page 71, May, 1964
              Esquire, Volume 61, page 14, June, 1964

See: AB41, AB144, AB195, AB205, AN71, AP183, AP185-190

F46   NIGHT OF THE IGUANA

M-G-M/Seven Arts, released October 5, 1964, 118 minutes
Available on video cassette (M-G-M/United)

Director: John Huston
Executive Prod.   Abe Steinberg
Producer: Ray Stark
Screenplay: Anthony Veiller and John Huston
Photography: Gabriel Figueroa
Editor: Ralph Kemplen
Art Director: Stephen Grimes
Music: Benjamin Frankel
Sound: Basil Fenton Smith and Leslie Hodgson

Based on the play by Tennessee Williams

Starring: Richard Burton (Rev. Laurence Shannon),
             Ava Gardner (Maxine Faulk), Deborah Kerr
             (Hannah Jelkes), Sue Lyon (Charlotte
             Goodall), James "Skip" Ward (Hank Prosner),
             Grayson Hall (Judith Fellows), Cyril
             Delevanti (Nonno), and Mary Boylan (Miss
             Peebles)

Story: Ava is a bawdy owner of a run-down Mexican
             resort hotel where a defrocked cleric
             (Burton) turns tourist guide. Conflicts
             arise between Ava, Burton, and Kerr, who
             plays a penniless drifter.

Reviews: Film Daily, Volume 124, page 3, July 1, 1964
             Hollywood Reporter, Volume 181, page 3,
                   July 1, 1964
             Variety, page 6, July 1, 1964
             Motion Picture Herald Prod. Digest,
                   July 8, 1964
             Life, Volume 57, page 11, July 10, 1964
             Boxoffice, Volume 85, page 2844,
                   July 13, 1964
             Time, Volume 84, page 86, July 17, 1964
             Films in Review, Volume 15, page 439,
                   August-September, 1964
             Sight and Sound, Volume 33, page 199,
                   August, 1964
             America, Volume III, page 61, August 15, 1964
             Commonweal, Volume 80, page 580,
                   August 21, 1964
             BFI Monthly Film Bulletin, Volume 31,
                   page 146, October, 1964
             Films and Filming, Volume 11, page 28,
                   October, 1964

See: AB51, AB81, AB91, AB104, AB117, AB118, AB155,
     AB161, AB172, AB235, AN72-73, AP184, AP190-201

F47   THE BIBLE

20th Century-Fox, released 1966, 175 minutes
Available on video cassette (Films Inc.)

Director:	John Huston
Producer:	Dino De Laurentiis
Screenplay:	Christopher Fry, Jonathan Griffin, Ivo Perilli, Vittorio Bonicelli
Photography:	Guiseppe Rotunno
Editor:	Ralph Kemplen
Art Direction:	Mario Chiari
Set Decoration:	Enzo Eusepi and Bruno Avesani
Special Effects:	Augie Lohman
Music:	Toshiro Mazazumi
Costumes:	Maria De Matteis
Choreography:	Katherine Dunham
Sound:	Fred Hynes

Starring: Michael Parks (Adam), Ulla Bergryd (Eve),
Richard Harris (Cain), John Huston (Noah
and God), Stephen Boyd (Nimrod), George C.
Scott (Abraham), Ava Gardner (Sarah),
Peter O'Toole (Three Angels), Zoe Sallis
(Hagar), Gabriele Ferzetti (Lot), Eleanor
Rossi Drago (Lot's wife), Franco Nero (Abel),
Alberto Lucantoni (Isaac)

Story: Huston narrates this epic translation of
the Old Testament. Ava plays Sarah, barren
wife of Abraham. After he takes Hagar to
bear him a child, Sarah is visited by an
Angel and told she will bear a child
(Isaac).

Reviews: Sight and Sound, Volume 35, page 199,
              August, 1966
          Christian Century, Volume 83, page 1083,
              September 7, 1966
          Film Daily, page 38, September 28, 1966
          Hollywood Reporter, page 3, September 28,
              1966
          Motion Picture Herald Prod. Digest,
              Pages 13, 26, September 28, 1966
          Variety, page 6, September 28, 1966
          New York Times, page 60, September 29, 1966
          Catholic World, Volume 204, page 64,
              October, 1966
          Films in Review, Volume 17, page 517,
              October, 1966
          Harper's Magazine, Volume 233, page 132,
              October, 1966
          New Yorker, Volume 42, page 184, October 1,
              1966

Saturday Review, Volume 49, page 34,
        October 1, 1966
Vogue, Volume 148, page 162, October 1, 1966
Newsweek, Volume 68, page 105, October 3,
        1966
Life, Volume 61, page 22, October 7, 1966
Time, Volume 88, page 119, October 7, 1966
America, Volume 115, page 433, October 8,
        1966
Illustrated London News, Volume 249, page 11,
        October 8, 1966
Christian Science Monitor, page 6, (Western
        Edition), October 10, 1966
Motion Picture Herald Prod. Digest,
        Page 614, October 12, 1966
Spectator, Volume 217, page 487, October 14,
        1966
Filmfacts, Volume 9, page 213-17,
        October 15, 1966
London Times, page 18, October 16, 1966
Look, Volume 30, page 104, October 18, 1966
Commonweal, Volume 85, page 79, October 21,
        1966
New Republic, Volume 155, page 30,
        October 22, 1966
BFI Monthly Film Bulletin, Volume 33,
        page 163, November, 1966
Films and Filming, Volume 13, page 8,
        November, 1966
Playboy, Volume 13, pages 32, 34, November,
        1966
Reporter, Volume 35, page 56, November 3,
        1966
Senior Scholastic, Volume 89, page 26,
        November 11, 1966
Christian Century, Volume 83, page 1410,
        November 16, 1966
Cinema, Volume 3, page 47, December, 1966
National Review, Volume 19, page 428,
        April 18, 1967
Film Quarterly, Volume 20, pages 11-22,
        Summer, 1967

See: AB10, AB17, AB20, AB32, AB91, AB148, AB153, AB172,
    AN75-76, AP202-213, AP214, AP216, AP228

F48 MAYERLING

M-G-M/Associated British/Warner-Pathe', released
October 5, 1970, 140 minutes
Available on video cassette (M-G-M/United)

Director: Terence Young
Producer: Robert Dorfmann
Screenplay: Terence Young
Photography: Henri Alekan

Music: Francis Lai

From the novel by Claude Anet; historical documentation
from The Archduke by Michael Arnold

Starring: Omar Sharif (Rudolf), Catherine Deneuve
             (Maria Vetsera), James Mason (Franz-Josef),
             Ava Gardner (Elizabeth), James Robertson
             Justice (Prince of Wales), Genevieve Page
             (Countess Larisch), Ivan Desny (Count
             Hoyos), Andrea Parisy (Stephanie), Fabienne
             Dali (Mizzi Kaspar), Maurice Teynac (Szeps),
             Moustache (Bratfisch), Bernard Lajarrige
             (Loschek), and Veronique Vendell (Lisl
             Stockau)

Story: Beautifully photographed tragedy of the
             real Austrian Crown Prince Rudolf who falls
             in love with a commoner. Ava plays the
             Prince's mother.

Reviews: New York Times, page 25, February 14, 1969
             Senior Scholastic, Volume 94, page 27,
                  February 14, 1969
             Look, Volume 33, page 66, February 18, 1969
             Life, Volume 66, page 10, February 21, 1969
             Time, Volume 93, page 87, February 21, 1969
             Holiday, Volume 45, page 31, March, 1969
             New Yorker, Volume 45, page 71, March 1, 1969
             America, Volume 120, page 288, March 8, 1969

See: AB110, AB172

F49   THE LIFE AND TIMES OF JUDGE ROY BEAN

First Artists Productions/National General, released
1972, 124 minutes
Available on video cassette (Films Inc.)

Director: John Huston
Producer: John Foreman
Assoc. Producer: Frank Caffey
Assoc. Director: Mickey McCardle
Screenplay: John Milius
Photography: Richard Moore
Editor: Hugh S. Fowler
Art Direction: Tambi Larsen
Set Decoration: Robert Benton
Music: Maurice Jarre
Song: Maurice Jarre, Marilyn and Alan
                    Bergman
Sound Editor: Keith Stafford
Sound Recording: Larry Jost

Starring: Paul Newman (Judge Roy Bean), Jacqueline
                Bisset (Rose Bewan), Ava Gardner (Lily
                Langtry), Tab Hunter (Sam Dodd), John
                Huston (Grizzly Adams), Stacy Keach
                (Bad Bob), Roddy McDowall (Frank Gass),
                Victoria Principal (Marie Elena),
                Anthony Zerbe (Hustler), Ned Beatty
                (Hector Crites), Jim Burk (Bart Jackson),
                Matt Clark (Nick the Grub), Steve Kanaly
                (Whorehouse Jim Luck), Bill McKinney
                (Fermel Paree), Francesca Jarvis
                (Mrs. Jackson), Karen Carr (Mrs. Grub),
                Jack Colvin (Pimp), and Howard Morton
                (Photographer)

Story: Long, dull semi-western loosely based on
                the real "hanging" judge who named his
                town after Lily Langtry. Ava portrays
                Langtry, who comes to town (in a
                fictional visit) after Bean's death.

Reviews: Filmfacts, Volume 15, page 607, 1972
                Hollywood Reporter, page 3, December 7,
                   1972
                Variety, page 20, December 13, 1972
                New York Times, Volume 52, page 1,
                   December 19, 1972
                Time, Volume 100, page 75, December 25,
                   1972
                Commonweal, Volume 97, page 327,
                   January 12, 1973
                New Yorker, Volume 48, pages 86-88,
                   January 13, 1973
                New Republic, Volume 168, page 26,
                   January 20, 1973
                Senior Scholastic, Volume 102, page 18,
                   February 12, 1973

See: AB60, AB70, AB86, AB91, AB144, AB161, AB169,
     AB172, AB181, AN77-81, AP219, AP221, AP223-224

F50   THE DEVIL'S WIDOW (formerly TAM LIN)

Commonwealth United, released September, 1972,
107 minutes
Available on video cassette (Ivy Films)

Director: Roddy McDowall
Producer: Alan Ladd, Jr., and Stanley Mann
Screenplay: William Spier
Photography: Billy Williams
Editor: John Victor Smith
Music: Stanley Myers
Designer: Don Ashton
Songs: The Pentangle

Starring: Ava Gardner (Michaela), Ian McShane (Tom),
             Stephanie Beacham (Janet), Cyril Cusack
             (Vicar), Richard Wattis (Elroy), David
             Whitman (Oliver), Madeline Smith (Sue),
             Fabia Drake (Miss Gibson), Sinead Cusack
             (Rose), Jennie Hanley (Caroline), Joanna
             Lumley (Georgia), Pamela Farbrother (Vanna),
             Bruce Robinson (Alan), Rosemary Blake
             (Kate), Michael Bills (Michael), Peter
             Henwood (Guy), Heyward Morse (Andy), Julian
             Barnes (Terry), Oliver Norman (Peter), and
             Virginia Tingwell (Lottie)

Story: "Arty" film about Ava's attempts to keep
             her much-younger lover and his crowd from
             leaving her clutches.

Reviews: Saturday Review, Volume 54, page 73,
                  November 27, 1971

F51   THAT'S ENTERTAINMENT

M-G-M, released 1974, 137 minutes
Available on video cassette (M-G-M/United)

Producer: Jack Haley, Jr. and Daniel Melnick

Starring: Fred Astaire, Gene Kelly, Elizabeth Taylor,
             James Stewart, Bing Crosby, Liza Minnelli,
             Donald O'Connor, Debbie Reynolds, Mickey
             Rooney, and Frank Sinatra

Story: Wonderful compilation of M-G-M Studio's
             biggest movie hits and stars, with the
             above-mentioned stars as hosts. Ava was
             seen in scenes from Show Boat.

Reviews: Variety, page 16, April 17, 1974
             Motion Picture Herald Prod. Digest, page 93,
                  April 24, 1974
             Time, Volume 103, page 71, May 20, 1974
             New York, Volume 7, page 90, May 27, 1974
             New Yorker, Volume 50, pages 104-107,
                  June 10, 1974
             Commonweal, Volume 100, page 361, June 28,
                  1974
             Saturday Review, Volume 1, page 25,
                  June 29, 1974
             Atlantic, Volume 234, pages 95-97,
                  July, 1974
             Dance Magazine, Volume 48, page 30,
                  July, 1974

New York Times, Section II, page 1,
        July 7, 1974
Films in Review, Volume 25, pages 435-437,
        August-September, 1974
BFI Monthly Film Bulletin, Volume 41,
        page 231, October, 1974
New Statesman, Volume 88, page 479,
        October 4, 1974
Christian Century, Volume 91, page 1042,
        November 6, 1974

See: AB161, AB202

F52   EARTHQUAKE

Univeral/MCA, released November, 1974, 129 minutes
Available on video cassette (Swank Films)

Director:	Mark Robson
Exec. Producer:	Jennings Lang
Producer:	Mark Robson
Screenplay:	George Fox and Mario Puzo
Photography:	Philip Lathrop
Special Effects:	Frank Brendel, Jack McMasters, and Albert Whitlock
Sound:	Melvin M. Metcalfe, Sr., and Ronald Pierce
Music:	John Williams

Starring: Charlton Heston (Stuart Graff), Ava Gardner
            (Remy Graff), George Kennedy (Patrolman
            Lew Slade), Lorne Greene (Sam Royce),
            Genevieve Bujold (Denise Marshall),
            Richard Roundtree (Quade), Marjoe Gortner
            (Jody), Barry Sullivan (Dr. Stockle),
            Victoria Principal (Rosa), Lloyd Nolan
            (Dr. Vance), Walter Matthau (Drunk), Monica
            Lewis (Royce's secretary), Gabe Dell (Miles'
            manager), Pedro Armendariz, Jr. (Slade's
            partner), Lloyd Gough (Cameron), John
            Randolph (Mayor), Kip Niven (Assistant
            Seismologist), Tiger Williams (Corry Marshall),
            Donald Moffat (Dr. Harvey Johnson), Jesse
            Vint (Buck), Alan Vint (Ralph), George
            Murdoch (Sid)

Story: Executive (Heston) and his jealous wife
            (Gardner) are caught with hundreds who
            are trapped when a tremendous earthquake
            strikes Los Angeles.

Reviews: American Cinematographer, Volume 55,
page 1325, November, 1974
Hollywood Reporter, page 3, November 13,
1974
Variety, page 18, November 13, 1974
Los Angeles Times, Section IV, page 1,
November 15, 1974
New York Times, page 20, November 16, 1974
New York Times, Section II, page 1,
November 24, 1974
Independent Film Journal, Volume 74,
page 5, November 27, 1974
Motion Picture Herald Prod. Digest, page 51,
November 27, 1974
New York, Volume 7, page 76, December 2,
1974
New Yorker, Volume 50, page 152-154,
December 2, 1974
Newsweek, Volume 84, page 104, December 2,
1974
Time, Volume 104, page 4, December 9, 1974
Village Voice, page 90, December 23, 1974
BFI Monthly Film Bulletin, Volume 42,
page 7, January, 1975
Films in Review, Volume 26, page 47,
January, 1975
Commonweal, Volume 102, page 52, April 11,
1975

See: AB58, AB85-86, AB100, AB109, AB145, AB172, AB221,
AN83-85, AP229-235

F53   PERMISSION TO KILL

Columbia/Warner, released 1975, 96 minutes

Director: Cyril Frankel
Producer: Paul Miles
Screenplay: Robin Estridge
Photography: Eddie Young

From the novel by Robin Estridge

Starring: Dirk Bogarde (Alan Curtis), Ava Gardner
(Katina Peterson), Bekim Fehmiu
(Alexander Diakim), and Timothy Dalton
(Charles Lord)

Story: Spy chief Bogarde tries to prevent Fehmiu
from returning to his dictator-controlled
country in this thriller.

See: AB101

F54   THE BLUE BIRD

20th Century-Fox/Len Films, USSR, released May, 1976,
100 minutes
Available on video cassette (Williams Films)

Director: George Cukor
Producers: Edward Lewis, Paul Maslansky, and
                     Alexander Archansky
Screenplay: Hugh Whitemore and Alfred Hayes
Photography: Freddie Young and Jonas Gritzus
Editor: Ernest Walter
Music: Irwin Kostal
Songs/Ballet: Andrei Petrov
Lyrics: Tony Harrison

Based on the play The Blue Bird by Maurice
Maerterlinck

Starring: Elizabeth Taylor (Mother, Maternal Love,
                     Witch, Light), Jane Fonda (Night), Ava
                     Gardner (Luxury), Cicely Tyson (Cat),
                     Robert Morley (Father Time), Harry Andrews
                     (Oak), Todd Lookinland (Twityl), Patsy
                     Kensit (Mytyl), Will Geer (Grandfather),
                     Mona Washbourne (Grandmother), George
                     Cole (Dog), Richard Pearson (Bread),
                     Nadia Pavlova (Blue Bird), George Vitzin
                     (Sugar), Margareta Terechova (Milk),
                     Oleg Popov (Fat Laughter), Leonid
                     Nevedomsky (Father), Valentina Ganilae
                     Ganibalova (Water), and Yevgeny Scherbakov
                     (Fire), with the Leningrad Kirov Ballet

Story: United States/Russia co-production about
                     children seeking the Blue Bird of
                     Happiness in this star-studded musical
                     fantasy.

Reviews: Films and Filming, pages 18-19, April,
                        1976
                     Hollywood Reporter, page 3, May 5, 1976
                     Variety, page 34, May 12, 1976
                     New York Times, Section II, page 17,
                        1976
                     Newsweek, Volume 87, page 111, May 17,
                        1976
                     Los Angeles Times, Section I, page 1,
                        May 19, 1976
                     New York, pages 75-76, May 24, 1976
                     New Yorker, Volume 52, pages 138-139,
                        May 24, 1976
                     Independent Film Journal, page 7,
                        May 28, 1976

Films in Review, Volume 27, page 377,
        June-July, 1976
Motion Picture Herald Prod. Digest, page 2,
        June 3, 1976
Time, Volume 107, page 67, June 14, 1976
Vogue, Volume 166, page 26, July, 1976
Film Comment, Volume 12, page 22, July-
        August, 1976

See: AB157, AB158-59, AN86-87, AN89, AP236-240,
    AP242, AP270

F55 THE CASSANDRA CROSSING

International Cine Productions/United Kingdom-USA,
released Avco Embassy Anglo-Italian 1976-1977
Available on video cassette (Films Inc.)

Director: George Pan Cosmatos
Producer: Carlo Ponti
Screenplay: Robert Katz, George Pan Cosmatos,
                     and Tom Mankiewicz
Photography: Enio Guarniere
Editor: Francois Bonnot and Joe Pollini
Prod. Designer: Aurelio Crugnola
Sound: Carlo Palmiere
Costumes: Andriana Berselli
Music: Jerry Goldsmith

Starring: Sophia Loren (Jennifer), Richard Harris
             (Chamberlain), Ava Gardner (Nicole), Burt
             Lancaster (MacKenzie), Martin Sheen
             (Navarro), Ingrid Thulin (Elena), Lee
             Strasberg (Kaplan), John Philip Law (Stack),
             Ann Turkel (Susan), O. J. Simpson (Father
             Haley), and Lionel Stander (Conductor)

Story: Disaster movie filmed in France and
             Switzerland about a plague-carrying train
             nearing a weakened bridge.

Reviews: New York Times, page 48, February 10, 1977
             New West, Volume 2, page 82, February 14,
                 1977
             New York, Volume 10, page 55, February 28,
                 1977
             Philadelphia, Volume 68, page 52, March, 1977
             Chicago, Volume 26, page 76, April, 1977
             Playboy, Volume 24, page 38, April, 1977
             Connecticut, Volume 40, page 53, May, 1977

See: AN90, AN93

F56 THE SENTINEL

Universal, released 1977, 93 minutes
Available on video cassette (Swank Motion and Twyman
Films)

Director: Michael Winner
Producer: Michael Winner and Jeffrey Konvitz
Screenplay: Michael Winner and Jeffrey Konvitz
Photography: Dick Kratina
Editor: Bernard Gribble and Terence Rawlings
Designer: Philip Rosenberg
Set Decorations: Ed Stewart
Special Effects: Albert Whitlock
Costumes: Peggy Farrell
Makeup: Dick Smith and Bob Laden
Hairstyles: Bill Farley
Sound: Ted Mason, Les Lazarowitz

Starring: Chris Sarandon (Michael Lerman), Cristina
                Raines (Alison Parker), Burgess Meredith
                (Charles Chazen), Arthur Kennedy
                (Monsignor Franchino), Jose Ferrer (Robed
                Figure), Ava Gardner (Miss Logan), Martin
                Balsam (Professor Buzinsky), John
                Carradine (Father Halloran), Eli Wallach
                (Detective Gatz), Sylvia Miles (Gerde),
                Christopher Walken (Rizzo), Deborah Raffin
                (Jennifer), Beverly D'Angelo (Sandra),
                Fred Stuthman (Alison's father), Hank
                Garrett (Brenner), William Hickey (Perry),
                and Reid Shelton (Priest)

Story: Ava plays a rental agent who finds an
                apartment for Alison, who needs to get away
                from her fiance. The house she rents is a
                gateway to hell. Alison has been sent there
                to be a new sentinel, to prevent the armies
                of hell from invading the world.

Reviews: Hollywood Reporter, page 3, February 11, 1977
                Los Angeles Times, Section I, page 23,
                     February 11, 1977
                New York Times, page 12, February 12, 1977
                Variety, page 24, February 16, 1977
                America, Volume 136, page 170, February 26,
                     1977
                Newsweek, Volume 89, page 92, February 28,
                     1977
                Time, Volume 109, page 78, Febraury 28, 1977
                BFI Monthly Film Bulletin, Volume 44, page 51,
                     March, 1977

Films and Filming, Volume 23, pages 47-49,
            March, 1977
Films and Filming, Volume 23, page 31,
            April, 1977
See: AB134, AB166, AN91-92, AP244-245

F57   CITY ON FIRE

Avco Embassy, released August, 1979, 101 minutes
Available on video cassette (Films Inc.)

Director: Alvin Rakoff
Producer: Claude Heroux
Exec. Producer: Sandy Howard and Harold Greenberg
Screenplay: Jack Hill, David P. Lewis, and
                   Celine LaFreniere
Photography: Rene Verzier
Designer: William McCrow
Art Director: Claude Marchand
Editor: Jean Pol Passe, Jacques Clairoux
Costumes: Yvon Duhaime
Music: William McCauley and Matthew McCauley

Starring: Barry Newman (Frank Whitman), Susan Clark
                   (Diana), Shelley Winters (Nurse), Leslie
                   Nielsen (Mayor), James Franciscus (Jimbo),
                   Ava Gardner (Maggie), Henry Fonda (Fire
                   Chief), Jonathan Welsh (Herman), and
                   Richard Donat (Captain)

Story: Disaster film about an arsonist who torches
                   a local oil refinery and the fire spreads
                   to the entire city.

Reviews: New York Times, Section III, page 11,
                   September 14, 1979
See: AB176

F58   THE KIDNAPPING OF THE PRESIDENT

Crown International/Sefel Pictures International,
released August, 1980, 113 minutes
Available on video cassette

Director: George Mendeluk
Producer: Joseph Sefel, George Mendeluk, and
                   John Ryan
Screenplay: Richard Murphy
Photography: Michael Molloy
Music: Paul Zaza

Based on the book by Charles Templeton

Starring: William Shatner (Jerry O'Connor), Hal
             Holbrook (President Adam Scott), Van Johnson
             (Vice President Ethan Richards), Ava Gardner
             (Betty Richards), Miguel Fernandes (Roberto
             Assanti), Cindy Girling (Linda), Michael J.
             Reynolds (MacKenzie), Elizabeth Shepherd
             (Joan O'Connor), Gary Reineke (Dietrich),
             Maury Chaykin (Harvey), Murray Westgate
             (Archie), Michael Kane (Herb), with: Jackie
             Burroughs, Aubert Pallascio, Virginia
             Podesser, Elias Zarov, Larry Duran, Patrick
             Brymar, Gershon Resnik, John Stocker,
             Chappelle Jaffe, and John Romaine

Story: Third World terrorists kidnap the President.
             Ava played the long-suffering wife of the
             Vice President.

Reviews: New York Times, Section III, page 12,
                  August 15, 1980

See: AP250, AP262

F59   PRIEST OF LOVE

Filmways Pictures Inc.-Enterprise Pictures, Ltd., released
October, 1981, 125 minutes
Available on video cassette (Images Films)

Director: Christopher Miles
Producer: Christopher Miles and Andrew Donally
Screenplay: Alan Plater
Photography: Ted Moore
Designers: Ted Tester and David Brockhurst
Editor: Paul Davies
Costumes: Anthony Powell
Music: Joseph James

Based on the book by Harry T. Moore and the writings of
D. H. Lawrence

Starring: Ian McKellen (D.H. Lawrence), Janet Suzman
             (Frieda Lawrence), Ava Gardner (Mabel Dodge
             Luhan), Penelope Keith (The Honorable
             Dorothy Brett), Jorge Rivero (Tony Luhan),
             John Gielgud (Herbert G Muskett), James
             Faulkner (Aldous Huxley), Mike Gwilym (John
             Middleton Murry), Massimo Ranieri (Pini),
             Marjorie Yates (Ada Lawrence), Jane Booker
             (Barbara Weekley), Wendy Alnutt (Maria
             Huxley), and Elio Pandolfi (Orioli)

Story: This film depicts the last years of author
                D. H. Lawrence and his relationship with
                his wife, Frieda, and publication of <u>Lady
                Chatterly's Lover</u>.

Reviews: <u>Variety</u>, page 3, September 30, 1981
                <u>Saturday Review</u>, Volume 8, page 60,
                    October, 1981
                <u>Los Angeles Times</u>, Section V, page 2,
                    October 6, 1981
                <u>New York Times</u>, Section III, page 1,
                    October 11, 1981
                <u>New Republic</u>, Volume 185, pages 20-21,
                    October 21, 1981
                <u>National Review</u>, Volume 33, page 1498,
                    December 11, 1981

TELEVISION

T1 A.D.

International Film Productions/Proctor and Gamble
Productions, NBC presentation March 31-April 4, 1985,
12 hours

Director: Stuart Cooper
Producer: John A. Martinelli and Vincenzo
                 Labella
Screenplay: Vincenzo Labella and Anthony
                 Burgess
Photography: Ennio Guarnieri
Editor: John A. Martinelli
Music: Lalo Schifrin
Costumes: Enrico Sabbatini

Starring: Anthony Edwards (Nero), Colleen Dewhurst
                 (Antonia), Ava Gardner (Agrippina), David
                 Hedison (Porcius Festus), John Houseman
                 (Gamaliel), Richard Kiley (Claudius),
                 James Mason (Tiberius), John McEnergy
                 (Caligula), Ian McShane (Sejanus),
                 Jennifer O'Neill (Messalina), Millie
                 Perkins (Mary), Denis Quilley (Peter),
                 Fernando Rey (Seneca), Richard Roundtree
                 (Serpenius), Susan Sarandon (Livilla),
                 Ben Vereen (Ethiopian), Tony Vogel
                 (Aquila), Jack Warden (Nerva), Anthony
                 Zerbe (Pontius Pilate), Neil Dickson
                 (Valerius), Cecil Humphreys (Caleb),
                 Amanda Pays (Sarah), Philip Sayer
                 (Saul/Paul), Dian Venora (Corinna), and
                 Michael Wilding, Jr. (Jesus)

Story: Epic mini-series about the conflict between
            the Jewish zealots, early Christians, and
            Roman Empire (years 30-69 A.D). This marked
            Ava's television movie debut.

See: AN97-98, AP264

T2   THE LONG HOT SUMMER

Leonard Hill Films, NBC presentation October 6-7, 1985,
4 hours

Director: Stuart Cooper
Producer: Leonard Hill, John Thomas Lenox, and
                Dori Weiss
Screenplay: Irving Ravetch and Harriet Frank, Jr.
Teleplay: Rita Mae Brown and Dennis Turner
Photography: Reed Smoot and Steve Yaconelli
Editor: Dann Cahn
Music: Charles Bernstein
Designer: Jan Scott

From the novel The Hamlet by William Faulkner

Starring: Don Johnson (Ben Quick), Jason Robards, Jr.
            (Will Varner), Judith Ivey (Noel Varner),
            Cybill Shepherd (Eula Varner), Ava Gardner
            (Minnie Littlejohn), William Russ (Jody
            Varner), Wings Hauser (Wilson Mahood),
            Alexandra Johnson (Agnes Stewart), Stephen
            Davies (Alan Stewart), Charlotte Stanton
            (Mrs. Stewart), William Forsythe (Isaac),
            James Gammon (Billy Quick), Rance Howard
            (Wilk), Bill Thurman (Houstin), Robert Wentz
            (Ratliff), Irma Hall (Cecilia Howlett),
            Joe Berryman (Deputy Hampton), Patricia
            Rendleman (Lisa), Norman Bennett (Auctioneer),
            and Jerry Haynes (Lew)

Story: Television mini-series remake of the 1958
            film about an ambitious drifter and the
            southern family into which he insinuates
            himself.

T3   HAREM

Highgate Pictures/New World TV, ABC presentation
February 9-10, 1986, 4 hours

Director: Billy Hale
Producer: Martin Manulis, Frank Doelger,
                     Helen Vernon and Michael Dryhurst
Screenplay: Karol A. Hoeffner
Photography: Donald M. Morgan and Brian West
Editor: John F. Link II, Peter Boita, and
                     Jason Krasucki
Designer: Simond Holland
Art Direction: Clinton Cavers
Music: John Scott

Starring: Nancy Travis (Jessica Gray), Art Malik
             (Pasha), Sarah Miles (Lady Ashley), Yaphet
             Kotto (Kislar), Julian Sands (Forest),
             Cherie Lunghi (Usta), Omar Sharif (Sultan
             Hasan), Ava Gardner (Kadin), and Georgine
             Anderson (Aunt Lilly)

Story: Ava plays a jealous harem grand dame in
             this exotic adventure mini-series about
             the kidnapping of an American woman who
             is then forced to join the harem.

T4   KNOTS LANDING

Television series first telecast December 20, 1979 on
CBS, Thursday evenings 10:00-11:00 p.m.

Producer: Lorimar Productions

Starring: Ted Shackelford (Gary Ewing), Joan Van Ark
             (Valene Ewing), Michele Lee (Karen Fairgate
             MacKenzie), Donna Mills (Abby Cunningham
             Ewing), Julie Harris (Lilimae Clements),
             Kevin Dobson (Mack MacKenzie), William
             Devane (Gregory Sumner), Teri Austin (Jill
             Bennett), Nicollete Sheridan (Paige
             Matheson), Michelle Phillips (Anne W.
             Matheson), Peter Reckell (Johnny Rourke);
             guest cast: Don Murray (Sid Fairgate),
             John Pleshette (Richard Avery), Constance
             McCashin (Laura Avery Sumner), James
             Houghton (Kenny Ward), Kim Lankford (Giner
             Ward), Tonya Crowe (Olivia Cunningham), Jane
             Elliot (Judy Trent), Allan Miller (Scooter
             Warren), Stephen Macht (Joe Cooper), Lisa
             Hartman (Ciji Dunne; Cathy Geary Rush),
             Jon Cypher (Jeff Munson), Alec Baldwin
             (Joshua Rush), Howard Duff (Paul
             Galveston), Ava Gardner (Ruth Galveston),
             Ruth Roman (Sylvia Lean), Red Buttons (Al
             Baker), Lynne Moody (Patricia Williams)

Story: This CBS night-time soap opera was a spin-off
          from the Friday night CBS series <u>Dallas</u>.
          Gary Ewing was the black sheep of the Ewing
          family in Dallas, so he moves to southern
          California with his wife. He fights an
          alcoholic past and gets involved in the
          neighborhood problems. Ava played the
          widow of a congressman. She brought a
          tongue-in-cheek mystery to her role.

          Ava appeared in the following episodes:

          "The Deluge"   February 28, 1984
          "A Piece of The Pie"   March 7, 1985
          "Four No Trump"   April 11, 1985
          "A Price to Pay"   May 2, 1985
          "One Day in a Row"   May 9, 1985
          "Vulnerable"   May 16, 1985

See: AB207, AB213, AB216, AB232, AN97, AP263

RADIO PRODUCTIONS

R1   "Lady in Distress," Suspense, CBS, May 1, 1947

R2   Bob Hope Show, Pepsodent Production, from the El
     Capitan Theatre in Hollywood. Ava Gardner won Most
     Promising New Star of 1947 at the 1947 Look
     Achievement Awards for Outstanding Achievement in
     the Motion Picture Industry; Bob Hope was M.C.;
     February 3, 1948

R3   "Flesh and Fantasy," Screen Guild Players, R. J.
     Reynolds. Ava appeared as Joan; May 26, 1949

R4   Hollywood Calling, Ava appeared as a guest; July 24,
     1949

R5   Chesterfield Supper Club, Liggett and Meyers
     Production. Ava appeared as guest, September 29,
     1949

R6   "The Bribe," <u>Camel Screen Guild Theatre</u>, R. J.
      Reynolds Production. Ava appeared as Elizabeth
      Hintten in the episode based on her film of the
      same name, on November 10, 1949.

R7   <u>Bob Hope Show</u>, Liggett and Meyers Production; Ava was
      a guest on March 6, 1951

R8   <u>Screen Directors' Guild Annual Awards</u>, from Beverly
      Hills. Ava presented award for John Huston to
      his assistant Jack Greenwood, on May 27, 1951

R9   <u>Bob Hope Show</u>, Liggett and Meyers Production; Ava was
      a guest on October 16, 1951

R10   "U.N. Featurette," <u>Weekend</u>; Ava was a guest on
      May 15, 1955

R11   "The Unicef Story," <u>United Nations</u>. Ava was a taped
      guest on December 11, 1956

R12   <u>Life and The World</u>, in cooperation with <u>Life</u> magazine.
      Ava appeared on taped dialogue from <u>The Sun Also
      Rises</u>, with her co-star Tyrone Power, on
      September 13, 1957

R13   <u>Command Performance</u>, #341, AFRS; Ava was M.C., with
      guests Ken Niles, Steve Allen, Jack Douglas, Herb
      Jeffries, June Foray, and Dink Trout

R14   <u>Jubilee, #226</u>, AFRS; Ava guest-starred along with
      Gene Norman, Jack McVea, Jack Teagarden, Judy
      Porter, Saul Davis, and Jean Louise

R15   <u>M-G-M Theatre of The Air</u>, #31, in syndicated episode
       "Chained," with Ava Gardner, Don Briggs, John
       Gibson, Ed Stokes and host Howard Dietz

SOUNDTRACKS/MUSICAL RECORDINGS

S1   "The More I Know of Love," sung by Eileen Wilson for
       Ava Gardner in <u>The Killers</u>, 1946

      See: AB 197

S2   "Don't Tell Me," sung by Eileen Wilson for Ava Gardner
       in <u>The Hucksters</u>, 1947

      See: AB 197

S3   "Speak Low," sung by Eileen Wilson for Ava Gardner
       in <u>One Touch of Venus</u>, 1948

S4   "How Am I To Know," sung by Ava Gardner on <u>Juke Box</u>
       <u>USA</u> 147 and <u>Turn Back the Clock</u> 594, 1951

S5   "Bill," sung by Annette Warren for Ava Gardner in
       <u>Show Boat</u>, 1951

      See: AB 197

S6   "Can't Help Lovin' Dat Man," sung by Annette Warren
       for Ava Gardner in <u>Show Boat</u>, SP-599, 1951

S7   "Bill," sung by Ava Gardner on soundtrack album
       <u>Show Boat</u>, M-G-M (M) E-559, (M) E-3230, (M) M-527
       (reissue), (M) M-527, and (S) MS-527, 1951

S8   "Can't Help Lovin' Dat Man," sung by Ava Gardner on
      soundtrack album Show Boat, M-G-M (M) E-559,
      (M) E-3230, (M) M-527 (reissue), (M) M-527, and
      (S) MS-527, 1951

      See: AB 197

S9   "Lovers Were Meant to Cry," sung by Ava Gardner (to
      Clark Gable) in Lone Star, 1952

      See: AB 197

S10   "Snows of Kiliminjaro," on the soundtrack album
      Music from Great Film Classics, London
      (S) SP-44144, 1952

S11   "The Killers," on soundtrack album Lust for Life,
      Decca (M) DL-10015 and (S) DL-710015, 1956

S12   The Sun Also Rises, soundtrack album, Kapp
      (M) K-DL-7001, 1957

S13   The Naked Maja, soundtrack album, United Artists
      (M) UAL-4031 and (S) UAS-5031, 1959

S14   On The Beach, soundtrack album, Roulette (M) R-25098,
      (S) SR-25098, 1959

S15   55 Days at Peking, soundtrack album, Columbia
      (M) CL-2028 and (S) CS-8828, 1963

S16   Night of The Iguana, soundtrack album, M-G-M,
      M-PR-4, (M) E-4247, and (S) SE-4247, 1964

S17   The Bible, soundtrack album, 20th Century,
      (S) TFS-4187, 1966

S18   The Life and Times of Judge Roy Bean, soundtrack album,
        Columbia (S) S-31948, 1972

S19   Earthquake, soundtrack album, MCA S-2081, 1973

S20   Those Glorious M-G-M Musicals, M-G-M, (S)-42-ST, 1973

S21   That's Entertainment, soundtrack album, MCA (S)-2-11002,
        1974

BIBLIOGRAPHY

ANNOTATED BOOKS

AB1   Hanna, David, <u>Ava, Portrait of a Star</u>, New York:
           G. P. Putnam's Sons, 1960

           Hanna was a writer-journalist who became Ava's
           press agent just previous to her signing as star
           of <u>The Barefoot Contessa</u>. He traveled the world
           with Ava, witnessing her stardom and caringly
           writing about her until he left her employment
           in 1964.

           See: F36

AB2   Gehman, Richard, <u>Sinatra and His Rat Pack</u>, New York:
           Belmont Books, 1961

           Ava's on-again, off-again relationship and marriage
           to Frank Sinatra are touched upon.

AB3   Hemingway, Leicester, <u>My Brother, Ernest Hemingway</u>,
           New York: Fawcett Crest, 1961

           The author cites his brother's friendship with the
           feisty movie star Ava Gardner.

AB4   Hopper, Hedda and Brough, James, <u>The Whole Truth</u>
           <u>and Nothing But</u>, New York: Doubleday, 1962

Gossip columnist Hopper wonders, in her interest of lovers Sinatra and Gardner, will they ever tie the knot?

AB5   Everson, William K., <u>The Bad Guys, A Pictorial History of The Movie Villain</u>, New York: Cadillac Publishing Company, 1964

The author gives his well-researched account of bad guys in films and states that Ava was a perfect gangster moll in <u>The Killers</u>.

See: F17

AB6   Graham, Sheilah, <u>The Rest of The Story</u>, New York: Coward-McCann, Inc., 1964

Sheilah Graham was competition for gossip columnists Hedda Hopper and Louella Parsons. She reported the tempestuous relationship of Ava Gardner and current lovers at the time.

AB7   Taylor, Elizabeth, <u>Elizabeth Taylor: An Informal Memoir</u>, New York: Harper and Row, Inc., 1964

Ms. Taylor considered Ava Gardner to be a truly beautiful woman.

AB8   Davis, Sammy Jr., <u>Yes, I Can, The Story of Sammy Davis, Jr.</u>, New York: Simon and Schuster, 1965

Sammy mentions the Hollywood <u>Confidential</u> magazine article that caused a sensation when rumors spread that he and Ava were having a love affair during an appearance they made at the Apollo in New York when Ava was plugging her film <u>The Barefoot Contessa</u>.

See: F36

AB9   Horne, Lena and Schickel, Richard, <u>Lena</u>, New York: New American Library, 1965

Lena mentions that Ava lived up the street from her and they had "coffee clatches" together.

AB10   Kael, Pauline, <u>Kiss Kiss, Bang Bang</u>, New York:
           Little, Brown and Company, 1965, 1968

        Ms. Kael reviews Ava's films and gives her glowing
        raves for her work in <u>The Killers</u>, <u>The Barefoot
        Contessa</u>, and <u>On The Beach</u>. However, she felt that
        Ava was "downright unglamorous as a woman who has
        lived too hard and drunk too much" in <u>On The Beach</u>.
        She pans <u>The Bible</u> but lauds Ava's acting in her role
        as Sarah. She found that Ava brought great passion
        to her role as the ill-fated wife of an Italian count
        in <u>The Barefoot Contessa</u>.

        See: F17, F41, F47

AB11   McCarthy, Clifford, <u>The Complete Films of Humphrey
           Bogart</u>, Secaucus, New Jersey: The Citadel Press,
           1965

        The author gives Ava a splendid review of her work
        in <u>The Barefoot Contessa</u>.

        See: F36

AB12   Michael, Paul, <u>Humphrey Bogart, The Man and His
           Films</u>, New York: Bobbs-Merrill Company, Inc.,
           1965

        Mr. Michael reports Bogart's dislike for Ava
        while filming <u>The Barefoot Contessa</u> because he
        felt she was a lazy actress.

        See: F36

AB13   Rooney, Mickey, <u>I.E., An Autobiography</u>, New York:
           G. P. Putnam's Sons, 1965

        Mickey acknowledges that Ava was the love of his
        life but their marriage was doomed because of the
        vast differences in their temperaments, expectations,
        etc.

AB14   Hyams, Joe, <u>Bogie, The Definitive Biography of
           Humphrey Bogart</u>, New York: New American Library,
           1966

        Bogart deliberately flubbed lines so that Ava would
        be uncomfortable during filming of <u>The Barefoot
        Contessa</u>.

        See: F36

AB15   Lamarr, Hedy, <u>Ecstasy and Me, My Life as a Woman</u>,
           New York: Fawcett Publications, Inc., 1966

Lamarr showed Frank Sinatra and Ava Gardner how to
enjoy the beaches and bay of Acapulco while they
were vacationing together.

AB16   Gerberg, Albert B., <u>Bashful Billionaire, The Story
        of Howard Hughes</u>, New York: Lyle Stuart, 1967

        The author included brief mention of Ava as one of
        the many beautiful women Howard Hughes was enchanted
        with during the 1940s.

AB17   Hirsch, Phil, <u>Hollywood Confidential</u>, New York:
        Pyramid Books, 1967

        Hirsch relates the passionate affair Ava had with
        George C. Scott while filming <u>The Bible</u> in Rome.

        See: F47

AB18   Simon, John Ivan, <u>Private Screenings</u>, New York:
        MacMillan Press, 1967

        He mentions Ava as being one of the lasting
        beauties of the M-G-M era.

AB19   Thomas, Bob, <u>King Cohn, The Life and Times of Harry
        Cohn</u>, New York: G. P. Putnam's Sons, 1967

        Ava begged Cohn to test Sinatra for the role of
        Maggio in <u>From Here to Eternity</u>.

AB20   Crist, Judith, <u>The Private Eye, The Cowboy, and The
        Very Naked Girl</u>, New York: Holt, Rinehart and
        Winston, 1968

        Judith Crist reviews the film <u>The Bible</u>. She
        refers to the still-beautiful face and better
        acting ability Ava brought to her role as Sarah.

        See: F47

AB21   Fredrik, Nathalie, <u>Hollywood and The Academy Awards</u>,
        Los Angeles, California: Award Publications, 1968

        Ava's acting in <u>Mogambo</u> won her plaudits and an
        Academy Award nomination for Best Actress.

        See: F34

AB22   Reed, Rex, <u>Do You Sleep In The Nude?</u> New York: New
        American Library, 1968

        Reed reprises his article written for <u>Esquire</u>
        magazine where he painted Ava as a hard-drinking,
        sulky has-been movie star.

AB23   Shaw, Arnold, <u>Sinatra, Twentieth-Century Romantic</u>,
        New York: Holt, Rinehart and Winston, 1968

        Shaw illustrates Ava's passionate affair, marriage,
        and breakup with Sinatra. It mentions that she
        dated Richard Condon, author of <u>The Manchurian
        Candidate</u>. Sinatra later starred in the excellent
        film classic based on the book.

AB24   Everson, William K., <u>A Pictorial History of The
        Western Film</u>, Secaucus, New Jersey: The Citadel
        Press, 1969

        The author mentions Ava in her role as the forlorn
        wife of a land baron in <u>Ride, Vaquero</u>, co-starring
        Robert Taylor and Anthony Quinn.

        See: F33

AB25   Reed, Rex, <u>Conversations in The Raw</u>, New York:
        New American Library, 1969

        Reed refers to Ava and her love life with husbands
        Mickey Rooney, Artie Shaw, and Frank Sinatra.

AB26   Thomas, Tony, Behlmer, Rudy, and McCarthy, Clifford,
        <u>The Films of Errol Flynn,</u> Secaucus, New Jersey:
        The Citadel Press, 1969

        Ava won good review for her role as Lady Brett
        Ashley in <u>The Sun Also Rises</u>, which was filmed in
        Pamploma, Paris, Biarritz, Morelia, and Mexico City.

        See: F39

AB27   Essoe, Gabe, <u>The Films of Clark Gable</u>, Secaucus,
        New Jersey: The Citadel Press, 1970

        Ava is credited for her roles in <u>The Hucksters</u>,
        <u>Lone Star</u>, and <u>Mogambo</u>, which starred Gable.

        See: F21, F30, F34

AB28   Knef, Hildegard, <u>The Gift Horse, Report on a Life</u>,
       New York: McGraw-Hill Book Co., 1970

       Knef mentions Ava and their high-spirited times
       while filming <u>The Sun Also Rises</u>.

       See: F39

AB29   Thompson, Howard, <u>The New York Times Guide to Movies
       on TV</u>, New York: Random House, 1970

       The author includes Ava's movies to date that
       appeared on television, with photos.

AB30   Zmijewsky, Steve, Ricci, Mark, and Zmijewsky, Boris,
       <u>The Complete Films of John Wayne</u>, Secaucus,
       New Jersey: The Citadel Press, 1970, 1983

       Mention is made of Ava's nonspeaking role in the
       romantic World War II film <u>Reunion in France</u>
       starring Joan Crawford and John Wayne.

       See: F3

AB31   Morella, Joe and Epstein, Edward Z., <u>Lana, The
       Public and Private Lives of Miss Turner</u>, New York:
       Lyle Stuart, Inc., 1970

       The authors relate the incident where Sinatra
       reportedly came home one day to find the two
       lovely movie stars in a compromising position.
       Actress Barbara Payton claimed to have been there,
       too. They also mention that Lana and Ava did a
       dance routine at a party hosted by the Duke of
       Manchester in London. They sang "Take Me Out To
       The Ball Game." It caused almost as much of a
       sensation as when Princess Margaret Rose did her
       famous can-can dance. Lana and Ava were to appear
       together in a film titled <u>My Most Intimate Friend</u>,
       which, curiously, never got made.

AB32   Reed, Rex, <u>Big Screen, Little Screen</u>, New York:
       MacMillan, 1971

       Rex Reed pans the movie <u>The Bible</u>, which he
       considered it and everyone in it dreadful.

       See: F47

AB33   Ringgold, Gene and McCarthy, Clifford, The Films of
            Frank Sinatra, Secaucus, New Jersey: The Citadel
            Press, 1971

        Highlighted was Ava's marriage to Sinatra from
        November 7, 1951 to their final divorce on July 5,
        1957 (although they had separated four years
        previously). Ava said, "When he was down, he was
        sweet, but when he got back up, he was hell."

AB34   Wilson, Earl, The Show Business Nobody Knows,
            New York, Cowles Book Company, Inc., 1971

        Wilson mentions the beautious Ava and her tempestu-
        ous life with Frank Sinatra.

AB35   Dietrich, Noah, Howard, The Amazing Mr. Hughes,
            New York: Fawcett Gold Medal Book, 1972

        Mr. Dietrich briefly relates Howard Hughes'
        infatuation with the young, nubile Ava Gardner.

AB36   Eells, George, Hedda and Louella, New York:
            G. P. Putnam's Sons, 1972

        Ava's sultry personality brought men into her
        life that fueled much gossip reported by the famous
        Louella Parsons and Hedda Hopper, both on the
        radio and in the press.

AB37   Eells, George, Malice in Wonderland, New York:
            Lorevan Publishing, Inc., 1972

        Eells wrote this sequel to Hedda and Louella,
        the two gossip reporters whose rivalry for press
        and air time were world-known. Ava's relationships
        are briefly discussed.

AB38   Parish, James Robert and Bowers, Ronald L., The
            M-G-M Stock Company - The Golden Era, New York:
            Arlington House, 1972

        Parish and Bowers provide a biography of Ava and
        a brief filmography.

AB39   Shipman, David, <u>The Great Movie Stars: The</u>
          <u>International Years</u>, New York: St. Martin's
          Press, 1972

       The author furnishes a limited biography of
       actress Ava Gardner.

AB40   Sirk, Douglas, <u>Sirk on Sirk; Interviews with</u>
          <u>Jon Holliday</u>, New York: Viking Press, 1972

       The interview includes a review of the movie
       <u>Hitler's Madman</u> in which Ava had a walk-on role.

       See: F9

AB41   Thomas, Tony, <u>The Films of Kirk Douglas</u>, Secaucus,
          New Jersey: The Citadel Press, 1972

       Thomas gives a glowing report on Ava's role in
       <u>Seven Days in May</u>.

       See: F45

AB42   Tomkies, Mike, <u>The Robert Mitchum Story</u>, Chicago,
          Illinois: Henry Regnery Company, 1972

       The author briefly mentions Mitchum's delight in
       working with Ava in <u>My Forbidden Past</u>. She was
       "like one of the boys" on the set and they shared
       a comfortable friendship.

       See: F28

AB43   Barbour, Alan G., <u>Humphrey Bogart</u>, New York:
          Galahad Books, 1973

       Barbour reviews Ava's good performance in <u>The</u>
       <u>Barefoot Contessa</u>.

       See: F36

AB44   Green, Stanley, <u>Starring Fred Astaire</u>, New York:
          Dodd, Mead Publishing, 1973

       <u>On The Beach</u> is the science-fiction film that
       featured Ava in a starring role. Astaire found
       her enchanting and easy to work with, and her
       performance proved middle age had not stopped
       her evolution as an actress.

       See: F41

AB45   Haskell, Molly, <u>From Reverence to Rape, The</u>
          <u>Treatment of Women in The Movies</u>, New York:
          Holt, Rinehart and Winston, 1973

Ava is mentioned as one of the most beautiful
actresses on the screen, whose sultriness was
admired by women as well as men.

AB46   Hyams, Joe, Mislaid in Hollywood, New York: Peter H.
           Wyden, Inc., 1973

Hyams' interview with Ava for Life magazine took
place over a several-month period. He found Ava
to be very complex. It had been rumored that the
two were lovers, but not confirmed.

AB47   Jorda, Rene, Clark Gable, New York: Galahad Books,
           1973

Ava is included in review of the three films she
made with Gable. It is noted that Gable let Ava
get good lines and scenes in Mogambo, to guarantee
her Oscar nomination.

See: F34

AB48   Kobal, John, Gods, Goddesses of The Movies, New York:
           Crescent Books, 1973

Ava's role in Mogambo is highlighted as well as her
beauty and performance in Pandora and The Flying
Dutchman. She was named the most beautiful woman
in the world in his review of Pandora.

See: F27, F34

AB49   Morella, Joe, Epstein, Edward Z., and Griggs, John,
           The Films of World War II, A Pictorial Treasury
           of Hollywood's War Years, Secaucus, New Jersey:
           The Citadel Press, 1973

Ava's roles as an extra are noted in the M-G-M
films Hitler's Madman and Reunion in France.

See: F3, F9

AB50   Rosen, Marjorie, Popcorn Venus, Women, Movies, and
           The American Dream, New York: Coward, McCann,
           and Geoghegan, Inc., 1973

Ava's performances and screen images in One Touch of
Venus, Pandora and The Flying Dutchman, and The
Barefoot Contessa helped to maintain the fantasy
creature syndrome whereby her beauty was so breath-
taking no man could resist her.

See: F23, F27, F36

AB51   Vermilye, Jerry, <u>Bette Davis</u>, New York: Pyramid
      Communications, Inc., 1973

      Bette Davis lost the role of Maxine Faulk to Ava
      in <u>Night of the Iguana</u>.

      See: F46

AB52   Wayne, Jane Ellen, <u>Robert Taylor</u>, New York: Manor
      Books, 1973

      Taylor worked together with Ava on three films.
      They shared an understanding friendship and he
      loved her wit, directness, and sexiness.

AB53   Bergen, Polly, <u>Polly's Principles</u>, New York:
      Peter Wyden, 1974

      During her teen years, Polly wanted to look like
      Ava. At the beginning of her career, she copied
      Ava's looks from magazines, including poses and
      makeup techniques.

AB54   Chaneles, Sol and Wolsky, Albert, <u>The Movie Makers</u>,
      Secaucus, New Jersey: Derbibooks, Inc., 1974

      The authors provide a one-page, indepth biography
      of Ava's career to date.

AB55   Corliss, Richard, <u>Talking Pictures</u>, New York:
      Overlook Press, 1974

      Corliss reports on a major film for Ava, <u>The
      Barefoot Contessa</u>.

      See: F36

AB56   Daltan, David, <u>James Dean: The Mutant King, A
      Biography,</u> New York: Straight Arrow Books, 1974

      Ava is mentioned as to her impact on the film
      community in the 1950s.

AB57   Edwards, Anne, <u>Judy Garland</u>, New York: Simon and
      Schuster, 1974

      Remarked upon is Ava's relationship with Mickey
      Rooney, frequent co-star of Judy Garland in
      musicals of the 1930s and 1940s.

AB58   Fox, George, Earthquake, The Story of a Movie,
           New York: New American Library, 1974

         The author cites Ava's lusty performance as well
         as her behavior on the set of the all-star cast
         of Earthquake, which featured Surround Sound.

         See: F52

AB59   Harris, Warren G., Gable and Lombard, New York:
           Simon and Schuster, 1974

         Ava is mentioned as Gable's co-star in Mogambo.

         See: F34

AB60   Higham, Charles, Ava: A Life Story, New York:
           Delacorte Press, 1974

         Well-researched biography of Ava Gardner that
         included filmography through 1972's The Life and
         Times of Judge Roy Bean.

         See: F49

AB61   Parish, James Robert and Stanke, Don E., The Glamour
           Girls, New York: Arlington House, 1974

         The authors' book on screen beauties of the thirties,
         forties and fifties includes and beautiful and
         sensual Ava Gardner in her role for the film Mogambo.

         See: F34

AB62   Parish, James Robert and Whitney, Steven, Vincent
           Price, Unmasked, New York: Drake Publishing, 1974

         This biography of the famous horror film actor
         includes their co-starring roles in The Bribe.
         Price considered Ava the most beautiful brunette
         in films. He appreciated her sense of humor.

         See: F24

AB63   Sheppard, Dick, Elizabeth, The Life and Career of
           Elizabeth Taylor, New York: Doubleday, 1974

         Ava is quoted: "Name me any actress who survived
         all that crap at M-G-M. Maybe Lana Turner.
         Certainly Liz Taylor. But they all hated acting
         as much as I do. All except for Elizabeth. She
         used to come up to me on the set and say, 'If only
         I could learn to be good.' And, by God, she
         made it."

AB64   Anger, Kenneth, <u>Hollywood Babylon</u>, New York: Dell
        Publishing, 1975

        Anger features many of the Hollywood <u>Confidential</u>
        magazine scandals, including Ava's.

AB65   Behlmer, Rudy and Thomas, Tony, <u>Hollywood's</u>
        <u>Hollywood, The Movies About The Movies</u>, Secaucus,
        New Jersey: The Citadel Press, 1975

        <u>The Barefoot Contessa</u> was about a movie star who
        rises from the depths of poverty to the heights of
        fame and fortune only to be killed by her jealous
        husband.   This film was loosely based on the lives
        Rita Hayworth and Aly Khan, with a little of Howard
        Hughes thrown in.

        See: F36

AB66   Druxman, Michael B., <u>Make It Again, Sam, A Survey of</u>
        <u>Movie Remakes</u>, New York: A. S. Barnes, 1975

        Movies in which Ava starred that were sequels to
        original works: <u>Show Boat</u> and <u>Mogambo</u> (<u>Show Boat</u>
        and Red Dust, respectively).

        See: F29, F34

AB67   Eames, John Douglas, <u>The M-G-M Story</u>, New York:
        Crown Publishers, 1975

        This book featured a synopsis of Ava's movies
        released from 1942 through 1960.

AB68   Fordin, Hugh, <u>The World of Entertainment,</u>
        <u>Hollywood's Greatest Musicals</u>, New York:
        Doubleday and Company, Inc., 1975

        <u>Show Boat</u> made Ava an international star in 1951.
        She was rated the highest in the previous showing
        at Bay Theatre, Pacific Palisades, California, on
        March 22, 1951, garnering 78% in popularity among
        the men and 80% among female viewers.   The film
        was completed at a cost of $2,295,429; it grossed
        $8,650,000.   Annette Warren was chosen to sing for
        Ava in the movie, although Ava made the sound
        recording for the album.

        See: F29

AB69   Frank, Gerald, _Judy_, New York: Harper and Row, 1975

      M-G-M aide Lester Peterson was the best man at Ava's
      1941 wedding to Mickey Rooney.

AB70   Hamblett, Charles, _Paul Newman, A Biography_, New York:
      W. H. Allen, 1975

      Ava is listed in the review and credits of the 1972
      film _The Life and Times of Judge Roy Bean_. Ava played
      Lily Langtry.

      See: F49

AB71   Hyams, Joe, _Bogart and Bacall_, A Love Story, New York:
      David McKay and Company, Inc., 1975

      The author touches upon the touchy working
      relationship Ava had with Bogart during filming of
      The Barefoot Contessa.

      See: F36

AB72   Kael, Pauline, _When The Lights Go Down_, New York:
      Holt, Rinehart and Winston, 1975

      The author reviews _The Snows of Kiliminjaro_, where
      Ava dies in Gregory Peck's arms. Kael mentions
      that, of newer actresses on the scene, Lonette
      McKee has the sexual brazenness like screen stars
      Susan Hayward and Ava Gardner had in their youths.

      See: F32

AB73   Morris, George, _Errol Flynn, A Pyramid Illustrated
      History of The Movies,_ New York: Pyramid
      Publications, 1975

      Ava's performance as an American ex-patriot in
      Spain was realistic and believable. She fared
      well with her co-stars Errol Flynn and Mel Ferrer.

AB74   Parish, James Robert and Stanke, Don E., _The
      Debonairs_, New York: Arlington House, 1975

      The authors depict Ava's roles in the films _The
      Great Sinner_, _My Forbidden Past_, and _The Little
      Hut_.

      See: F25, F28, F40

AB75   Quirk, Lawrence J., _The Films of Robert Taylor_,
         Secaucus, New Jersey: The Citadel Press, 1975

         Ava's legendary beauty was the only thing that
         saved her wooden performance in _Knights of the_
         Round Table. She fared better in her co-starring
         role in their first movie together, _The Bribe_.
         Ride, Vaquero teamed the two sensational actors
         together in brilliant Technicolor.

         See: F24, F33, F35

AB76   Rovin, Jeff, _A Pictorial History of Science Fiction_
         Films, Secaucus, New Jersey: The Citadel Press,
         1975

         Rovin paints a flattering picture of Ava and her
         believable performance in _On The Beach_.

         See: F41

AB77   Scherman, David E., _Life Goes To The Movies_,
         New York: Time-Life Books, 1975

         Ava in a bubble bath from 1948 is featured in a
         section on bathing beauties in the movies. In
         the segment "But Some Made It Big," Ava's
         marriages and the films _The Hucksters_, _Mogambo_,
         and _The Barefoot Contessa_ are mentioned.

         See: F21, F34, F36

AB78   Thomas, Tony, _The Films of The Forties_, Secaucus,
         New Jersey, The Citadel Press, 1975

         Lauded are Ava's sultry performances in _The Killers_,
         as Kitty Collins, and _The Hucksters_, as Jean
         Ogilvie.

         See: F17, F21

AB79   Wortley, Richard, _Erotic Movies_, New York: Crown
         Publishers, 1975

         Ava's well-endowed cleavage is included.

AB80   Zec, Donald, _Sophia, An Intimate Biography_, New York:
         Pinnacle Books, 1975

         Zec relates Ava and Frank's parting of the ways
         and his co-starring with Sophia Loren in _The Pride_
         and The Passion, which filmed in Europe. Ava had
         been considered for the role.

AB81   Bacon, James, <u>James Bacon's Hollywood Is a Four</u>
        <u>Letter Word</u>, Chicago, Illinois: Contemporary
        Books, 1976

        Bacon informs his readers that Frank and Ava got
        drunk and shot out all the street lights of a town
        outside of Palm Springs. Sinatra paid to get them
        replaced and to keep the story out of the papers.
        While filming <u>Night of The Iguana</u>, Ava took up
        with a 21-year-old beach boy who publicly beat her.
        Elizabeth Taylor said in a press conference that
        she considered Ava Gardner to be more beautiful
        than she.

        See: F46

AB82   Bawden, Liz-Anne, <u>The Oxford Companion to Film</u>,
        New York-London: Oxford University Press, 1976

        The author provides a brief biography of Ava
        Gardner.

AB83   Brode, Douglas, <u>The Films of The Fifties</u>, Secaucus,
        New Jersey: The Citadel Press, 1976

        Reviewed is the 1959 United Artists film <u>On The</u>
        <u>Beach</u>. The author mentions that Ava's role as
        Moira Davidson provides the pathos needed for the
        tale of survivors of the world's nuclear holocaust.

        See: F41

AB84   Hanna, David, <u>Hollywood Confidential</u>, New York:
        Nordon Publications, Inc., 1976

        Hanna, a publicist who had been Ava's confidente
        and traveling companion from 1954-1960, writes of
        the lush and decadent life that Ava lived while at
        the height of her beauty and fame. He mentions that
        Ava's father was a sharecropper. An interesting
        tidbit told of Greta Garbo's meeting with Ava and
        the fact that the two doffed their bathing suit
        tops for an after-lunch swim at Greta's.

AB85   Heston, Charlton, <u>The Actor's Life, Journals 1956-76</u>,
        New York: Simon and Schuster, 1976, 1978

        Charlton Heston did not like Ava Gardner very much
        during filming of <u>55 Days at Peking</u> and <u>Earthquake</u>.
        He felt she lacked professionalism.

        See: F44, F52

AB86   Kael, Pauline, <u>Reedling</u>, New York: Little Brown,
           1976

        Ms. Kael examines and profiles the performances
        Ava gave in the films <u>Earthquake</u> and <u>The Life and
        Times of Judge Roy Bean</u>.

        See: F49, F52

AB87   Kleiner, Dick, <u>Hollywood's Greatest Love Stories</u>,
           New York: Simon and Schuster, 1976

        The author relates the passionate affair, marriage,
        and divorce of Ava Gardner and Frank Sinatra.

AB88   Madden, Nelson, <u>The Real Howard Hughes Story, His
           Life and Death, 1905-76</u>, New York: Manor Books,
           1976

        Ava's rocky romance with the elusive billionaire
        is depicted in this biography of Howard Hughes.

AB89   Parish, James Robert and Stanke, Don E., <u>The
           Swashbucklers</u>, Carlstad, New Jersey: Rainbow
           Books, 1976

        Ava's roles are described in the films <u>The Little
        Hut</u> and <u>Bhowani Junction</u>. It is also mentioned
        that Ava was originally considered for the role in
        the 1952 movie <u>Scaramouche</u>.

        See: F38, F40

AB90   Parish, James Robert, <u>The Tough Guys</u>, Carlstad,
           New Jersey: Rainbow Books, 1976

        Ava's supporting performances are highlighted
        in this book that features 1940s and 1950s
        movie villains and heroes, among them her co-
        stars Burt Lancaster, Robert Mitchum, and
        Robert Taylor.

AB91   Pratley, Gerald, <u>Cinema of John Huston</u>, New York:
           A. S. Barnes Publishing Inc., 1976, 1977

        Pratley gives long reviews of Huston's films that
        also featured Ava, whom Huston thought to be a very
        underrated actress. Films Ava did for Huston were
        <u>Night of The Iguana</u>, <u>The Bible</u>, and <u>The Life and
        Times of Judge Roy Bean</u>.

        See: F46, F47, F49

AB92   Ragan, David, <u>Who's Who In Hollywood 1900-1976</u>,
        New York: Arlington House, 1976

        Provided are a brief biography and filmography
        to date of Ava Gardner.

AB93   Romero, Gerry, <u>Sinatra's Women</u>, New York: Manor
        Books, 1976

        The author recreates Ava's role in Frank Sinatra's
        life.

AB94   Seuling, Barbara, <u>The Loudest Screen Kiss and Other
        Little-Known Facts About The Movies</u>, New York:
        Doubleday, 1976

        The photos taken by Ava's brother-in-law were
        spotted by an M-G-M employee who brought them to
        the attention of Louis B. Mayer, head of M-G-M
        Studios. Mayer said of Ava's screen test, "She
        can't talk, she can't act, she's terrific."

AB95   Shipman, David, <u>Great Movie Stars</u>, New York: A&W
        Visual Library, 1976

        Ava's life and films are briefly touched upon in
        this book that features the most popular stars
        in cinema.

AB96   Tornabene, Lyn, <u>Long Live The King, A Biography of
        Clark Gable</u>, New York: Simon and Schuster, 1976

        While filming <u>The Hucksters</u>, Ava had announced
        her ambition to marry the king of the movies. She
        was slated to make a movie with Gable that never
        took place. On her first wedding anniversary with
        Frank Sinatra, Ava in Africa playing the Jean
        Harlow role in <u>Mogambo</u>. During wrap-up of the
        film in London, she dressed in a $3,000 ball gown
        and prepared fried chicken dinner for Gable,
        Robert Taylor, the Alan Ladds, John Huston, and
        Lana Turner.
        See: F21, F34

AB97   Vermilye, Jerry and Ricci, Mark, <u>The Films of
        of Elizabeth Taylor</u>, Secaucus, New Jersey:
        The Citadel Press, 1976

AB98   Winnington, Richard, <u>Film Criticism and Caricatures,</u>
        <u>1943-53</u>, New York: Barnes and Noble Books, 1976

        Ava's exquisite beauty as the siren in <u>Pandora and</u>
        <u>The Flying Dutchman</u>, who is drawn towards a
        mysterious man, is described, although the film
        received marginal reviews.

        See: F27

AB99   Crowther, Bosley, <u>Vintage Films</u>, New York: G. P.
        Putnam's Sons, 1977

        <u>New York Times</u> movie critic Crowther mentions that
        Ava had a cameo role in the film <u>Around the World</u>
        <u>in 80 Days</u>.

        See: F37

AB100   Fitzgerald, Michael G., <u>Universal Pictures</u>,
        Westport, Connecticut: Arlington Publishers, 1977

        The studio's vintage movies in which Ava's roles
        are depicted and provided with photographs are
        <u>The Killers</u>, <u>Singapore</u>, and <u>Earthquake</u>.

        See: F17, F22, F52

AB101   Halliwell, Leslie, <u>Halliwell's Film Guide, A Survey</u>
        <u>of 8,000 English-Language Movies</u>, New York:
        Charles Scribner's Sons, 1977

        Halliwell's indepth research includes synopses of
        Ava's films and performances from her parts in <u>We</u>
        <u>Were Dancing</u> through <u>Permission to Kill</u>.

        See: F1, F53

AB102   Hirschhorn, Clive, <u>Films of James Mason</u>, Secaucus,
        New Jersey: The Citadel Press, 1977

        <u>Pandora and The Flying Dutchman</u> are characterized
        in this book, starring Ava as Pandora Reynolds
        and James Mason as the Flying Dutchman. Hirschhorn
        believed Ava was spectacularly ravishing and
        believable in her role.

        See: F27

AB103   Kass, Judith, <u>Ava Gardner</u>, New York: Pyramid
        Publishers, 1977

        The author's biography of Ava contains lavish
        photographs, as well as a current biography of
        the beautiful actress.

AB104   Keyes, Evelyn, <u>Scarlett O'Hara's Younger Sister</u>,
          New York: Lyle Stuart, Inc., 1977

         Keyes was married to John Huston when <u>Night of The
         Iguana</u> was being filmed in Mexico. She had also
         been an ex-wife of Ava's ex-husband, Artie Shaw,
         about whom they compared notes. It was expected
         that there would be much stress for the cast and
         crew during filming of the Tennessee Williams
         story, but all got along famously.

         See: F46

AB105   Kobal, John, <u>Rita Hayworth, Portrait of a Love
          Goddess</u>, New York: W. W. Norton and Company,
          <u>Inc.</u>, 1977, 1978

         Kobal remarks that Rita Hayworth's life with Aly
         Khan is the basis for Ava's movie <u>The Barefoot
         Contessa</u>.   It was said that Rita lost out to Ava
         for the role. Ava was slated to star in <u>Fire Down
         Below</u>, which went to Rita.

         See: F36

AB106   Krueger, Miles, <u>Show Boat: The Story of a Classical
          American Musical</u>, New York: Oxford University
          Press, 1977

         Ava's poignant role as the tragic Julie in the
         much-loved musical film is delineated.

AB107   Lewis, Arthur H., <u>Those Philadelphia Kellys</u>,
          New York: William Morrow and Company, Inc., 1977

         Ava Gardner was the only movie star invited to
         attend the marriage of actress Grace Kelly to
         Prince Rainier of Monaco in 1956.

AB108   Peary, Gerald and Shatzkin, Robert, <u>Classic
          American Novels in The Movies</u>, New York: F.
          Ungar Publishing Company, 1977

         <u>The Sun Also Rises</u> was one of the filmed versions
         of an Ernest Hemingway novel. Ava starred as
         Lady Brett Ashley in the film.

         See: F39

AB109   Rovin, Jeff, <u>The Films of Charlton Heston</u>,
          Secaucus, New Jersey: The Citadel Press, 1977

Heston co-starred with Ava in <u>55 Days at Peking</u> and
<u>Earthquake</u>. <u>55 Days at Peking</u> was a colossal flop.
<u>Earthquake</u> was a critical failure but box-office hit.

See: F44, F52

AB110   Sharif, Omar with Guinehard, Marie-Therese, <u>The
         Eternal Male</u>, New York: Doubleday, 1977

During filming of <u>Mayerling</u> in 1966, Omar and Ava
became pals. He thought of Ava as being lonely
and perpetually frustrated in love because she was
too demanding even though she was "infinitely
feminine."

See: F48

AB111   Bacall, Lauren, <u>Lauren Bacall, By Myself</u>, New York:
         Alfred A. Knopf, 1978

Bacall recalls the time she brought a coconut cake
to Ava to present to Frank Sinatra on his birthday.
She was all set to dislike the glamorous Ava, but
Lauren found her to be very down-to-earth and
pleasant.

AB112   Benny, Mary Livingstone with Marks, Hilliard and
         Borie, Maurice, <u>Jack Benny</u>, New York: Doubleday,
         1978

In 1972, Mary and Jack Benny took Ava with them
to the Joe Frazier boxing match in London.

AB113   Collins, Joan, <u>Past Imperfect</u>, London: Coronet
         Books, 1978

Collins was known as Britain's answer to Ava
Gardner because of their similarity in coloring
and posture.

AB114   Csida, Joseph and Csida, June Bundy, <u>American
         Entertainment, A Unique History of Popular
         Show Business</u>, New York: Watson-Duptill
         Publications, 1978

Ava is mentioned in the chapter "No Scarcity
of Hits."

AB115   Freedland, Michael, <u>The Two Lives of Errol Flynn</u>,
          New York: Bantam Books, 1978, 1980

          Her role as Lady Ashley Brett is remembered along
          with Flynn's in the film <u>The Sun Also Rises</u>, in
          this expose of the life and films of Errol Flynn.

          See: F39

AB116   Harris, Jay B., <u>TV Guide - The First 25 Years</u>,
          New York: Simon and Schuster, 1978

          The author mentions the marriage of Ava to the
          popular TV personality Frank Sinatra.

AB117   Kaminsky, Stuart M., <u>John Huston - Maker of Magic</u>,
          New York: Houghton Mifflin, 1978

          <u>Night of The Iguana</u> was one of the movies Kaminsky
          features in this indepth filmography of actor-
          director John Huston. Huston's passion for hiring
          Ava and providing her with roles that suited her
          mid-life career is evident in his praise of Ava
          for taking the roles.

          See: F46

AB118   Madsen, Axel, <u>John Huston, A Biography</u>, New York:
          Doubleday, 1978

          While filming <u>Night of The Iguana</u>, John Huston
          tried to make his wife Evelyn Keyes jealous of
          the attention he paid Ava, particularly at
          the wrap-up party. Huston presented cast members
          with gold-plated derringers. There is also a
          reference to Helen Lawrenson's <u>Show</u> magazine
          article where Ava kicked a <u>Life</u> magazine
          photographer (Gjon Mili). Her description of
          Ava's behavior was "her customary self--amiable
          as an adder."

          See: F46

AB119   Marill, Alvin H., <u>Robert Mitchum on Screen</u>,
          Cranbury, New Jersey: A. S. Barnes and Co., Inc.,
          1978

          Marill depicts <u>My Forbidden Past</u> as "a dreary
          Nineteenth Century costume melodrama that teamed
          Mitchum with Ava Gardner." It is also noted that
          the film was made in 1949 but not released until
          the spring of 1951, by Howard Hughes.

          See: F28

AB120   Peary, Danny, Close-Ups, New York: Workman Publishing,
         1978

         The author includes a short biography, refers to
         The Snows of Kiliminjaro with Gregory Peck, and
         lists her movies. The segment on Ava is written
         by novelist-poet Richard Elman (who wrote Taxi
         Driver), who had met Ava in an elevator years
         previously but didn't have the courage to talk to
         her. The piece was actually a confession of his
         lust for her ever since he first saw her on screen.

         See: F32

AB121   Shaheen, Jack G., Nuclear War Films, Chicago,
         Illinois: Southern Illinois University Press, 1978

         Shaheen provides a synopsis and review of the film
         On The Beach.

         See: F41

AB122   Spoto, Donald, Stanley Kramer - Film Maker, New York:
         G. P. Putnam's Sons, 1978

         Director Stanley Kramer's thought-provoking film
         based on Nevil Shut's novel On The Beach is lauded
         for its intelligence as well as its realistic
         portrayals by Ava Gardner and the other cast members.

         See: F41

AB123   Arce, Hector, The Secret Life of Tyrone Power,
         New York: William Morrow and Company, 1979

         Arce asserts that Ava and other American actors
         who worked on The Sun Also Rises stayed in Europe
         to get a tax break.

         See: F39

AB124   Cassiday, Bruce, Dinah! New York: Franklin Watts,
         Inc., 1979, 1980

         Dinah Shore was a radio singer and actress in the
         1940s. She was up for the role of Julie in Show
         Boat that eventually went to Ava. It was thought
         that Ava's role as Jean Ogilvie in The Hucksters
         was a fictionalized Dinah Shore.

         See: F21, F29

AB125   Ford, Dan, Pappy: The Life of John Ford, New Jersey:
         Prentice-Hall, 1979

         Ford directed Mogambo, which was one of his few
         nonwestern films. At first, he intimidated Ava
         with his overwhelming personality. When she

realized he could be bluffing, she stood up to him. They became friends thereafter.

See: F34

AB126   Guiles, Fred Lawrence, <u>Tyrone Power, The Last Idol</u>, New York: Doubleday, 1979

Darryl Zanuck wanted Ava alone for the role of Lady Brett Ashley in the film <u>The Sun Also Rises</u>. Hemingway, who was a close friend of Ava's and lived nearby in Spain, was appalled at the screenplay.

See: F39

AB127   Hotchner, A. E., <u>Sophia, Living and Loving, Her Own Story</u>, New York: William Morrow, 1979

The author mentions that Ava was considered for the role Sophia won in the film <u>The Pride and The Passion</u> that co-starred her estranged husband, Frank Sinatra.

AB128   Levy, Alan, <u>Forever Sophia</u>, New York: Grosset and Dunlap, Inc., 1979

Sophia briefly talks about the beauty of Ava Gardner and her unhappy marriage to Frank Sinatra.

AB129   Linet, Beverly, <u>Ladd, The Life, The Legend, and The Legacy of Alan Ladd</u>, New York: Arbor House, 1979

After attending a gala at the British Royal Palace, Ava cooked southern fried chicken for a celebrity entourage, dressed in an evening gown.

AB130   Matthews, J. H., <u>Surrealism and American Feature Films</u>, New York: Twayne Publishers, 1979

The lavish and spectacular photography in the film <u>Pandora and The Flying Dutchman</u> were enhanced by the beauty of Ava Gardner.

See: F27

AB131   Merritt, Jeffrey, <u>Day by Day: The Fifties</u>, New York: <u>Facts on File</u>, 1979

The following dates were listed with corresponding
events in Ava's life: July 19, 1951 (premier in
New York of Showboat); November 7, 1951 (Ava and
Sinatra marry in Germantown, Pennsylvania);
December 9, 1951 (Ava and Sinatra robbed of $16,800
in jewelry in London); September 29, 1954 (The
Barefoot Contessa premiers in New York); and
December 17, 1959 (On The Beach premiers in New York).

See: F29, F36, F41

AB132   Placed, J. A., The Non-Western Films of John Ford,
         Secaucus, New Jersey: The Citadel Press, 1979

Ava's fine, Oscar-winning performance is highlighted
in the review of the film Mogambo.

See: F34

AB133   Quirk, Lawrence J., The Films of Robert Taylor,
         Secaucus, New Jersey: The Citadel Press, 1979

Featured were the three films in which Ava
co-starred with Taylor: The Bribe, Ride, Vaquero,
and Knights of The Round Table. Taylor said of
Ava: "A good Joe, comfortable to be around."

See: F24, F33, F35

AB134   Reed, Rex, Travolta to Keaton, New York: William
         Morrow and Company, Inc., 1979

Reed's piece on Ava tells of her reclusiveness;
she lives in an old Victorian home in London. He
felt that Ava was a good actress and that she was
cast as a real estate agent in The Sentinel
because she looked like a real agent.

See: F56

AB135   Wlashin, Ken, The Illustrated Encyclopedia of The
         World's Great Movie Stars and Their Films, From
         1900 to The Present Day, New York: Crown
         Publishers, 1979

In the brief biography on Ava Gardner, she is
referred to as "The World's Most Beautiful Woman,"
which was also conferred to her on posters
advertising the film The Barefoot Contessa (this
poster can be seen in Frank Sinatra's film Not As
a Stranger). Ava's name is also mentioned in the
biographies of Bogart, Gable, and Sinatra.

See: F36

AB136   Bojarski, Richard, The Films of Bela Lugosi,
         Secaucus, New Jersey: The Citadel Press, 1980

         In the feature on Ghosts On The loose, it is
         mentioned that Ava Gardner plays a young newlywed
         who brightens up the lives of the Bowery Boys.
         See: F10

AB137   Clarens, Carlos, Crime Movies, An Illustrated
         History, New York: W. W. Norton and Co., 1980

         Ava's role as Kitty Collins is featured in the
         piece on The Killers.

         See: F17

AB138   Davis, Sammy Jr., Hollywood In a Suitcase, New York:
         William Morrow, 1980, 1981

         Sammy was a member of Frank Sinatra's rat pack while
         Sinatra was married to Ava. Ava's friendship with
         Sammy made the gossip columns because of their
         racial differences.

AB139   Elmo, Don, The Giant Book of Trivia, New York:
         Unisystems, Inc., 1980

         Ava was featured in the "Femme Fatales" segment.
         It is mentioned that Ava's role as the statue
         that comes to life in the film One Touch of Venus
         was originally done by Mary Martin on Broadway.

         See: F23

AB140   Freedland, Michael, Gregory Peck, New York: William
         Morrow, 1980

         Ava co-starred in two films with Peck: The Great
         Sinner and On The Beach. Peck admired Ava's
         beauty and appreciated her earthy personality.

         See: F25, F41

AB141   Higham, Charles, Errol Flynn, The Untold Story,
         New York: Doubleday, 1980, 1981

         In the spring of 1957, Errol Flynn and Ava met
         at Hotel Bamer in Morelia, Mexico to start filming
         The Sun Also Rises.

         See: F39

AB142 Huston, John, <u>An Open Book</u>, New York: Alfred A.
           Knopf, Inc., 1980, 1981

       Huston elaborates on the joy he felt working with
       Ava, whom he considered to be an accomplished,
       underrated actress.

AB143 Linet, Beverly, <u>Susan Hayward: Portrait of a
           Survivor</u>, New York: Atheneum Books, 1980

       The author asserts that Ava was included in the
       many liaisons Hayward's first husband, actor Jess
       Barker, had during their stormy marriage.

AB144 Magill, Frank, <u>Magill's American Film Guide</u>,
           Volumes I-5, New Jersey: Salem Press, 1980-1983

       Noted film reviewer Magill chronicles Ava's films
       and gives favorable credit to her performances in
       <u>Bhowani Junction</u>, <u>The Killers</u>, <u>The Life and Times
       of Judge Roy Bean</u>, <u>Mogambo</u>, <u>Night of The Iguana</u>,
       <u>On The Beach</u>, <u>Seven Days in May</u>, <u>Show Boat</u>, and
       <u>The Sun Also Rises</u>.

       See: F17, F29, F34, F38, F39, F41, F46, F49

AB145 Magill, Frank, <u>Magill's Survey of Cinema</u>, Series I-
           VI, New Jersey: Salem Press, 1980

       Magill continues his series of movie reviews and
       includes Ava's performances in <u>Around the World in
       80 Days</u> (cameo) and <u>Earthquake</u>.

       See: F37, F52

AB146 Medved, Harry and Medved, Michael, <u>The Golden Turkey
           Awards</u>, New York: Perigee Books, 1980, 1981

       The star-studded cast of <u>Earthquake</u> included
       58-year-old Lorne Greene as the father of
       52-year-old Ava Gardner.

       See: F52

AB147 Phillips, Gene, <u>Hemingway and Film</u>, New York: Ungar
           Publishers, 1980

       The author credits Ava's fine performance in <u>The
       Snows of Kiliminjaro</u>.

       See: F32

AB148   Pickard, Roy, <u>The Award Movies, A Complete Guide</u>
          <u>From A to Z</u>, New York: Schocken Books, 1980

          In encyclopedia form are included Ava's movies
          <u>The Barefoot Contessa</u>, <u>The Bible</u>, <u>The Killers</u>,
          <u>Knights of The Round Table</u>, <u>Mogambo</u>, <u>On The Beach</u>,
          and <u>The Snows of Kiliminjaro</u>.

          See: F17, F32, F34-36, F41, F47

AB149   Robertson, Patrick, <u>Guiness Film Facts and Feats</u>,
          London: Guiness Books, 1980

          The author informs readers that Ava played herself
          in the film <u>The Band Wagon</u> and that she had
          originally failed her first screen test.

          See: F31

AB150   Springer, John, <u>Forgotten Films to Remember</u>,
          Secaucus, New Jersey: The Citadel Press, 1980

          Springer compiles and chronicles many movies of
          the 1940s and 1950s that have become true
          classics because of the stories, photography,
          and acting. He features Ava's films <u>The Great</u>
          <u>Sinner</u> (for its photography); <u>Bhowani Junction</u>
          (for its political statement and Ava's acting);
          and <u>The Sun Also Rises</u> (for recreating a classic
          Hemingway work).

          See: F25, F38, F39

AB151   Stempel, Tom, <u>Screenwriter, The Life and Times of</u>
          <u>Nunnally Johnson</u>, New York: A. S. Barnes, 1980

          Nunnally Johnson appreciated Ava's talents and
          she considered him a friend. The author touches
          upon her work on the film <u>The Angel Wore Red</u>,
          co-starring Henry Fonda.

          See: F43

AB152   Winters, Shelley, <u>Shelley, Also Known as Shirley</u>,
          New York: William Morrow, 1980, 1981

          Amid Shelley's confessions of multiple liaisons
          with her male co-stars, she mentions Ava and her
          contribution to M-G-M Studios plus Ava's
          co-starring role in <u>The Naked Maja</u> with Shelley's
          then-husband Anthony Franciosa.

          See: F42

AB153   Campbell, Richard H. with Pitts, Michael R., The
         Bible On Video, A Checklist 1897-1980, New Jersey:
         Scarecrow Press, 1981

         The authors acknowledge that George C. Scott and
         Ava Gardner stood out in their roles as Abraham and
         Sarah, respectively, in the 1966 John Huston film
         The Bible (La Bibbia).

         See: F47

AB154   Cross, Robin, The Big Book of B Movies, or How Low
         was My Budget? New York: St. Martin's Press, 1981

         Cross delineates Ava's role and performance in one
         of her first big parts, Three Men In White.

         See: F15

AB155   Ferris, Paul, Richard Burton, The Actor, The Lover,
         The Star, New York: Coward, McCann and Geoghegan,
         1981

         Ava's initial fear in accepting the role of Maxine
         Faulk in Night of The Iguana then her eventual
         comfort with her character and protrayal are
         recalled.

         See: F46

AB156   Godfrey, Lionel, Cary Grant, The Light Touch,
         New York: St. Martin's Press, 1981

         Sophia Loren replaced Ava on the film The Pride and
         The Passion, which co-starred Grant along with
         Frank Sinatra.

AB157   Guiles, Fred L., Jane Fonda, The Actress in Her Time,
         New York: Doubleday, 1981, 1982

         Jane Fonda found it interesting and enjoyable working
         with two of the screen greats, Elizabeth Taylor and
         Ava Gardner while filming The Blue Bird in Russia.

         See: F54

AB158   Hirschhorn, Clive, The Hollywood Musical, New York:
         Crown Publishers, 1981

         Interesting book containing the musicals in which
         Ava starred for M-G-M and Universal: One Touch of
         Venus, Show Boat, The Band Wagon, and The Blue Bird.

         See: F23, F29, F31, F54

AB159   Kelley, Kitty, <u>Elizabeth Taylor, The Last Star</u>,
        New york: Simon and Schuster, 1981

        Elizabeth Taylor wanted the role Ava won in the film
        <u>The Barefoot Contessa</u>. While filming <u>The Blue Bird</u>
        in the Soviet Union, Taylor and Gardner shared a
        bathroom in their small living quarters on the lot.

        See: F36, F54

AB160   Lamparski, Richard, <u>Lamparski's Hidden Hollywood,</u>
        <u>Where The Stars Lived, Loved, and Died</u>, New York:
        Simon and Schuster, 1981

        The author lists Ava's first Hollywood address at
        the Hollywood Wilcox Hotel at Selma and Wilcox,
        across the street from the post office.

AB161   Magill, Frank, <u>Magill's Survey of Cinema, Series II</u>,
        Volumes 3-5, New Jersey: Salem Press, 1981

        The author chronicles films to date that include
        Ava's cameo in <u>That's Entertainment</u> and <u>The Band Wagon</u>
        plus her performances in <u>Mogambo</u>, <u>The Sun Also Rises</u>,
        <u>Night of The Iguana</u>, and <u>The Life and Times of Judge</u>
        <u>Roy Bean</u>.

        See: F31, F34, F39, F46, F49, F51

AB162   Osborne, Jerry and Hamilton, Bruce, <u>First Edition</u>
        <u>Sound Tracks and Original Cast</u>, Phoenix, Arizona:
        O'Sullivan Woodside and Company, 1981

        The authors provide information on recordings done
        for the movies and include several of her films.
        <u>Show Boat</u> credits Ava's voice on the soundtrack.

        See: F29

AB163   Pickard, Roy, <u>Who Played Who In The Movies</u>, New York:
        Schocken Books, 1981

        The author describes Ava's performance as Queen
        Guinivere in <u>Knights of The Round Table</u> as
        "controlled sensuality."

        See: F35

AB164   Quinlan, David, <u>The Illustrated Directory of Film</u>
        <u>Stars</u>, New York: Hippocrene Books, 1981

        Ava is featured in a short biography and list of
        her films to date. She is also mentioned in the
        biographies of Mickey Rooney and Frank Sinatra.

AB165   Thomson, David, <u>A Biographical Dictionary of Film</u>,
         New York: William Morrow, 1981

         This book contains a brief biography of actress
         Ava Gardner.

AB166   Bookbinder, Robert, <u>The Films of The Seventies</u>,
         Secaucus, New Jersey: The Citadel Press, 1982

         The authors chose <u>The Sentinel</u> as one of the most
         memorable movies of the 1970s. Ava portrayed
         real estate agent Miss Logan, for which she
         garnered favorable reviews in this eerie, cult
         movie.

         See: F56

AB167   Daniell, John, <u>Ava Gardner</u>, New York: St. Martin's
         Press, 1982

         Daniell furnishes a biography and filmography that
         features many movie stills from Ava's film career.

AB168   Flamini, Roland, <u>Ava</u>, New York: Coward, McCann and
         Geoghegan, 1982

         Flamini's book was generally regarded as a rehash
         of tabloid-style news on Ava's life; it included
         no filmography, references, bibliography, or index
         to substantiate some of his claims.

AB169   Garfield, Brian, <u>Western Films</u>, New York: Rawson
         Associates, 1982

         Included in this lengthy book on film oaters
         is Ava's contribution to the scenery in <u>Lone
         Star</u>, <u>Ride, Vaquero</u>, and <u>The Life and Times of
         Judge Roy Bean</u>.

         See: F30, F33, F49

AB170   Goldstein, Norm, <u>Frank Sinatra, O'l Blue Eyes</u>,
         New York: Holt, Rinehart and Winston, 1982

         Ava met Frank Sinatra at the premier of <u>Gentlemen
         Prefer Blondes</u> at the end of 1949 in New York.
         They married at the home of Lester Sachs the day
         after Sinatra's final divorce decree from Nancy
         was received. It is also mentioned that while
         Ava sat for sculptor Josef Nicolosi for the statue
         of Venus for the film <u>One Touch of Venus</u>, she
         dropped her top to give "a touch of realism."

         See: F23

AB171   Jewell, Richard B., and Harbin, Vernon, The RKO Story,
        New York: Arlington House, 1982

        The only film Ava did for RKO Studios was My Forbidden
        Past, where she was sumptuously dressed and woodenly
        directed in this rather short feature film co-starring
        Robert Mitchum.

        See: F28

AB172   Kael, Pauline, 5001 Nights at The Movies - A Guide
        From A-Z, New York: Holt, Rinehart and Winston, 1982

        In this edition, Kael gives surprisingly good reviews
        of Ava's performances in the following films: The
        Barefoot Contessa ("ornate and garrulous; it's classic
        camp"); The Bible ("sprawling epic with breathtaking
        conceptions and moments of beauty"); Earthquake
        ("the picture is swill but it isn't a cheat"); The
        Killers ("director does wonders with Ava Gardner");
        The Life and Times of Judge Roy Bean ("Ava as Lily
        Langtry provides only highlight"); Mayerling ("The
        choice was Ava Gardner--a star famous for beauty and
        underacting--to play Sharif's mother, the Empress,
        seems inspired"); Mogambo ("entertaining--Gardner
        had never seemed happier"); Night of The Iguana
        ("sentimental, dumb"); On The Beach ("Ava is lovable
        wildflower who has lived too hard and drunk too
        much"); One Touch of Venus ("ravishing in a
        bowdlerized version of a Broadway show"); Pandora and
        The Flying Dutchman ("Ava looking unspeakably
        luscious--The Barefoot Contessa but without as much
        talk"); and Show Boat ("Ava at her most beautiful
        as Julie, looks as if she's dying to parody her lines").

        See: F17, F23, F27, F29, F34, F36, F41, F46, F47, F49

AB173   Magill, Frank, Magill's Cinema Annual 1982, 1983,
        New Jersey: Salem Press, 1982

        The author chronicles Ava's good performances in
        The Barefoot Contessa and The Snows of Kiliminjaro
        and Ava's creditable job in a not-well-received
        Priest of Love.

        See: F32, F36, F59

AB174   Slide, Anthony, Selected Film Criticisms, New Jersey:
        Salem Press, 1982

        Slide critiques Ava's films The Snows of Kiliminjaro
        and Show Boat.

        See: F29, F32

AB175   Sealy, Shirley and Williamson, Bruce, <u>The Celebrity Sex Register</u>, New York: Simon and Schuster, 1982

This expose contains a list of Ava's lovers: Mario Cabre, Walter Chiari, Luis Miguel Dominguin, Howard Duff, Howard Hughes, Mickey Rooney, George C. Scott, Artie Shaw, Fred Sidewater, Frank Sinatra, Philip Yordan ("Quite simply the most boring woman I have ever known"), Turhan Bey, Clark Gable ("no bullshit buddy"), and Stewart Granger. Ava's quotes about her lovers: Howard Hughes ("just the ticket for a girl like me from the deep south and lazy") and Sinatra ("was great in bed...the quarreling started on the way to the bidet").

AB176   Strick, Philip, <u>The Great Movie Actresses</u>, New York: William Morrow, 1982

Ava has worked with many of the greats in directing, such as Fred Zinnemann (<u>Kid Glove Killer</u>), William Goldbeck (<u>Three Men in White</u>), Siodmak (<u>The Killers</u>), Robson (<u>The Little Hut</u>), Arthur Lewin (<u>Pandora and The Flying Dutchman</u>), Rakoff (<u>City of Fire</u>), Joseph Mankiewicz (<u>The Barefoot Contessa</u>), Vincent Sherman (<u>Lone Star</u>), and George Cukor (<u>Bhowani Junction</u>), as well as John Huston.

See: F4, F15, F17, F27, F30, F36, F38, F40, F57

AB177   Thompson, Verita with Shepherd, Donald, <u>Bogie and Me</u>, New York: St. Martin's Press, 1982

Ms. Thompson had a long-time clandestine affair with Humphrey Bogart. She corroborates the story of Bogart's needling of Ava during the filming of <u>The Barefoot Contessa</u>. She quotes him as saying Ava was a "Grabtown Gypsy."

See: F36

AB178   Trent, Paul and Lawton, Richard, <u>The Image Makers, Sixty Years of Hollywood Glamour</u>, New York: Crown Publishers, 1982

Ava is mentioned and featured in movie stills from her films <u>The Hucksters</u> and <u>Bhowani Junction</u>.

See: F21, F38

AB179   Turner, Lana, <u>Lana, The Lady, The Legend, The Truth</u>, New York: E. P. Dutton, Inc., 1982

Lana talks about her long-time friendship with Ava, including the fact that they were both married to

Artie Shaw. Lana refutes the tale that was a
scandalized account of Sinatra finding the two lovely
stars in bed together. She asserts that they were,
in fact, in the kitchen eating fried chicken with
Ben Cole.

AB180   Dick, Bernard F., <u>Joseph L. Mankiewicz</u>, New York:
        Twayne Publishers, 1983

        Mankiewicz directed Ava in her fine performance for
        <u>The Barefoot Contessa</u>. He found Ava to be a
        hardworking, punctual, and totally professional star.

        See: F36

AB181   Hardy, Phil, <u>The Western</u>, New York: William Morrow,
        1983

        Ava is credited in the performances she gave in <u>Lone
        Star</u>, <u>Ride, Vaquero</u>, and <u>The Life and Times of Judge
        Roy Bean</u>.

        See: F30, F33, F49

AB182   Hirschhorn, Joel, <u>Consumer Guide Editors Rating The
        Movie Stars</u>, New York: Crown Publishers, 1983

        Ava received 2½ stars in the editors' rating.
        A minimal biography and limited filmography include
        the quote from Joseph Mankiewicz: "Ava is the most
        sittingest actress I've ever worked with."

AB183   Lentz, Harris M., <u>Science Fiction, Horror and
        Fantasy Film and Television Credits</u>, Volume 1,
        North Carolina: McFarland and Company, 1983

        <u>On The Beach</u> is included in this volume, although
        it seems rather out of place with the other horror
        films featured. Ava's role is briefly recounted.

        See: F41

AB184   Lloyd, Ann and Fuller, Graham, <u>The Illustrated Who's
        Who of The Cinema</u>, New York: MacMillan Publishing
        Co., Inc., 1983

        This book provides a limited biography and list of
        Ava's films.

AB185   Mordden, Ethan, <u>A Look at the Women Who Made Hollywood</u>,
        New York: St. Martin's Press, 1983

        Ava Gardner is one of the beauties given credit as
        establishing a lasting career.

AB186   Sennett, Ted, <u>Great Hollywood Movies</u>, New York:
        Harry N. Abrams, Inc., 1983

        The dark-haired temptress Ava Gardner is mentioned
        for her contribution to the movie industry. It
        features photographs from <u>Mogambo</u> and <u>The Killers</u>.

        See: F17, F34

AB187   Thomas, Bob, <u>Golden Boy, The Untrold Story of William
        Holden</u>, New York: St. Martin's Press, 1983

        Highlighted is the story of Ava frying chicken for
        a celebrity party after a gala in London. The
        author also relates the story of Ava skinny dipping
        at a party at Paul and Ruth Clemens' home.

AB188   Walker, Alexander, <u>Joan Crawford, The Ultimate Star</u>,
        New York: Harper and Row, 1983

        While filming <u>Reunion in France</u>, Ava was noticed in
        her bit role by Louis B. Mayer: "I told them she'd
        be a star. The idiots have no flair. I told them."

        See: F3

AB189   Bradford, Sarah, <u>Princess Grace</u>, New York: Stein and
        Day, 1984

        Grace Kelly and Ava Gardner became fast friends
        while working with Clark Gable on <u>Mogambo</u>. Their
        friendship lasted through Kelly's marriage to Prince
        Rainier of Monaco until her death in 1982. Ava was
        the only movie star invited to attend the important
        events in Grace's life: her marriage, her eldest
        daughter's first marriage, and Grace's funeral.

        See: F34

AB190   Eells, George, <u>Robert Mitchum, An Unauthorized
        Biography</u>, New york: Franklin Watts, Inc., 1984

        Mitchum called Ava Gardner "Honest Ave" because
        "she doesn't have to pad her bust."

AB191   Griggs, John, <u>The Films of Gregory Peck</u>, Secaucus,
          New Jersey, The Citadel Press, 1984

          Ava co-starred with Peck in <u>The Great Sinner</u>, <u>On The
          Beach</u>, and <u>The Snows of Kiliminjaro</u>. Her role in
          <u>The Great Sinner</u> was based on the real Polina Suslov,
          mistress of Dostoevsky in 1962 who shared his love for
          gambling, to the detriment of both their lives.

          See: F25, F32, F41

AB192   Haining, Peter, <u>Raquel Welch</u>, New York: St. Martin's
          Press, 1984, 1985

          Ava was considered for a role in a film that was to
          be produced by Raquel's production company, Tilda.
          She was to play Raquel's mother because she still
          was beautiful looking at the age of 46. The screen-
          play was written by Elizabeth Kata (author of <u>A Patch
          of Blue</u>).

AB193   Hayes, David and Walker, Brent, <u>The Films of The
          Bowery Boys</u>, Secaucus, New Jersey: The Citadel
          Press, 1984

          The author's featured Ava's comedic role in <u>Ghosts
          On The Loose</u>.

          See: F10

AB194   Higham, Charles, <u>Audrey, The Life of Audrey Hepburn</u>,
          New York: MacMillan Publishing Company, 1984

          Audrey Hepburn and Ava adored eachother and spent
          time shopping together during the European shooting
          of <u>The Sun Also Rises</u>, which co-starred Audrey's
          husband, Mel Ferrer. Ava was dating Peter Viertel
          during this time after she broke up with Walter
          Chairi.

          See: F39

AB195   Hunter, Allan, <u>Burt Lancaster, The Man and His Movies</u>,
          New York: St. Martin's Press, 1984

          Burt and Ava smoldered together in <u>The Killers</u>.
          Twenty years or so later they appeared in the
          political intrigue <u>Seven Days in May</u>.

          See: F17, F45

AB196   Leigh, Janet, There Really was a Hollywood, New York:
         Doubleday, 1984

         Ava gave Janet a bridal shower before her wedding
         to Tony Curtis. Ava and Frank Sinatra made a
         Christmas appearance at the London Colosseum, at a
         benefit appearance for National Playing Fields
         Association sponsored by the International Variety
         Club. When the rest of the entourage left (including
         Tony Curtis, Janet Leigh, Rhonda Fleming, Dorothy
         Kristen, Jimmy Van Heusen, Jimmy McHugh, and John
         Haskell), Sinatra and Ava had a fight and decided
         not to go.

AB197   Warner, Alan, Who Sang What On The Screen, Australia:
            Angus H. Robertson Publishing, 1984

         Ava sang "Lovers Were Meant to Cry" to Clark Gable
         in Lone Star.   Eileen Wilson sang for Ava (as
         Pepper) and did a rendition of "Don't Tell Me" in
         The Hucksters. Wilson again dubbed the singing
         for Ava in One Touch of Venus, singing "Speak Low"
         to Dick Haymes. Wilson sang for Ava but was credited
         for singing "The More I Know of Love" for the film
         The Killers. Annette Warren sang "Bill" for the film
         Show Boat (Ava provided her own voice on the sound-
         track version).

         See: F17, F21, F23, F29, F30

AB198   Woodward, Ian, Audrey Hepburn, New York: St. Martin's
            Press, 1984

         It is mentioned that Alberto de Rossi was the Italian
         make-up artist for Ava, Audrey Hepburn, and
         Elizabeth Taylor.

AB199   Arden, Eve, Three Faces of Eve, New York: St. Martin's
            Press, 1985

         Arden co-starred with Ava in One Touch of Venus.
         She felt Ava was truly one of the most beautiful
         creatures on the face of the earth with a real
         down-to-earth personality. She also believed that
         Ava had a haunting sadness about her when she played
         with Eve's children on visits to her home.

         See: F23

AB200 Bookbinder, Robert, Classics of The Gangster Film,
         Secaucus, New Jersey: The Citadel Press, 1985

       The author provides a critique of performances in
       the 1946 movie The Killers.

       See: F17

AB201 Drosnin, Michael, Citizen Hughes, New York: Holt,
         Rinehart and Winston, 1985

       Ava's short-lived, stormy love relationship with
       Howard Hughes is noted.

AB202 Giroux, Robert, 500 Best American Films to Buy, Rent,
         or Videotape, New York: First Pocket Books, 1985

       The author indicates that the following films were
       available to date: The Band Wagon, The Killers,
       On The Beach, Show Boat, and That's Entertainment.

       See: F17, F29, F31, F41, F51

AB203 La Guardia, Robert and Arceri, Gene, Red, The
         Tempestuous Life of Susan Hayward, New York:
         MacMillan, 1985

       Susan Hayward considered Ava to be lazy and
       unprofessional. She was very jealous of Ava
       Gardner.

AB204 Morley, Sheridan, The Other Side of The Moon, A
         Biography of David Niven, New York: Harper and
         Row, 1985

       Ava shared the screen with Niven in The Little Hut
       and 55 Days at Peking. His gentlemanly behavior
       helped Ava give relatively good performances in
       less-than-well-received movies.

       See: F40, F44

AB205 Munn, Michael, Kirk Douglas, A Biography, New York:
         St. Martin's Press, 1985

       Douglas claims he bowedout of the film The Great
       Sinner. Frankenheimer encouraged Ava to appear in
       the movie Seven Days in May after a six-year absence
       from the screen.

       See: F25, F45

AB206 Ragan, David, <u>Movie Stars of the 40s</u>, Englewood
          Cliffs, New Jersey: Prentice-Hall, 1985

       Ava's biography mentions her marriages to Mickey
       Rooney and Frank Sinatra.

AB207 Schmering, Christopher, <u>The Soap Opera Encyclopedia</u>,
          New York: Ballantine Books, 1985

       Ava appeared on <u>Knots Landing</u> as Ruth Galveston. She
       proved to be a highlight of the night-time soap
       opera by trying to bust up relationships in the
       story line.

       See: T1

AB208 Sinatra, Nancy, <u>Frank Sinatra, My Father</u>, New York:
          Doubleday, 1985

       Nancy relates her first meeting with the beautiful
       new stepmother as being awesome yet not intimidating.
       Ava gave Nancy her first lipstick.

AB209 Thomas, Tony, <u>Howard Hughes in Hollywood</u>, Secaucus,
          New Jersey: The Citadel Press, 1985

       Howard Hughes was infatuated with the lovely movie
       star, who fit his idea of the perfect female.

AB210 Wallis, Donald, <u>Variety's Complete Science Fiction
          Reviews</u>, New York: Garland Publishing, 1985

       Ava and Gregory Peck made a good romantic team,
       according to the author, for their roles in <u>On
       The Beach.</u>

       See: F41

AB211 Douglas, Melvyn and Arthur, Tom, <u>See You at The Movies</u>,
          <u>The Autobiography of Melvyn Douglas</u>, Lanham,
          Maryland: University Press of America, Inc., 1986

       Douglas felt his love scenes with Ava in <u>My Forbidden
       Past</u> were nothing to write home about until he saw
       the raw erotic magnetism picked up by the camera and
       projected on the film.

       See: F28

AB212 Francisco, Charles, <u>David Niven: Endearing Rascal</u>,
          New York: St. Martin's Press, 1986

The author mentions Ava for her roles in the silly
film <u>The Little Hut</u> and the epic loser <u>55 Days at
Peking</u>.

See: F40, F44

AB213   Friedrich, Otto, <u>City of Nets</u>, New York: Harper and
         Row, 1986

Ava's segments include her relationship with Howard
Hughes, being new to Hollywood, courting Artie Shaw,
and appearing on <u>Knots Landing</u>.

See: T1

AB214   Kelley, Kitty, <u>His Way, the Unauthorized Biography of
         Frank Sinatra</u>, New York: Bantam, 1986

Kelley includes all the gossip, scandal, and tidbits
from interviews and publications written about
Sinatra's life, including his marriage to Ava Gardner.

AB215   Quinlan, David, <u>Quinlan's Illustrated Directory of
         Film Stars</u>, New York: Hippocrene Books, Inc., 1986

Quinlan features short biography and listing of Ava's
movies.

AB216   Terrace, Vincent, <u>Encyclopedia of Television Series,
         Pilots, and Specials, The Index of Who's Who in
         Television, Volume III, 1934-84</u>, New York: Zoetrope,
         1986

Featured are the episodes on <u>Knots Landing</u> that
Ava appeared in (dates, time, network, etc.).

See: T1

AB217   Vinson, James, <u>Actors and Actresses, The International
         Dictionary of Films and Filmmakers</u>, Volume 3,
         Chicago, Illinois, St. James Press, 1986

Vinson includes a mundane biography of Ava gardner.

AB218   Altman, Rick, <u>The American Film Musical</u>, Indiana:
         Indiana University Press, 1987

Ava's rise to stardom is touched upon.

AB219   Boller, Hal F., and Davis, Ronald L., Hollywood
         Anecdotes, New York: William Morrow and Company,
         1987

         Included are the tidbits: Ava trained as a
         secretary; she stayed out late; she was referred
         to as a beautiful sex symbol of Hollywood.

AB220   Spada, James, Grace, The Secret Lives of a Princess,
         New York: Doubleday, 1987

         Spada paints an unprincessly picture of Grace Kelly.
         Ava is remembered as her friend.

AB221   Thomson, David, Warren Beatty and Desert Eyes,
         New York: Doubleday, 1987

         The author tells of a commercial announcement Ava
         did to promote the film Earthquake. In a Paris
         nightspot, Ava's look-alike is spotlighted.

         See: F52

AB222   Wayne, Jane Ellen, Gable's Women, Englewood Cliffs,
         New Jersey: Prentice-Hall, 1987

         In the background information given about Gable's
         co-star in The Hucksters, Lone Star, and Mogambo,
         Ava's birthplace is indicated to be Boon Hill,
         North Carolina.

         See: F21, F30, F34

AB223   Brodge, Douglas, Lost Films of The Fifties,
         Secaucus, New Jersey: The Citadel Press, 1988

         The author feels that Ava Gardner had never looked
         more radiant than in the film Pandora and The
         Flying Dutchman.

         See: F27

AB224   Crane, Cheryl with Jahr, Cliff, Detour, A Hollywood
         Story, New York: William Morrow, 1988

         Crane, daughter and only child of actress Lana
         Turner, recounts her mother's lasting friendship
         with Ava.

AB225 Douglas, Kirk, The Ragman's son, An Autobiography,
       New York: Simon and Schuster, 1988

       Although not written in great detail, Douglas claims
       to have had an affair with Ava Gardner at the height
       of her career.

AB226 Quinlan, David, Wicked Women of The Screen, The Lives
       and Careers of The Great On-Screen Schemers,
       Seducers, Double Crossers, and Temptresses,
       New York: St. Martin's Press, 1988

       Ava's role as the young singer/gangster moll in
       The Killers is credited as having an impact on the
       film world.

       See: F17

AB227 Reynolds, Debbie and Columbia, David Patrick, Debbie,
       My Life, New York: William Morrow, 1988, 1989

       As one of M-G-M Studio's great entertainers, Debbie
       Reynolds holds court in her book and provides many
       anecdotes of the greats she had worked with or been
       associated with by virtue of being a studio member,
       including Ava Gardner. She refers to Ava's initial
       shyness at the studio then to her rise to stardom.

AB228 Torme, Mel, It Wasn't All Velvet, New York: Viking
       Penguin, Inc., 1988

       Mel Torme had a beautiful voice that melted a lot of
       young actresses' hearts as well as the public fans.
       As a newcomer to films, he met the luscious Ava
       Gardner, with whom he shared romantic dates.

AB229 Davis, Sammy Jr., and Boyer, Jane and burt, Why Me?
       New York: Farrar, Strauss and Giroux, 1989

       Sammy writes about the pining love that Frank Sinatra
       carried for Ava after their break-up, when Sinatra
       still sang love songs to her at his musical
       engagements, even though she wasn't there to
       appreciate them.

AB230 Grobel, Lawrence, The Hustons, New York: Scribner's
       Sons, 1989

       Ava's friendship with John Huston is discussed.

After Ava made <u>The Killers</u>, Huston wanted very much to get romantically involved with Ava. They ended up being good friends instead.

See: F17

AB231   Higham, Charles and Moseley, Roy, <u>Cary Grant, A</u>
        <u>Lonely Heart</u>, Orlando, Florida: Harcourt Brace
        Jovanovich, 1989

According to the authors, Ava supposedly had an affair with writer Joe Hyams while he conducted lengthy interviews with her that were later published in <u>Life</u> magazine.

AB232   Klain, Jane, <u>International Television and Video</u>
        <u>Almanac</u>, New York: Quickley Publishing Company,
        1989

This reference book erroneously lists Ava as having appeared on <u>Falcon Crest</u>, instead of <u>Knots Landing</u>.

See: T1

AB233   Leaming, Barbara, <u>If This was Happiness, A Biography</u>
        <u>of Rita Hayworth</u>, New York: Viking Press, 1989

On the New Year's Eve party following Rita's divorce from Orson Welles, Ava found a sleeping Rita and covered her up. She proposed hiring a limo to take Rita home, but Rita ended up staying there until the next day.

AB234   Robinson, Jeffrey, <u>Rainier and Grace, An Intimate</u>
        <u>Portrait</u>, New York: Atlantic Monthly Press, 1989

While filming <u>Mogambo</u>, Grace and Ava wanted to attend a pantomime show in town. Ava passed herself off as Gable's secretary and got tickets. Clark Gable was lividly angry, but Grace thought the situation was hilarious. Although Ava was separated from Sinatra at the time, she sat beside him at the wedding of Prince Rainier and Grace Kelly.

See: F34

AB235   Wayne, Jane Ellen, <u>Ava's Men: The Private Life of</u>
        <u>Ava Gardner</u>, New York: St. Martin's Press, 1989

The author exhaustively chronicles Ava's liaisons.

See: AP277

AB236   Winters, Shelley, <u>Shelley II, The Middle of My Century</u>,
        New York: Simon and Schuster, 1989

        Shelley's jealousy of the beautiful Ava Gardner (who
        co-starred with her then-husband, Anthony Franciosa,
        in <u>The Naked Maja</u>) is very evident in her second
        confessional. Shelley claims that during shooting,
        Ava had to have the best cameraman, crew, makeup
        people, etc., because Ava was just a spoiled M-G-M
        baby on loan. She captions a photograph of Franciosa
        and Gardner: "Don't they look beautiful together?
        Wouldn't it have been nice if they had been making the
        same movie? Ava was doing <u>The Naked Maja</u> and he was
        doing <u>Goya</u>." She also coveted Ava's role of Maxine
        Faulk in <u>Night of The Iguana</u>. She quotes Ava as saying
        (in Rome), "In peacetime, Italians feed the cats of
        Rome. In wartime, cats feed the people."

        See: F42, F46

UNANNOTATED BOOKS

UB1   Blum, Daniel, <u>Screen World 1950-58</u>, New York: Biblo
      and Tannen, 1950-58

UB2   Blum, Daniel and Kobal, John, <u>A New Pictorial History
      of The Talkies</u>, New York: G. P. Putnam's Sons,
      1958, 1968, 1973, 1982

UB3   Flynn, Errol, <u>My Wicked, Wicked Ways</u>. New York: G. P.
      Putnam's Sons, 1959

UB4   Goodman, Ezra, <u>The Fifty Year Decline and Fall of
      Hollywood</u>, New York: Simon and Schuster, 1961

UB5   Williams, Tennessee, <u>Night of The Iguana</u>, New York:
      New American Library, 1961

UB6   Fenin, George N. and Everson, William K., <u>The Western</u>,
      New York: Grossman Publishers, 1962, 1973

UB7   Schickel, Richard, <u>Stars</u>, New York: Dial, 1962

UB8   Dahl, Arlene, <u>Always Ask a Man</u>, New York: Prentice-Hall,
      1965

UB9   Halliwell, Leslie, The Filmgoer's Companion, New York:
       Avon Books, 1965

UB10   Willis, John, Screen World 1966, Volume 17, New York:
       Crown Publishers, 1966   .

UB11   Dickens, Homer, The Films of Marlene Dietrich,
       Secaucus, New Jersey: The Citadel Press, 1968

UB12   Levant, Oscar, The Unimportance of Being Oscar,
       New York: Simon and Schuster, 1968

UB13   Quirk, Lawrence J., The Films of Joan Crawford,
       Secaucus, New Jersey: The Citadel Press, 1968

UB14   Guiles, Fred Lawrence, Norma Jean, The Life of
       Marilyn Monroe, New York: McGraw Hill Publishers,
       1969

UB15   Weaver, John T., Forty Years of Screen Credits,
       1929-69, Volume 1:A-J, New Jersey: Scarecrow
       Press, 1970

UB16   Willis, John, Screen World 1970, New York: Crown
       Publishers, 1970

UB17   Salem, James M., A Guide to Critical Reviews, Part IV:
       The Screenplay from The Jazz Singer to Dr.
       Strangelove, Volume I/II, New Jersey: The Scarecrow
       Press, 1971

UB18   Vermilye, Jerry, Burt Lancaster, Hollywood's Magic
       People, New York: Falcon Enterprises, 1971

UB19   Willis, John, Screen World 1971, Volume 22, New York:
       Crown Publishers, 1971

UB20   Hunt, Todd, Reviewing For The Mass Media, New York:
       Chilton Publishers, 1972

UB21   Sadoul, Georges, Dictionary of Films, University of
       California Press, 1972

UB22   Willis, John, Screen World 1972, Volume 23, New York:
        Crown Publishers, 1972

UB23   Bayer, William, The Great Movies, New York: Grosset
        and Dunlap, Inc., 1973

UB24   Green, Stanley, Starring Fred Astaire, New York: Dodd,
        Mead Publishers, 1973

UB25   Willis, John, Screen World 1973, Volume 24, New York:
        Crown Publishers, 1973

UB26   Berle, Milton and Frankel, Haskel, Milton Berle,
        New York: Delacorte Press, 1974

UB27   Gross, Martina A., The Nostalgia Quiz Book #2,
        New York: Arlington House, Inc., 1974

UB28   Harrison, Rex, Rex, New York: Dell Publishing Co.,
        Inc., 1974

UB29   Kazan, Elia and Ciment, Michel, Kazan on Kazan,
        New York: Viking Press, 1974

UB30   Ringgold, Gene, The Films of Rita Hayworth, The
        Legend and Career of a Love Goddess, Secaucus,
        New Jersey: The Citadel Press, 1974

UB31   Tyler, Parker, A Pictorial History of Sex in Films,
        Secaucus, New Jersey: The Citadel Press, 1974

UB32   Agan, Patrick, Is That Who I Think It Is? Volume 1,
        New York: Ace Books, 1975

UB33   Austin, David, Scott, Robert, and Snyder, Harry, A
        Pictorial History of Sex in The Movies, New York:
        The Hamlin Publishing Group, Ltd., 1975

UB34   Benchley, Nathaniel, Humphrey Bogart, Boston,
        Massachusetts: Little Brown & Co., 1975

UB35   Fleming, Karl and Fleming, Anne Taylor, The First
        Time, New York: Simon and Schuster, 1975

UB36   Hanna, David, _The World of Jacqueline Susann_, New York:
        Manor Books, Inc., 1975

UB37   Niven, David, _Bring On The Empty Horses_, New York:
        G. P. Putnam's Sons, 1975

UB38   Webster, Ned, _Penny Crossword Puzzles_, #27, New York:
        Pocket Books, 1975

UB39   Willis, John, _Screen World 1975_, Volume 26, New York:
        Crown Publishers, 1975

UB40   Galella, Ron, _Off-Guard_, New York: Crown Publishers,
        1976

UB41   Lamparski, Richard, _Lamparski's Whatever Became of...?_
        New York: Bantam Books, 1976

UB42   Parish, James Robert and De Carl, Lennard, _Hollywood
        Players: The Forties_, New York: Arlington House,
        1976

UB43   Saltz, Donald, _The Bantam Trivia Quiz Book 2_, New York:
        Bantam Books, 1976

UB44   Valentino, Lou, _The Films of Lana Turner_, Secaucus,
        New Jersey: The Citadel Press, 1976

UB45   Vance, Malcolm, _Tara Revisited_, New York: Award
        Books, 1976

UB46   Willis, John, _Screen World 1976_, Volume 27, New York:
        Crown Publishers, 1976

UB47   Casper, Joseph Andrew, _Vincente Minnelli and The
        Film Musical_, New York: A. S. Barnes, 1977

UB48   Exner, Judith, _My Story, as Told to Ovid Demaris_,
        New York: Grove Press, Inc., 1977

UB49   Kreidl, John F., <u>Nicholas Ray, Guide to References</u>
       <u>and Resources</u>, New York: Twayne Publishers, 1977

UB50   La Guardia, Robert, <u>Monty - A Biogrpahy of Montgomery</u>
       <u>Clift</u>, New York: Avon Books, 1977

UB51   Parish, James Robert and Stanke, Don E., <u>The All-</u>
       <u>Americans</u>, New York: The Arlington House, 1977

UB52   Quirk, Lawrence J., <u>The Films of Ronald Colman</u>,
       Secaucus, New Jersey: The Citadel Press, 1977

UB53   Willis, John, <u>Screen World 1977</u>, Volume 28, New York:
       Crown Publishers, 1977

UB54   Erens, Patricia, <u>The Films of Shirley MacLaine</u>, New
       York: A. S. Barnes, 1978

UB55   Godfrey, Lionel, <u>Paul Newman, Superstar</u>, New York:
       St. Martin's Press, 1978

UB56   Geist, Kenneth L., <u>Pictures Will Talk, The Life and</u>
       <u>Films of Joseph L. Mankiewicz</u>, New York: Scribner
       Publishing Company, 1978

UB57   Parish, James Robert, Mank, Gregory, and Stanke, Don,
       <u>The Hollywood Beauties</u>, New York: The Arlington
       House, 1978

UB58   Stallings, Penny with Mandelbaum, Howard, <u>Flesh and</u>
       <u>Fantasy</u>, New York: St. Martin's Press, 1978

UB59   Suid, Lawrence H., <u>Guts: Glory</u>, New York: Addison
       Wesley Press, 1978

UB60   Thomas, Bob, <u>Joan Crawford: A Biography</u>, New York:
       Simon and Schuster, 1978

UB61   Truffaut, Francois, <u>The Films of My Life</u>, New York:
       Simon and Schuster, 1978

UB62   Willis, John, <u>Screen World 1978</u>, Volume 29, New York:
       Crown Publishers, 1978

UB63   Agan, Patrick, The Decline and Fall of The Love
       Goddesses, Los Angeles, California: Pinnacle Books,
       1979

UB64   Colombo, John Robert, Popcorn in Paradise, The Wit
       and Wisdom of Hollywood, New York: Holt, Rinehart,
       and Winston, 1979

UB65   Katz, Ephraim, The Film Encyclopedia, New York:
       Thomas Y. Crowell Publishers, 1979

UB66   Marx, Kenneth S., Star Stats, Who's Whose in
       Hollywood, Los Angeles, California: Price, Stern,
       Sloan Publishers, Inc., 1979

UB67   Moreno, Eduardo, The Films of Susan Hayward, Secaucus,
       New Jersey: The Citadel Press, 1979

UB68   Schary, Dore, Heyday, New York: Berkley Books, 1979

UB69   Scheuer, Steven H., The Television Annual 1978-79,
       New York: MacMillan Publishing Co., Inc., 1979

UB70   Speed, F. Maurice, Film Review 1979-80, New York:
       Elsevier-Dutton, 1979

UB71   Taylor, Theodore, Jule, The Story of Composer Jule
       Styne, New York: Random House, 1979

UB72   Thomas, Tony and Solomon, Aubrey, The Films of 20th
       Century-Fox, Secaucus, New Jersey: The Citadel
       Press, 1979

UB73   Tierney, Gene with Herskowitz, Mickey, Self-Portrait,
       New York: Wyden Books, 1979

UB74   Willis, John, Screen World 1979, Volume 30, New York:
       Crown Publishers, 1979

UB75   Basten, Fred E., Glorious Technicolor, The Movies'
       Magic Rainbow, New York: A. S. Barnes, 1980

UB76   Denis, Christopher P., The Films of Shirley MacLaine,
       Secaucus, New Jersey: The Citadel Press, 1980

UB77   Gurvitz, Ian, _The Great TV and Movie Quiz_, New York:
        Prestige Books, Inc., 1980

UB78   Kobal, John, _Film-Star Portraits of The Fifties_,
        New York: Dover Publications, 1980

UB79   Lane, Hana Umlauf, _The World Almanac Book of Who_,
        New Jersey: Prentice-Hall, 1980

UB80   Mailer, Norman, _Of Women and Their Elegance_,
        New York: Simon and Schuster, 1980

UB81   Michael, Paul, _The Great American Movie Book_,
        New Jersey: Prentice-Hall, 1980

UB82   Newquist, Roy, _Conversations with Joan Crawford_,
        New York: Berkley Books, 1980

UB83   Reagan, Nancy with Libby, Bill, _Nancy_, New York:
        William Morrow & Co., 1980

UB84   Strait, Raymond and Robinson, Terry, _Lanza, His
        Tragic Life_, New Jersey: Prentice-Hall, 1980

UB85   Strasberg, Susan, _Bittersweet,_ New York: G. P.
        Putnam's Sons, 1980

UB86   Willis, John, _Screen World 1980_, Volume 31, New York:
        Crown Publishers, 1980

UB87   Bronaugh, Robert Brett, _The Celebrity Birthday Book_,
        New York: Jonathan David Publishers, 1981

UB88   Bumgardner, C. W., _Movie Trivia Quiz Book_, New York:
        Ventura Associates, Inc., 1981

UB89   Connor, Jim, _Ann Miller - Tops in Taps, An Authorized
        Pictorial History_, New York: Franklin Watts
        Publishing, 1981

UB90   Fisher, Eddie, _Eddie, My Life, My Loves_, New York:
        Harper and Row, 1981

UB91   Green, Stanley, Encyclopedia of The Musical Film,
       New York: Oxford University Press, 1981

UB92   Howard, Brett, Lana, Los Angeles, California:
       Holloway House Publishing Company, 1981

UB93   Kaplan, Mike, Variety International Show Business
       Reference, Volume 292, New York: Garland Reference
       Library of the Humanities, 1981

UB94   McCambridge, Mercedes, A Quality of Mercy, New York:
       Times Books, 1981

UB95   Willis, John, Screen World 1981, Volume 32, New York:
       Crown Publishers, 1981

UB96   Allyson, June with Leighton, Frances Spatz, June
       Allyson, New York: G. P. Putnam's Sons, 1982

UB97   Brown, Jay A., Rating The Movies, Skokie, Illinois:
       Publications International Ltd., 1982-87

UB98   Carey, Gary, Judy Holliday, An Intimate Life Story,
       New York: Seaview Books, 1982

UB99   Crawley, Tony, Screen Dreams, The Hollywood Pinup,
       New York: G. P. Putnam's Sons, 1982

UB100 Dallinger, Nat, Unforgettable Hollywood, New York:
       William Morrow and Company, Inc., 1982

UB101 Pero, Taylor and Rovin, Jeff, Always, Lana, New York:
       Bantam Books, 1982

UB102 Willis, John, Screen World 1982, Volume 33, New York:
       Crown Publishers, 1982

UB103 Di Orio, Al, Barbara Stanwyck, A Biography, New York:
       Berkley Books, 1983

UB104 Moger, Art, Hello! My Real Name Is..., Secaucus,
       New Jersey: The Citadel Press, 1983

UB105   Simonet, Thomas, <u>Oscar: A Pictorial History of The</u>
         <u>Academy Awards</u>, Chicago, Illinois: Contemporary
         Books, 1983

UB106   Spoto, Donald, <u>The Dark Side of Genius: The Life of</u>
         <u>Alfred Hitchcock</u>, New York: Little, Brown and
         Company, 1983

UB107   Willis, John, <u>Screen World 1983</u>, Volume 34, New York:
         Crown Publishers, 1983

UB108   Yates, Paula, Blondes, <u>A History From The Earliest</u>
         <u>Roots</u>, New York: G. P. Putnam Publishing Group,
         1983

UB109   Clinch, Minty, <u>Burt Lancaster</u>, New York: Stein and
         Day, 1984

UB110   Dickens, Homer, <u>The Films of Barbara Stanwyck</u>,
         Secaucus, New Jersey: The Citadel Press, 1984

UB111   Einstein, Xavier, <u>Trivia Mania</u>, New York: Zebra
         Books, 1984

UB112   Rovin, Jeff, <u>Joan Collins, The Unauthorized Biography</u>,
         New York: Bantam Books, 1984

UB113   Stacy, Jan and Syversten, Ryder, <u>The Great Book of</u>
         <u>Movie Villains</u>, Chicago, Illinois: Contemporary
         Books, Inc., 1984

UB114   Willis, John, <u>Screen World 1984</u>, Volume 35, New York:
         Crown Publishers, 1984

UB115   Windeler, Robert, <u>Burt Lancaster</u>, New York:
         St. Martin's Press, 1984

UB116   Kaplan, Mike, <u>Variety Who's Who In Show Business</u>,
         New York: Garland Publishing, Inc., 1985

UB117   Limbacher, James L., <u>Feature Films: Directory of</u>
         <u>Feature Films on 16mm and Videotape Available</u>
         <u>for Rental, Sale, and Lease</u>, New York: R. R.
         Bowker Company, 1985

UB118   O'Neill, Terry, Legends, New York: Viking Pres, 1985

UB119   Russell, Jane, Jane Russell, An Autobiography - My
        Past and My Detours, New York: Franklin Watts,
        Inc., 1985

UB120   Summers, Anthony, Goddess, The Secret Lives of
        Marilyn Monroe, New York: New American Library,
        1985

UB121   Variety Presents: The Complete Book of Major U.S.
        Show Business Awards, New York: Garland Reference
        Library of The Humanities, 1985

UB122   Willis, John, Screen World 1985, Volume 36, New York:
        Crown Publishers, 1985

UB123   Alpert, Hollis, Burton, New York: G. P. Putnam's
        Sons, 1986

UB124   Bergan, Ronald, The United Artists Story, New York:
        Crown Publishers, 1986

UB125   Buckley, Gail Lumet, The Hornes, New York: Alfred A.
        Knopf, 1986

UB126   Dyer, Richard, Stars, London, England: BFI Publishers,
        1986

UB127   Heide, Robert and Gilman, John, Starstruck, The
        Wonderful World of Movie Memorabilia, New York:
        Doubleday Publishing Company, 1986

UB128   Linet, Beverly, Star Crossed, The Story of Robert
        Walker and Jennifer Jones, New York: G. P.
        Putnam's Sons, 1986

UB129   Lippe, Richard, Actors and Actresses, The
        International Dictionary of Films and Film
        Makers, Volume III, Chicago, Illinois:
        St. Martin's Press, 1986

UB130   Martin, Mick and Porter, Marsha, Video Movie Guide,
        New York: Ballantine Books, 1986

UB131   Parish, James Robert and Terrace, Vincent, Actors'
        Television Credits Supplement III, New Jersey:
        Scarecrow Press, 1986

UB132   Pitts, Michael R., Western Movies, A TV and Video
        Guide to 4200 Genre Films, North Carolina:
        McFarland and Company, 1986

UB133   Willis, John, Screen World 1986, Volume 37, New York:
        Crown Publishers, 1986

UB134   Brooks, Tim, The Complete Directory to Prime Time TV
        Stars, 1946-Present, New York: Random House, 1987

UB135   Norman, Barry, The Story of Hollywood, New York:
        Signet Book, 1987

UB136   Van Doren, Mamie with Aveilhe, Art, Playing The Field,
        New York: G. P. Putnam's Sons, 1987

UB137   Willis, John, Screen World 1987, Volume 38, New York:
        Crown Publishers, 1987

UB138   Edwards, Anne, Shirley Temple: American Princess,
        New York: William Morrow and Company, 1988

UB139   Europa Publications Unlimited, International Who's Who,
        1988-89, Beverly Hills, California: Jerry Martin-
        Morris Agency, 1988

UB140   Gam, Rita, Actors: A Celebration, New York:
        St. Martin's Press, 1988

UB141   Jenkins, Graham with Tuern, Barry, Richard Burton, My
        Brother, New York: Harper and Row Publishers, 1988

UB142   Marquis, Who's Who in America, Wilmette, Illinois:
        MacMillan Directory Division, 1988

UB143   Monaco, James, Who's Who In American Film Now,
        1975-80, New York: Zoetrope, 1988

UB144   Newman, Kim, <u>Nightmare Movies</u>, New York: Harmony
        Books, 1988

UB145   Wayne, Jane Ellen, <u>Crawford's Men</u>, New Jersey:
        Prentice-Hall, Inc., 1988

UB146   Briggs, Melvyn, <u>Richard Burton, A Life</u>, Boston,
        Massachusetts: Little, Brown and Company, 1989

UB147   Da, Lottie and Alexander, Jan, <u>Bad Girls of The
        Silver Screen</u>, New York: Carroll and Graf
        Publications, Inc., 1989

UB148   Kael, Pauline, <u>Hooked</u>, New York: E. P. Dutton, 1989

UB149   Mandelbaum, Howard and Myer, Eric, <u>Forties Screen
        Style</u>, New York: St. Martin's Press, 1989

UB150   Mitchum, John, <u>Them Ornery Mitchum Boys</u>, Pacifica,
        California: Creatures at Large Press, 1989

ANNOTATED PERIODICALS

AP1   "Milestones," Time, January 19, 1942

        Movie actor Joe Yule, Jr. (Mickey Rooney), age 21,
        marries Hollywood newcomer from North Carolina,
        Ava Gardner, age 19, in Ballard, California.

AP2   Isaacs, Hermine Rich, Theatre Arts, October, 1946

        Ava Gardner, Burt Lancaster, and Edmond O'Brien
        are moderately unfamiliar players that bring a
        touch of welcome countenance in the suitably
        fantastic gangster story, The Killers.

        See: F17

AP3   "Soaps, Success and Gable," Newsweek, July 19, 1947

        Ava walked off with a good portion of the footage
        as a small-time singer waiting for her chance at
        the big time in The Hucksters, co-starring Clark
        Gable.

        See: F21

AP4   "Cinema," Time, July 21, 1947

        Ava is lush as the nightclub singer in The
        Hucksters.

        See: F21

AP5   "Hellinger's Hemingway," <u>Newsweek</u>, September 9,
          1946

          Ava Gardner plays an icy gun-moll in the
          powerful, exciting movie <u>The Killers</u>.

          See: F17

AP6   "M-G-M Hawks Gable in <u>The Hucksters</u>," <u>Life</u>,
          July 28, 1947

          Ava Gardner helps provide a spot of excellence
          in <u>The Hucksters</u>, even though the love story is
          stupefyingly dull.

          See: F21

AP7   Hartung, Philip T., <u>Commonweal</u>, August 1, 1947

          The only bright spot in the below-standard, silly
          film <u>The Hucksters</u> is Ava's role as the singer
          in love with the unknowing Gable.

          See: F21

AP8   O'Hara, Shirley, <u>New Republic</u>, August 11, 1947

          <u>The Hucksters</u> does not show Ava to her advantage,
          although the film is worthwhile.

          See: F21

AP9   Palmer, C., <u>Silver Screen</u>, September, 1947

          Ava Gardner is the farmer's number one daughter
          in an article that tells of Ava's lowly beginnings
          in North Carolina to her rise to stardom with her
          recent film releases.

AP10   "Pearl of a Villain," <u>Newsweek</u>, September 29, 1947

          For her role in <u>Singapore</u>, Ava is given lines
          that even the great Katharine Hepburn couldn't
          make convincing, although she is attractive in
          her attempt.

          See: F22

AP11   "Cinema," Time, October 6, 1947

Ava is deep-chested in Singapore, a quiet, polished
frenzy about nothing. The first 200 women to come
to the box office at the premier won a string of
pearls each.

See: F22

AP12   Martin, Pete, "Tarheel Tornado," Saturday Evening
          Post, June 5, 1948

When Ava Gardner first came to Hollywood, no one
could understand her. She dropped her "g's" "like
magnolia blossoms."

AP13   Bowers, L., "Venus Modern Style," Silver Screen,
          July, 1948

One Touch of Venus starred the voluptuous Ava
Gardner, who brought the statue of Venus to life
in the most lively and lovely way.

See: F23

AP14   "Slight Touch of Venus," Newsweek, September 20,
          1948

Ava is more than adequate in being able to fill
the Grecian equivalent of a sarong in One Touch
of Venus.

See: F23

AP15   "Cinema," Time, September 27, 1948

Ava is lush in One Touch of Venus, a dry comedy
translated from the sprightly Broadway show that
starred Mary Martin.

See: F23

AP16   "What Have You Done to Our Child?" Theatre Arts,
          October, 1948

In One Touch of Venus, Ava is handsome to
perfection; however, she lacks Mary Martin's
charm. Ava is richly endowed with natural charms
that personify the goddess of love.

See: F23

AP17   Howe, H., "The Story of Ava Gardner," <u>Photoplay</u>,
        December, 1948

        The author provides an up-to-date biography of
        the beautiful young movie star whose popularity
        is growing with each picture.

AP18   "Ava Returns Home," <u>Photoplay</u>, January, 1949

        Ava Gardner returned home to Smithfield and posed
        for photographs with the local mayor, who gave
        her the key to the city. Thereafter, she called
        home "Grabtown."

AP19   "Cinema," <u>Time</u>, February 7, 1949

        In <u>The Bribe</u>, Ava beautifully embodies her role
        but hardly acted.

        See: F24

AP20   McCarten, John, <u>New Yorker</u>, February 12, 1949

        In <u>The Bribe</u>, Ava is a steamy torch singer, who
        teams with a hamming Charles Laughton in the
        footless, violent film.

        See: F24

AP21   "Grade C Bribe," <u>Newsweek</u>, February 14, 1949

        Ava Gardner is as discontented as she is
        curvacious in <u>The Bribe</u>.

        See: F24

AP22   Hatch, Robert, <u>New Republic</u>, February 21, 1949

        Ava plays the prize girl in <u>The Bribe</u>, the film
        that makes the cast seem to have taken a bribe
        in order to appear in it.

        See: F24

AP23   Lockhart, Jane, <u>Rotarian</u>, June, 1949

        You've seen it all before in the standard Hollywood
        romance, <u>The Bribe</u>, with Ava as a siren.

        See: F24

AP24   McCarten, John, <u>New Yorker</u>, July 9, 1949

         Beautiful Ava Gardner joins Gregory Peck in <u>The
         Great Sinner</u>, a calamitous endeavor on the evils
         of gambling.

         See: F25

AP25   Hartung, Philip T., <u>Commonweal</u>, July 15, 1949

         Boring performances hinder the pretentious film
         <u>The Great Sinner</u>.

         See: F25

AP26   "Cinema," <u>Time</u>, July 18, 1949

         In <u>The Great Sinner</u>, Ava Gardner acted as if she
         were stranded in a sedate costume party.

         See: F25

AP27   Lockhart, Jane, <u>Rotarian</u>, October, 1949

         Ava Gardner turns in an able peformance in <u>The
         Great Sinner</u>, although the film is probably
         confusing in its moral implications.

         See: F25

AP28   "New Films," <u>Newsweek</u>, December 26, 1949

         Revealingly gowned Ava Gardner provides an
         elementary motive for the infidelity of the
         husband and meets an untimely death in <u>East Side,
         West Side</u>.

         See: F26

AP29   "Cinema," <u>Time</u>, January 30, 1950

         <u>East Side, West Side</u> is a showcase for Ava's
         blissfully pneumatic figure. The movie was
         filmed as if a reader were actually turning the
         pages of the book it was based on.

         See: F26

AP30   Brown, Thomas Gilbert, <u>Library Journal</u>, February 1,
        1950

        Marcia Davenport's novel was transferred to the
        screen in a workmanlike manner. Ava wears her
        siren's dress comfortably.

AP31   Poster, William, <u>Nation</u>, February 18, 1950

        Every member of the cast of <u>East Side, West Side</u>
        utter their lines as if they meant every word
        they say. The film is too calculated and has too
        many subplots.

        See: F26

AP32   Swanson, P., "Don't Be Unhappy," <u>Photoplay</u>,
        March, 1950

        Ava Gardner gives her philosophy on life in a
        brief interview that brings her fans up to date
        on happenings in her world.

AP33   "Home Town Girl," <u>Good Housekeeping</u>, April, 1950

        Film star Ava Gardner tells of her life in the
        south, from her roots to her rise to fame.

AP34   Martin, Pete, <u>Saturday Evening Post</u>, May, 1951

        Ava talked to Martin about her financial status.
        Her expenses were eating away at her $50,000 a
        year salary.

AP35   Carlile, T., "The Truth About Ava," <u>Photoplay</u>,
        January, 1951

        The down-to-earth Ava Gardner proves that
        even her great beauty hasn't changed her basic
        personality.

AP36   O'Leary, D., "Making Friends in Hollywood," <u>Silver</u>
        <u>Screen</u>, March, 1951

        The beautiful screen star Ava Gardner is popular
        with the cast and crew of her films.

AP37   Walbridge, Earle F., <u>Library Journal</u>, March 1, 1951

        Although Ava Gardner is exquisite in <u>My Forbidden</u>
        <u>Past</u>, there is too much mumbo jumbo in the author's
        Creole gumbo, which also applies to the film.

        See: F28

AP38   "Current Feature Films," <u>Christian Century</u>,
        March 19, 1952

        <u>Pandora and The Flying Dutchman</u> is a visually
        beautiful but somehow unmoving film, with Ava
        Gardner and James Mason as two famous legends
        whose philosophical overtones are not always clear.

        See: F27

AP39   Morris, J., "Ava Faces a Problem," <u>Silver Screen</u>,
        April, 1951

        Ava's popularity and demand make it difficult for
        her to have a real home life.

AP40   "New Films," <u>Newsweek</u>, May 7, 1951

        Ava is lush but stiff in her role of Barbara
        Beaurevel in <u>My Forbidden Past</u>.

        See: F28

AP41   "Moss-hung Script," <u>Time</u>, May 14, 1951

        Actress Ava Gardner gets able support from actor
        Melvyn Douglas, who plays a scoundrel with relish,
        and handsome variety of low-necked costumes get
        able support from Ava Gardner.

AP42   Walbridge, Earle F., _Library Journal_, May 15, 1951

Ava's beauty and speech are admirable in the wordy
but peculiarly empty _Pandora and The Flying
Dutchman_.

see: F27

AP43   "Cinema," _Time_, May 28, 1951

Ava Gardner is beautiful in the unmercifully long
Technicolor pastiche of symbolism _Pandora and The
Flying Dutchman_.

See: F27

AP44   Alpert, Hollis, _Saturday Review_, June 9, 1951

In _Show Boat_, Ava's lugubrious role as Julie, who
hits the bottle hard after losing her man, becomes
progressively slack-lipped and red-eyed.

See: F29

AP45   Linden, Michael, _Library Journal_, June 15, 1951

Ava Gardner is pictorially exciting in _Show Boat_,
however, less so as a tragedienne. She is very
good in lip-synching the renditions of "Bill"
and "Can't Help Loving That Man."

See: F29

AP46   Hartung, Philip T., _Commonweal_, June 29, 1951

Ava is extremely effective in _Show Boat_. The way
she puts over a song could melt any heart of stone.

See: F29

AP47   Maxwell, E., "The Gardner-Sinatra Jigsaw,"
       Photoplay, July, 1951

Frank Sinatra has been seen squiring around town the
beautious actress Ava Gardner for some time now. It
is rumored they will wed.

AP48   "New Films," _Newsweek_, July 2, 1951

Visually and strictly on her own, Ava Gardner makes
a stunning Julie in _Show Boat_.

See: F29

AP49   "Cinema," _Time_, July 2, 1951

         Ava Gardner has no trouble looking her part as the
         sensuous Julie in _Show Boat_.

         See: F29

AP50   McCarten, John, _New Yorker_, July 28, 1951

         Ava is given such close scrutiny on the screen in
         Show Boat that her handsome face often looks like
         "a relief map of Yugoslavia." Her lip-synching is
         so rare that she might as well be reciting another
         song.

         See: F29

AP51   "Show Boat Dancers," _Life_, July 30, 1951

         Ava Gardner is lovely looking when she isn't
         singing in the musical _Show Boat_.

         See: F29

AP52   "I'm through With Romance," _Movie Magazine_,
            August, 1951

         Ava denies ever saying it or feeling it.

AP53   "Current Feature Films," _Christian Century_,
            August 1, 1951

         The performances of the entire cast of _Show Boat_
         are creditable.

         See: F29

AP54   "Farmer's Daughter," _Time_, September 3, 1951

         The interview delves into Ava's beginnings
         as a tomboy on a tobacco farm to her change of
         life as a worldly international movie star,
         who still considers herself a "down home" girl.

AP55   "How Ava Gardner Fooled Hollywood," _Photoplay_,
            October, 1951

         Ava Gardner fooled Hollywood by making tinseltown
         believe she was never shy and unsophisticated.

AP56   "Well,' said Frankie, 'we finally made it.'" Life,
        November 19, 1951

        Life magazine presented a selection of wedding
        pictures as a public service to those seeking
        pointers on how to face the camera on those
        occasions.

AP57   McCarten, John, New Yorker, December 15, 1951

        Ava is presented as being as hard to cultivate
        as ragweed in Pandora and The Flying Dutchman, a
        lunatic adaptation of the legend of the old sailor
        who couldn't lie peacefully in his grave until he
        found a woman willing to give her life for him.
        The movie should have won the "Incoherence Award
        of 1951."

        See: F27

AP58   "New Films," Newsweek, December 17, 1951

        Ava Gardner wears dresses cut low enough to
        satisfy the "most exigent" in Pandora and The
        Flying Dutchman.

        See: F27

AP59   "Cinema," Time, January 21, 1952

        In Lone Star, Ava is a lot of woman as the Austin,
        Texas editor who covers the fight for Texas
        statehood.

        See: F30

AP60   Waterbury, R., "The Life and Loves of Ava Gardner,"
        Photoplay, February, 1952

        Waturbury rehashes the short, tempestuous
        marriages to superstar Mickey Rooney and swing
        bandleader Artie Shaw. Her newlywed status as
        Mrs. Frank Sinatra is given best wishes for a
        lasting relationship.

AP61   McCarten, John, New Yorker, February 9, 1952

        Lone Star features Ava Gardner as a lady editor
        who, at first, does not get along with adventurer
        Clark Gable.

        See: F30

AP62   "New Films," Newsweek, February 11, 1952

        Ava ambiguously sings "Lovers Were Meant to Cry"
        to Clark Gable, on his patio, in Lone Star.

        See: F30

AP63   Rogers, V., "What About Ava's Career," Silver Screen,
            March, 1952

        With Ava's marriage to Frank Sinatra underway,
        it was wondered if the beautiful star would give
        up her career in favor of having a family.

AP64   "Notes and Recommendations," Holiday, March, 1952

        The principal lure to the discerning moviegoer
        of the film Pandora and The Flying Dutchman is the
        beauty and vitality of Ava Gardner.

        See: F27

AP65   Hartung, Philip T., Commonweal, March 7, 1952

        Ava Gardner and Clark Gable become romantically
        involved in Lone Star, a rousing horse opera with
        little, if any, historical value.

        See: F30

AP66   "Current Feature Films," Christian Century, April 2,
            1952

        Ava is good as the woman editor who needs to be
        convinced that Texas needs to become annexed in
        this less-than-historical document.

AP67   Clarke, S., "Why They are The Battling Sinatras,"
            Photoplay, June, 1952

        Hot-tempered Italian singer Frank Sinatra and the
        jealousy for his lovely actress wife, Ava Gardner,
        have served the press and public with notice that
        they do not lead sedate lives off-screen.

AP68   Rowland, R. C., "I Can Take It On The Chin," <u>Silver
        Screen</u>, September, 1952

        Beautiful star Ava Gardner may consider herself
        basically lazy, but she can take her career and
        life's hard knocks in stride.

AP69   McCarten, John, <u>New Yorker</u>, September 20, 1952

        The performances of the African fauna in <u>The Snows
        of Kiliminjaro</u> were more interesting than the main
        characters.

        See: F32

AP70   "New Films," <u>Newsweek</u>, September 29, 1952

        Ava Gardner and co-stars Gregory Peck and Susan
        Hayward provide pretentious characterizations in
        the meandering, maudlin romantic interpretation
        of Hemingway's story <u>The Snows of Kiliminjaro</u>.

        See: F32

AP71   Cahoon, Herbert, <u>Library Journal</u>, October 1, 1952

        Ava Gardner gives a surprisingly fine performance
        as Cynthia in the exciting <u>The Snows of
        Kiliminjaro</u>.

        See: F32

AP72   "The Snows of Success - Hollywood Shows How to Hop Up
        Hemingway," <u>Life</u>, October 6, 1952

        20th Century-Fox spent $3 million on this outstanding
        mixture of stars, scenery, sex and sentimentality,
        <u>The Snows of Kiliminjaro</u>.

        See: F32

AP73   Alpert, Hollis, <u>Saturday Review</u>, October 11, 1952

        Ava brings some fancy spots as a girl with a soul
        and on the loose in the long, pretentious <u>Snows of
        Kiliminjaro</u>.

        See: F32

AP74   "Current Feature Films," <u>Christian Century</u>,
         November 19, 1952

         <u>The Snows of Kiliminjaro</u> provides negative
         characters in a movie whose conclusions are as
         vague and uninspiring as they.

         See: F32

AP75   "Ava and Her Times," <u>Newsweek</u>, November 24, 1952

         Ava Gardner and her current comings and goings
         are featured in this article.

AP76   "New Bather, Same Gable," <u>Life</u>, January 26, 1953

         Gardner is cast as a girl no better than she has
         to be in <u>Mogambo</u>. However, Ava's bath is more
         refined than Jean Harlow's was in <u>Red Dust</u>--Ava's
         had a nearly modern shower while Harlow took hers
         in a rain barrel.

         See: F34

AP77   "Why is a Movie Star?" <u>Look</u>, February 10, 1953

         The popular international star Ava Gardner is
         interviewed.

AP78   Attwood, W., "London Memo from William Attwood,
         Subject: Ava," <u>London</u>, March, 1953

         Attwood informs the European fans what upcoming
         projects Ava Gardner is soon to appear in.

AP79   Wilson, Earl, "My Pal, Ava," <u>Silver Screen</u>,
         June, 1953

         News columnist Wilson made interviewing a
         pleasure for the otherwise "hounded" actress.

AP80   "Glamour in Africa: Filming <u>Mogambo</u>," <u>Look</u>,
         June 2, 1953

         Ava Gardner is briefly interviewed on her
         role in the new film <u>Mogambo</u>, a remake of
         <u>Red Dust</u>.

         See: F34

AP81   Alpert, Hollis, <u>Saturday Review</u>, July 18, 1953

Ava is lovely and gives an able performance in the otherwise lackluster western <u>Ride, Vaquero</u>.

See: F33

AP82   "New Feature Films," <u>Newsweek</u>, July 27, 1953

<u>Ride, Vaquero</u> is an interesting variation of the classic western film <u>Shane</u>. In a strange interlude, Ava kisses Robert Taylor and is rewarded with a slap across the face.

See: F33

AP83   "Cinema," <u>Time</u>, July 27, 1953

Miscast in <u>Ride, Vaquero</u>, Ava is exquisitely bored. She makes her role seem drab.

See: F33

AP84   Balling, F. D., "Just Because of Ava," <u>Silver Screen</u>, August, 1953

Ava Gardner brings to her roles much of her own home-grown good sense and nonthreatening beauty that make her a delight.

AP85   Walsh, Moira, <u>America</u>, August 1, 1953

Ava Gardner and Robert Taylor have roles that effectively obscure <u>Ride, Vaquero's</u> historical implications.

See: F33

AP86   Hartung, Philip T., <u>Commonweal</u>, August 7, 1953

<u>Ride, Vaquero</u> is a pretentious film where Ava and Robert Taylor make their romantic interludes only so-so.

See: F33

AP87   "Man, Who Wouldn't Look at Ava?" <u>Look</u>, October 6, 1953

Ava's exquisite beauty on and off the screen enure her to her fans.

AP88   McCarten, John, <u>New Yorker</u>, October 10, 1953

Ava is a toothsome, lissome actress who appears
in the African adventure film <u>Mogambo</u>, that never
quite takes itself seriously.

See: F34

AP89   Knight, Arthur, <u>Saturday Review</u>, October 10, 1953

Ava Gardner is acid and amusing in the once-famous
Jean Harlow manner. Her bright, crackling lines
in <u>Mogambo</u> keep her synthetic role vivid and alive.

See: F34

AP90   "New Feature Films," <u>Newsweek</u>, October 12, 1953

Ava is very fetching and turns up as a delightful
comedienne in <u>Mogambo</u>.

See: F34

AP91   "Cinema," <u>Time</u>, October 12, 1953

<u>Mogambo</u> dialogue seems to date back to an earlier
era than the original film, <u>Red Dust</u>. Ava romps
with a baby elephant and other wildlife.

See: F34

AP92   Owen, Alice G., <u>Library Journal</u>, October 15, 1953

Ava has sparkling lines in the exotic, romantic
<u>Mogambo</u>, set amid big game.

See: ·F34

AP93   Hartung, Philip T., <u>Commonweal</u>, October 16, 1953

Ava Gardner tosses up wisecracks with a flare
in <u>Mogambo</u>, her best role to date.

See: F34

AP94   Walsh, Moira, <u>America</u>, October 17, 1953

<u>Mogambo</u> is an expensive, stylish, visually absorbing
"piece of trash." However, Ava Gardner gets help
from the snappy dialogue that succeeds in making her
role as a shady lady with a heart of gold seem real.

See: F34

AP95   Farber, Manny, Nation, November 21, 1953

Mogambo wasn't good enough to dislike. However, Ava
Gardner, for the first time, acts as if she were
happy in the film.

See: F34

AP96   Gervasi, Ran, American Weekly, January 1, 1954

In this Sunday supplement, Ava supposedly "confessed
all." Gervasi described Ava as if she were a
refugee from a psychiatrist's couch.

AP97   Hine, Al, Holiday, January, 1954

Ava did the lazy-legged, sensual siren to
perfection in Mogambo.

See: F34

AP98   Walbridge, Earle F., Library Journal, January 15,
       1954

The handsome, conventional film Knights of The
Round Table featured a totally miscast Ava Gardner.

See: F35

AP99   Walsh, Moira, America, January 16, 1954

Ava Gardner's Guinevere lends a 20th Century
ingenue note to the love affair between Sir
Lancelot (Robert Taylor) and the queen in Knights
of The Round Table.

See: F35

AP100 McCarten, John, New Yorker, January 16, 1954

In Knights of The Round Table, Ava's unemotional
yet dignified air created an atmosphere of chaste
feelings in her affair with Lancelot.

See: F35

AP101 Alpert, Hollis, Saturday Review, January 16, 1954

Ava Gardner is silly in her role as Guinevere
in the otherwise handsomely-produced costume
epic Knights of The Round Table.

See: F35

AP102   "New Feature Films," <u>Newsweek</u>, January 18, 1954

          Ava Gardner is overly placid as Guinevere in the
          cautious but colorful epic <u>Knights of The Round
          Table</u>.

          See: F35

AP103   "Cinema," <u>Time</u>, January 25, 1954

          In the flashily entertaining, double-width comic
          strip <u>Knights of The Round Table</u>, Ava leans from
          a casement in a way that explains a lot of things
          the ancient "lays left unexplained."

          See: F35

AP104   Hartung, Philip T., <u>Commonweal</u>, January 29, 1954

          <u>Knights of The Round Table</u> is a filmed pageant;
          the story reads better, the film seldom strikes
          a note of reality.

          See: F35

AP105   Arnold, M., "Lonesome on Top of The World,"
               <u>Photoplay</u>, February, 1954

          Now that Ava Gardner is a megastar of the
          filmdom, will she stay as down-to-earth as
          before?

AP106   "Ava Gardner, Beauty," <u>Vogue</u>, February, 1954

          A beautiful portrait of Ava highlights an
          interview that features Ava's beauty secrets.

AP107   Kass, Robert, <u>Catholic World</u>, March, 1954

          Ava Gardner, Robert Taylor, and Mel Ferrer are
          pallid and over-solemn in <u>Knights of The Round
          Table</u>.

          See: F35

AP108   Reid, L., "Don't Let Ava Fool You," <u>Silver
               Screen</u>, March, 1954

          She may have appeared in some less-than-great
          films, but she is emerging as an actress to
          be reckoned with.

AP109   Duncan, David, "A New Light on Ava," Life, April 12,
         1954

         Ava is busy filming her latest movie in Rome, The
         Barefoot Contessa. She is learning to dance the
         flamenco and has earned the respect of the cast
         and crew for her tireless, hard work and sense of
         humor.

         See: F36

AP110   "End of The Affair," Time, June 21, 1954

         Ava settled in for a six-week wait for a divorce
         in Zephyr Cove, on Lake Tahoe's Nevada shore. She
         seemed weak from her trip home from Italy,
         especially after being hospitalized earlier for
         two kidney stones. The studio suspended Ava for
         stalling on her decision to not appear in Love Me
         or Leave Me. Ava is quoted, "Men are necessary,
         definitely not evil." Regarding her pending
         divorce, she stated, "He takes what he has, I
         take what I have."

AP111   Harvey, E., "Ava Gardner Plays the Gypsy--Filming
             of The Barefoot Contessa," Colliers, July 23,
             1954

         Ava is photographed rehearsing her flamenco dance
         on a location set for the film The Barefoot
         Contessa.

         See: F36

AP112   "Star Without Shoes," Cue, August 14, 1954

         Ava Gardner, star of The Barefoot Contessa, is no
         stranger to the comforts of bare feet. On or
         off screen, she prefers to be without shoes.

         See: F36

AP113   "Ava's Latest," Newsweek, October 4, 1954

         Ava is excellent in her role as Maria Vargas in
         The Barefoot Contessa, with is "literate and
         littered with some very good people."

         See: F36

AP114   Hartung, Philip T., Commonweal, October 8, 1954

          The Barefoot Contessa is a curious mesh of
          brilliant dialogue, melodrama, fine acting,
          witty satire, and an unusual subject matter.

          See: F36

AP115   McCarten, John, New Yorker, October 9, 1954

          The author feels that The Barefoot Contessa is a
          melodrama with "half-baked symbolism" with seedy
          gags. Ava, as the barefoot lady, is as insensitive
          to her surroundings as novocain.

          See: F36

AP116   Rogow, Lee, Saturday Review, October 16, 1954

          In The Barefoot Contessa, Ava is magnificently
          photographed and revealed as one of the most
          breathtakingly beautiful creatures on earth.
          She plays her part with a mature beauty and
          tragic fire that are very appealing.

          See: F36

AP117   "Cinema," Time, October 18, 1954

          Ava is pictured "at home with her feet in the
          dirt" for her role in The Barefoot Contessa, a
          film that is not much more than an international
          soap opera.

          See: F36

AP118   Walsh, Moira, America, October 30, 1954

          The cast is manipulated to elicit all their
          potentialities in The Barefoot Contessa.

          See: F36

AP119   Kass, Robert, Catholic World, November, 1954

          Ava is stunning as Maria Vargas in the
          otherwise awkwardly put-together, unpleasant
          The Barefoot Contessa.

          See: F36

AP120   "The Month's Best," <u>Coronet</u>, November, 1954

Ava is the beautiful cabaret dancer who becomes an
international success in <u>The Barefoot Contessa</u>.
Miss Gardner brings to the role a realistic
portrayal of a movie maker and continental
character.

See: F36

AP121   Lardner, J., "Public Love," <u>Newsweek</u>, December 13,
    1954

Ava Gardner is truly one of the world's most
popular film stars in the business today.

AP122   La Barre, H., "Ava in Pakistan," <u>Cosmopolitan</u>,
    March, 1956

<u>Bhowani Junction</u> is currently filming in Pakistan.
Ava will be taking on a multifaceted character
that will show her acting skills to her advantage.

See: F38

AP123   "Wrecks, Riot and Romance," <u>Life</u>, May 21, 1956

Ava Gardner survives them on all <u>Bhowani Junction</u>.
The camera noses through the story with a reporter's
curious eye.

See: F38

AP124   Cahoon, Herbert, <u>Library Journal</u>, June 1, 1956

<u>Bhowani Junction</u> is a good film that informs the
American public of other world cultures and
problems. Ava Gardner's role aids in cutting
through the political unrest of the film.

See: F38

AP125   McCarten, John, <u>New Yorker</u>, June 2, 1956

It is impossible to believe that anybody in this
film really represents the different political
factions in India. Ava's performance in <u>Bhowani
Junction</u> is less than credible alone in the fact
that she loses her phonetic balance.

See: F38

AP126   Knight, Arthur, <u>Saturday Review</u>, June 2, 1956

For her role in <u>Bhowani Junction</u>, "no man in his right mind would pass up the beautiful Ava Gardner for war in Sandhurst."

See: F38

AP127   "Cinema," <u>Time</u>, June 4, 1956

The shape of Asia is obscured by the shape of Ava in <u>Bhowani Junction</u>. Ava is Hollywood's idea of what every dying man needs. She does heavy breathing and uses her eyes to get sympathy, but who can tell what her real feelings are.

See: F38

AP128   Hartung, Philip T., <u>Commonweal</u>, June 8, 1956

<u>Bhowani Junction</u> is a fascinating, semi-historical panorama of India's turbulent times. The complexities of the role were difficult for Ava Gardner, but she looks like a million dollars in her fancy costumes.

See: F38

AP129   Walsh, Moira, <u>America</u>, June 9, 1956

Ava is a "fetching lassie" in any nationality in the extremely interesting <u>Bhowani Junction</u>.

See: F38

AP130   "New Feature Films," <u>Newsweek</u>, June 11, 1956

Ava Gardner is surprisingly effective as the distraught Cheechee Anglo-Indian social outcast in the sensitive, historical spectacular <u>Bhowani Junction</u>. The only drawback were the love scenes between Ava and Stewart Granger. In reality, the mores would not condone any display of affection outside the confines of the home.

See: F38

AP131   Hyams, Joe, "The Private Hell of Ava Gardner,"
          <u>Look</u>, November 27, 1956

Hyams chronicles the off-screen life of the flamboyant Ava Gardner. The first of two installments for the magazine show Ava to be haunted by her lifestyle.

AP132   Hyams, Joe, "Ava Gardner: In Search of Love," <u>Look</u>,
         December 11, 1956

         In this second installment for <u>Look</u> magazine,
         Hyams explains Ava's intense need to have love
         although she drives it away with possessiveness.
         Hyams also mentions that Ava's loneliness has
         driven her to the bottle.

AP133   Finlay, James Fenlon, <u>Catholic World</u>, April, 1957

         <u>The Little Hut</u> is a boring, vulgar film that has
         Ava terribly miscast. Her role as an English
         society girl represents an acting chore for
         which she was never intended by nature or
         inclination.

         See: F40

AP134   Nichols, Mark, "Barefoot Girl with Dressing,"
         <u>Coronet</u>, April, 1957

         <u>The Little Hut</u> is briefly mentioned in this
         article that describes her life to date. Ava
         loves living in her modest, two-bedroom home
         in Madrid, Spain. Her sense of humor serves
         her well. Her career has more inherent drama
         than her movie roles.

         See: F40

AP135   Knight, Arthur, <u>Saturday Review</u>, April, 1957

         Ava does not help <u>The Little Hut</u>, a tasteless,
         witless film.

         See: F40

AP136   Waterbury, Ruth, "Ava Gardner's Dry Tears,"
         <u>Photoplay</u>, April, 1957

         Lonely, lovely movie actress Ava Gardner
         hides her tears behind a happy facade.

AP137   Speicher, Charlotte Bilkey, <u>Library Journal</u>,
         May 1, 1957

         The wonderful talents of three fine performers
         (Ava Gardner, David Niven, and Stewart Granger)
         cannot salvage the glossy mistake <u>The Little Hut</u>.

         See: F40

AP138   McCarten, John, <u>New Yorker</u>, May 11, 1957

In <u>The Little Hut</u>, Ava and the others never come
into focus in this witless picture, full of
double-entendres.

See: F40

AP139   "Palmy," <u>Newsweek</u>, May 13, 1957

Ava Gardner and her co-stars are right for their
roles in the limp, romantic triangle they must
project in <u>The Little Hut</u>.

See: F40

AP140   "Cinema," <u>Time</u>, May 27, 1957

<u>The Little Hut</u> is a silly movie where we are
supposed to believe that, when two men and a
beautiful woman are stranded on an island,
all they do is talk.

See: F40

AP141   Hamburger, Philip, <u>New Yorker</u>, August 31, 1957

In <u>The Sun Also Rises</u>, Ava plies her trade with a
vengeance as Lady Brett Ashley. The film includes
superb photography, swift scenes, and some suggestion
of the desperately damned generation written about
by Ernest Hemingway.

See: F39

AP142   "Cinema," <u>Time</u>, September 2, 1957

Ava turns in the most realistic performance of her
career in <u>The Sun Also Rises</u>.
See: F39

AP143   Walsh, Moira, <u>America</u>, September 7, 1957

Ava Gardner plays the nymphomaniac in <u>The Sun
Also Rises</u>, a film that demonstrates that
Hemingway does not take kindly to the screen.

See: F39

AP144   Alpert, Hollis, <u>Saturday Review</u>, September 7, 1957

Ava seems to enjoy her role in <u>The Sun Also Rises</u>, doing well by her lines. However, Alpert wonders if a casting game was played in choosing who could play the part (he suggests June Allyson, Joan Crawford, or Esther Williams could have done as well as Lady Brett).

See: F39

AP145   "Hemingway of The 20s," <u>Newsweek</u>, September 9, 1957

Gardner is statuesque but distant in her portrayal of Lady Brett Ashley in <u>The Sun Also Rises</u>.

See: F39

AP146   Hartung, Philip T., <u>Commonweal</u>, September 13, 1957

<u>The Sun Also Rises</u> has almost no plot, although Ava Gardner looks stunning in the styles of the Twenties.

See: F39

AP147   "Hemingway's Lost Souls," <u>Life</u>, September 16, 1957

Photos of Ava Gardner enhance the article about <u>The Sun Also Rises</u>, a film that fails to catch the excitement and haunted gaiety of the 1920s.

See: F39

AP148   Roth, Philip, <u>New Republic</u>, September 30, 1957

For her role in <u>The Sun Also Rises</u>, Ava is not very good. She resembles a cross between the Snow Queen and Ann rutherford in <u>Andy Hardy</u>.

See: F39

AP149   Joyce, A., "The Woman Behind the Headlines," <u>Photoplay</u>, October, 1957

Ava Gardner's gaiety and nightlife are quite different from her sedate, lonely homelife.

AP150   Speicher, Charlotte Bilkey, <u>Library Journal</u>,
            October 1, 1957

            <u>The Sun Also Rises</u> is well-acted and intelligently
            conceived, with Ava Gardner as the loveless American
            beauty who finds solace in alcohol and affairs.

            See: F39

AP151   Hatch, Robert, <u>Nation</u>, October 12, 1957

            Ava Gardner suffers the disadvantage of being
            presented as the woman no man can resist in <u>The
            Sun Also Rises</u>--not very much of a story. She
            gives the impression of being a good-natured,
            not very experienced American working girl on an
            awful binge.

            See: F39

AP152   Finley, James Fenlon, <u>Catholic World</u>, November,
            1957

            Ava and the other cast members are excellent
            psychiatric couch candidates in <u>The Sun Also
            Rises</u>, which tells of their neurotic behaviors
            and sordid lifestyles that do not endear them
            to the audience.

            See: F39

AP153   Graves, R., "Toast to Ava Gardner," <u>New Yorker</u>,
            April 26, 1958

            Ava Gardner was included on its list of all-time
            great movie stars.

AP154   Whitcomb, J., "Goya: Artistic Violence Makes an
            Exciting Movie," <u>Cosmopolitan</u>, January, 1959

            Spanish painter Goya is the subject of Ava
            Gardner's latest film, <u>The Naked Maja</u>, where
            great beauty is shown to advantage.

            See: F42

AP155   "Cinema," <u>Time</u>, April 6, 1959

            Ava Gardner is beautiful but vapid in <u>The Naked
            Maja</u>, which contains too many atrocities on
            history.

            See: F42

AP156   Hartung, Philip T., Commonweal, April 24, 1959

Ava walked through her role, giving a dreadful
performance in the old-fashioned melodrama The
Naked Maja.

See: F42

AP157   "New Feature Films," Newsweek, April 20, 1959

Ava Gardner has an "I don't care" attitude as the
Duchess of Alba in The Naked Maja, with which her
audience will identify in this stinker.

See: F42

AP158   Walsh, Moira, Catholic World, June, 1959

The Naked Maja sets back for about twenty years
the production of movies about artists. Ava
Gardner and Anthony Franciosa, under the direction
of Henry Koster, give totally inept performances.

See: F42

AP159   McCarten, John, New Yorker, June 20, 1959

The Naked Maja is a posthumous libel on the painter,
Goya. Ava seems confused in her role.

See: F42

AP160   Knight, Arthur, Saturday Review, October 24, 1959

Ava Gardner looks downright unglamorous for the
first time in her career in On The Beach. She
reveals unsuspected depths of character.

See: F41

AP161   "Film Review," McCall's, November, 1959

Ava brings a gentle reality to her role as Moira
Davidson in On The Beach, the story of the end of
world following a nuclear explosion.

See: F41

AP162   Watson, B., "Haunted," Photoplay, November, 1959

Miss Gardner is haunted by her lack of a lasting
love.

AP163   "Dire Drama on The Death of The World," _Life_,
           November 30, 1959

           Director Stanley Kramer molded Ava Gardner, an
           international glamour girl, into a hard,
           used-up woman grown worldly and pitiful before
           the stark fact of unlimited death. She gives a
           fine performance in _On The Beach_.

           See: F41

AP164   Nichols, Mark, _Coronet_, December, 1959

           Ava Gardner gives a powerful, convincing
           performance in _On The Beach_, as an Australian
           play girl who finds temporary refuge in the
           arms of Gregory Peck, another one of the handful
           of survivors following the dropping of a nuclear
           warhead.

           See: F41

AP165   Beaufort, John, _Christian Science Monitor_,
           December, 1959

           On The Beach matches the somber warning of its
           theme with the jolting impact of its dramatic
           force. Ava is excellent as Moira Davidson.

           See: F41

AP166   Kauffmann, Stanley, _New Republic_, December 14, 1959

           Ava Gardner captures a true sense of hunger and
           self-disgust as the heartsick drunk she portrays
           in Stanley Kramer's _On The Beach_.

           See: F41

AP167   Walsh, Moira, _America_, December 19, 1959

           On The Beach provides apt and effective situations
           for Ava to realistically play the high-strung,
           hard-drinking Australian woman in love with a
           married man.

           See: F41

AP168   "New Feature Films," _Newsweek_, December 21, 1959

           Miss Gardner has never looked worse nor been more
           effective than in _On The Beach_.

           See: F41

AP169   Hartung, Philip T., Commonweal, December 25, 1959

On The Beach is the year's scariest and most
compelling film. Ava Gardner gives a surprisingly
good performance as a restless party girl.

See: F41

AP170   "Cinema," Time, December 28, 1959

On The Beach is an unrealistic film where the script
imagines the world's end as the scene in which Ava
Gardner stands and wistfully waves goodbye to Gregory
Peck and we see the sun sadly set into the
contaminated dawn.

See: F41

AP171   Hatch, Robert, Nation, January 2, 1960

The reviewer failed to estimate the impact of horror,
pity, and terror evoked in the hallucinatory
realism of On The Beach. Director Stanley Kramer's
way of filming let actress Ava Gardner shine.

See: F41

AP172   McCarten, John, New Yorker, January 2, 1960

Ava Gardner is a local wildflower who joins the rest
of the cast as being hardly able to represent real
people who are the only survivors of the annihilation
of the world in On The Beach.

See: F41

AP173   Schall, James V., Catholic World, May, 1960

Ava Gardner gives an excellent "Italian aura" (similar
to Anna Magnani) in her role as the heroine Moira
Davidson in On The Beach, specifically in her need
to be loved. This film is a compassionate appeal
to all men to think realistically about the nuclear
destruction of the world.

See: F41

AP174   "New Feature Films," Time, September 12, 1960

The Angel Wore Red is a turbid, Kleenex-sopper
with Ava Gardner and Dirk Bogarde in unbelievable
parts.

See: F43

AP175   "New Feature Films," Newsweek, September 12, 1960

The Angel Wore Red is a heavy-handed drama. Ava
Gardner looks worldly-worn as the prostitute in
love with a priest.

See: F43

AP176   Hartung, Philip T., Commonweal, September 30, 1960

The Spanish Civil War of 1936 was reduced to a
bumbling, confusing romantic film The Angel Wore Red.
Ava's scenes were silly as the prostitute who can't
realize her love for the priest is a lost cause.

See: F43

AP177   Walsh, Moira, America, October 1, 1960

Ava Gardner is the prostitute with a heart of gold
who has strong regenerative instincts in The Angel
Wore Red, based on The Fair Bride by Bruce Marshall.
The film handles the religious issues with adequate
insight without offensiveness.

See: F43

AP178   Jaffe, Rona, "Private Demons of Ava Gardner," Good
        Housekeeping, March, 1961

Ava developed psychosomatic stomach pains and
feelings of inferiority, so she went to see a
psychiatrist. Ava admitted that, if she had had
a baby, she would have become too bored to care
about it later.

AP179   Miron, C., "Ava at 38," Photoplay, June, 1961

As Ava Gardner nears middle age, she is still quite
beautiful. She looks forward to playing more
"meaty" character roles in the future.

AP180   Todd, R., "Did Ava Strike Out with Roger?" Photoplay,
        January, 1962

Rumors were afloat that movie star Ava Gardner was
secretly dating baseball great Roger Maris.

AP181   "Cinema," Time, May 31, 1963

For her role in 55 Days at Peking, Ava "goes to work
in a hospital like a Pekinese Scarlett O'Hara, pawning
her emeralds for food and drugs." She dies early on
in the film, which then drags eternally. In a photo
from the film, the caption reads, "Ava Gardner winged
by a boxer."

See: F44

AP182   "Nobody Eats Rats," Newsweek, June 3, 1963

In a surprising bit of realism to 55 Days at Peking,
Ava Gardner dies an hour or so before the end of this
long film.

See: F44

AP183   Knebel, Fletcher, Look, November 19, 1963

Ava Gardner and the rest of the cast in Seven Days
in May provide portrayals that made the White House
pleased and the Pentagon irritated.

See: F45

AP184   Lawrenson, Helen, "The Nightmare of The Iguana,"
         Show, January, 1964

Miss Lawrenson recalls the acid-tongued Ava Gardner
behavior during filming of Night of The Iguana in
Mexico. Her hard drinking did not endear Ava to
the press, which she detested for hounding her.

See: F46

AP185   Knight, Arthur, Saturday Review, February 1, 1964

Ava commendably plays a beat-up Washington
socialite in the powerful, frenetic political
thriller Seven Days in May.

See: F45

AP186   "Cinema," Time, February 21, 1964

The actors in Seven Days in May deliver their stilted
dialogue as if it were written as a prep-school essay.
The film is more farfetched than a campaign promise.

See: F45

AP187   Gill, Brendan, New Yorker, February 22, 1964

         Seven Days in May is an almost perfect thriller,
         with a cast to match. Although marvelous, it is
         not to be taken too seriously.

         See: F45

AP188   "Plot on The Potomac," Newsweek, February 24, 1964

         Ava Gardner is poutingly pretty in the dull thriller,
         Seven Days in May, about the possible military over-
         throw of the government.

         See: F45

AP189   Kauffmann, Stanley, New Republic, March 7, 1964

         Ava is no longer fresh-faced, but she is more
         attractive than ever in Seven Days in May.

         See: F45

AP190   MacDonald, Dwight, Esquire, June, 1964

         For her role in Seven Days in May, Ava repeats the
         battered yet gallant and decent alcoholic "woman
         of a certain age" she specialized in since On The
         Beach. She's no worse or no better than she was
         in the glamour-girl parts of her youth.

         See: F41, F45

AP191   Callahan, Richard, Life, July 10, 1964

         Ava's performance in Night of The Iguana was a
         revelation. She can act and all but runs away
         with the picture.

         See: F46

AP192   "Cinema," Time, July 17, 1964

         John Huston keeps Night of The Iguana clipping
         along and lets his actors, especially Ava Gardner,
         shine.
         See: F46

AP193   "Movie Review," Films in Review, August-September,

         Ava is a rampant tramp in Night of The Iguana,
         a film that's all horseplay and no hard work.

         See: F46

AP194 Walsh, Moira, _America_, August 15, 1964

Ava Gardner is the earthy hotel proprietess who projects compassion in this effective and powerful, moving Tennessee Williams story, _Night of The Iguana._

See: F46

AP195 Hartung, Philip T., _Commonweal_, August 21, 1964

For her role in _Night of The Iguana_, Ava is given her best part to date as the wilful, hoydenish hotelkeeper. Her character is the most moved and changed by the film's end.

See: F46

AP196 "New Feature Films," _Newsweek_, August 15, 1964

Ava Gardner reverted to her southern drawl for her role in _Night of The Iguana_. "A great woman played a great woman."

See: F46

AP197 Oliver, Edith, _New Yorker_, August, 1964

Ava was absolutely splendid as Maxine Faulk in _Night of The Iguana_.

see: F46

AP198 Birmingham, Stephen, _Cosmopolitan_, November, 1964

Birmingham reports the entourage that arrived in Mexico to film _Night of The Iguana_. Rumors were rampant that the leading ladies and guest/family members would cause great strife during their stay.

See: F46

AP199 Lawrenson, Helen, _Show_, November, 1964

"Ava Gardner was amiable as an adder and acted as spoiled as a medieval queen" during filming of _Night of The Iguana_.

See: F46

AP200 "Movie Greats," _Current Biography Yearbook_, March, 1965

Ava's brief biography and photo are included.

AP201   Vincent, M., "Ava Gardner," Films in Review, June/
        July, 1965

        Ava Gardner's roles are briefly mentioned as well
        as describing her newest role in Night of The
        Iguana.

        See: F46

AP202   Peters, Edward H., Catholic World, October, 1966

        The Bible included many impressive and beautiful
        scenes, but it could have been shortened. Ava
        was good in her role as Sarah, although the film
        wasn't an over-literal interpretation of the Bible.

        See: F47

AP203   Kotlowitz, Robert, Harper's Magazine, October, 1966

        Kotlowitz felt The Bible was sacred, profane, and
        "plain peculiar." Ava Gardner remains one of the
        world's beautiful women. However, when he sees her,
        all he can think of is Mickey Rooney. "That is the
        penalty of publicized stardom; if you want to act,
        you have to go about it in other ways."

        See: F47

AP204   Gill, Brendan, New Yorker, October 1, 1966

        Ava acts as if she were indifferent to her fate in
        The Bible, a hammy screen version of the Book of
        Genesis.

        See: F47

AP205   "Huston's Gospel," Newsweek, October 3, 1966

        Ava, as Sarah in The Bible, makes a moving display
        of time-ravaged beauty.

        See: F47

AP206   "Cinema," Time, October 7, 1966

        Among the stars dimmed for the occasion in The Bible
        are George C. Scott and Ava Gardner, as Abraham and
        Sarah, "The ancient, barren pair who crawl abed
        hopefully cooing Songs of Solomon."

        See: F47

AP207   Walsh, Moira, <u>America</u>, October 8, 1966

Ava Gardner and George C. Scott provide the most
fully realized Biblical sequence in <u>The Bible</u>,
which provided a great deal of history of the
Hebrew customs and psychology of the time.

See: F47

AP208   Cox, Harvey, <u>Look</u>, October 18, 1966

Ava put on a bathrobe as well as did Peter O'Toole
during filming of the terribly boring <u>The Bible</u>.

See: F47

AP209   Hartung, Philip T., <u>Commonweal</u>, October 21, 1966

Ava Gardner stands out in her role as Sarah in
<u>The Bible</u>. She has never looked lovelier.

See: F47

AP210   Kael, Pauline, <u>New Republic</u>, October 22, 1966

John Huston tries to do too much with too little
in the epic film <u>The Bible</u>. The story of Abraham
and Sarah acts and sounds like an acted-out TV
Bible story.

See: F47

AP211   Maxwell, James A., "Heaven and Earth in Two
        Dimensions," <u>Reporter</u>, November 3, 1966

<u>The Bible</u> provides a simple, uncomplicated approach
to portraying stories from The Bible. Ava Gardner
has somewhat "Semitic" features that come as a
shock, since all the other cast members look
"anglo-Saxon." However, she turned in an
excellent performance.

See: F47

AP212   Madsen, Axel, <u>Cinema</u>, December, 1966

The story of Abraham and Sarah in the film <u>The
Bible</u> was photographed in deep Rembrandt hues
of muted Technicolor.

See: F47

AP213   Linet, Beverly, <u>Who's Who in Hollywood</u>, 1967

        Ava Gardner continues to be one of the most popular
        movie stars, even as she nears the age of 40.

AP214   Russell, Francis, <u>National Review</u>, April 18, 1967

        Ava Gardner and George C. Scott wander through the
        Sahara in the pretentious interpretation of stories
        from <u>The Bible</u>.

        See: F47

AP215   Reed, Rex, "Ava: Life in The Afternoon," <u>Esquire</u>,
            May, 1967

        Reed presents Ava as a raucous, earthy star, still
        a knock-out after twenty years of moviemaking.
        She's not afraid to be honest.

AP216   Farber, Stephen, <u>Film Quarterly</u>, Summer, 1967

        Farber recounts Pauline Kael's panning of <u>The Bible</u>
        even though she liked Ava's performance.

        See: F47

AP217   Brennan, Terry, "And They Said It Wouldn't Last,"
            <u>Movie Life Yearbook</u>, 1968

        This magazine features a reprise of Ava's tumultuous
        life with Frank Sinatra in a short bit.

AP218   Caldwell, R., "Twilight of a Goddess," <u>Ladies Home
            Journal</u>, July, 1972

        Still-beautiful actress Ava Gardner has moved from
        Spain to an apartment in Ennismore Gardens,
        Kensington, England, which she shares with her dog.

AP219   "Film Review," <u>Film Facts</u>, December, 1972

        Ava is a welcome to the screen in her cameo role
        as Lily Langtry in <u>The Life and Times of Judge Roy
        Bean</u>.

        See: F49

AP220   Thompson, Thomas, "Liz Taylor is 40!", _Life_,
            February 25, 1972

         Thompson's article on the newly-turned forty-year
         old actress prompted her to expound, "Ava is truly
         beautiful."

AP221   "Cinema," _Time_, December 25, 1972

         None of the cast of _The Life and Times of Judge Roy
         Bean_ measures up to the performance done by Bruno,
         the bear.

         See: F49

AP222   Coughlan, Janice, _Who's Who in Movies_, 1973

         Legendary actress Ava Gardner is included in the
         section on international movie stars.

AP223   Westerbeck, Colin L., Jr., _Commonweal_, January 12,
            1973

         The Life and Times of Judge Roy Bean is a ludicrous,
         much too long film. Ava Gardner and Jackie Bisset
         were stars John Huston had promised to pay for their
         services.

         See: F49

AP224   Kael, Pauline, _New Yorker_, January 13, 1973

         The Life and Times of Judge Roy Bean is a logy,
         thick-skinned film, with Ava Gardner in a walk-on
         reminiscent of "The Westener."

         See: F49

AP225   Pearce, Ruth, _TV Movie Star Directory_, 1974

         A bit biography on the popular movie and television
         stars of the day includes Ava Gardner.

AP226   Beylie C., and Braucourt, Ecran, _Paris_, August-
            September, 1974

         Ava Gardner is one of the seven major international
         motion picture stars featured in this issue.

AP227   "Newsmakers," <u>Newsweek</u>, October 21, 1974

Although she will never be a great actress like
Garbo, Hepburn, or Davis, Ava Gardner is more sensitive and responsive than Turner, Hayworth, or Novak.
According to biography by Charles Higham, Ava may
have lived hard, but she seems more accessible and
likeable of the great movie stars.

AP228   Scott, V., "Ava," <u>Ladies Home Journal</u>, November,
   1974

Ava was glad to get the part in <u>The Bible</u>, because
it paid $50,000. She used the money to pay for
a vacation in Acapulco.

See: F47

AP229   Miller, Burton, <u>American Cinematographer</u>, November,
   1974

Ava wore an elegant beige suit in the film <u>Earthquake</u>.
Each actor had six different versions of each
wardrobe change. Both Ava and Genevieve Bujold
were good sports. Although they were "roughed up,"
they never let their physical appearance interfere
with the action called for in the script.

See: F52

AP230   Crist, Judith, "Snap, Crackle, Pop," <u>New York</u>,
   December 2, 1974

Ava gives a credible performance in <u>Earthquake</u>.
See: F52

AP231   Kael, Pauline, <u>New Yorker</u>, December 2, 1974

Ava Gardner's name lifts <u>Earthquake</u> out of the
Universal action-picture category. She is featured
as a beat-out, blowzy, shrill woman who loses her
husband to a younger, prettier woman (Bujold).
She was just another old star hired to beef up the
movie's star power.

See: F52

AP232   "Quake and Shake," <u>Newsweek</u>, December 2, 1974

All the top cast members are unbelievable in their
roles in <u>Earthquake</u>.

See: F52

AP233   "Cinema," _Time_, December 9, 1974

Loving patrons paid good money to see a bad movie,
Earthquake. "In the ugliest convention of the
genre, the camera lingers sadistically on the ruins
of a legendary beauty, Miss Gardner, as if
deglamorizing her could compensate for all the
film's other dishonesties and ineptitudes."

See: F52

AP234   Buckley, Michael, _Films in Review_, January, 1975

Ava Gardner was miscast in _Earthquake_, either as
Charlton Heston's wife or Lorne Greene's daughter,
although she still looks attractive in this
entertaining special effects extravaganza.

See: F52

AP235   Westerbeck, Colin L., Jr., _Commonweal_, April 11,
         1975

The depressing, overdone film _Earthquake_ was
another disaster film that did not have to be made.
Ava was a graspy, nagging, overweight wife of
Heston.

See: F52

AP236   Bielecki, Stanley, _Films and Filming_, April, 1976

Photographs from _The Blue Bird_ show Ava in her role
as Luxury, "with all the various other exotics."

See: F54

AP237   "Film Review," _Newsweek_, May 17, 1976

Ava Gardner perfectly embodies vulgar opulence
at Luxury in _The Blue Bird_, an insipid turkey.

See: F54

AP238   Simon, John, _New York_, May 24, 1976

Histrionically and visually, Ava Gardner is a
penury performer in _The Blue Bird_. Her still-
shapely legs are the "final vision of her last
remaining asset," and totally unnecessary to be
shown in the context of this film.

See: F54

AP239   Gilliatt, Penelope, New Yorker, May 24, 1976

Ava Gardner, as Luxury in The Blue Bird, riding a
horse and wearing a red velvet cloak, presides over
cream cakes and gets caught up in a sensuous adult
orgy that actually looks like "a free-expression
period in a progressive school."

See: F54

AP240   Bodeen, Dewitt, Films in Review, June-July, 1976

In The Blue Bird, Ava is gorgeously seductive as
Luxury, comparisoned in crimson velvet as the
sorceress of all ages. This film will "perch in
your memory as a happy treasure."

See: F54

AP241   Bernard, Andre, "Ava Gardner," Paris, 1976

Movie star Ava Gardner is the subject of this
entire magazine, replete with photographs of her
career and life.

AP242   Cocks, Jay, "Gilded Cage," Time, June 14, 1976

In The Blue Bird, Ava helps camp it up like a movie
queen on an overseas promotional junket.

See: F54

AP243   Roeder, B., "Newsmakers," Newsweek, November 1,
         1976

Ava is shown walking her dog in London. When
asked how she likes living the secluded life in
her Knightsbridge flat, she said, "To me, sanity
is more important than stardom."

AP244   "Cinema," Time, February 28, 1977

The Sentinel is a mumbo jumbo of blood and guts, with
Ava as a rental agent who tells the heroine the
house she's looking for a room in hasn't been lived
in for years.

See: F56

AP245   Bielecki, Stanley, <u>Films and Filming</u>, March, 1977

Ava Gardner plays Miss Logan in <u>The Sentinel</u>, the
real estate agent for the house in Brooklyn which
produces more for its tenants than running hot
and cold water.

See: F56

AP246   Donohue, Quinn, "Ava, Beauty in Exile," <u>Hollywood
Studio Magazine</u>, October, 1979

Ava has chosen to live the last few years in
Spain then England. Her fans respect her wishes
for privacy, yet she is accorded their best wishes
to again return to the screen.

AP247   Banks, Tom, "The New Ava Gardner Carolina Museum,"
<u>Hollywood Studio Magazine</u>, October, 1979

Ava's home state of North Carolina is the site of
the museum that holds much memorabilia of the
still-popular movie star.

AP248   Jacobs, Norman and O'Quinn, Kerry, "Screen Greats,"
<u>Hollywood Nostalgia</u>, 1980

Among the great screen stars of the past fifty
years was Clark Gable. He considered Ava a pal
and co-starred with her in more than one picture,
<u>Mogambo</u> and <u>Lone Star</u>.

See: F30, F34

AP249   Barrett, Rona, "Hollywood's Golden Age of Glamour -
The Fifties," <u>Rona Looks At</u>, Spring, 1980

Without a doubt one of the most beautiful brunettes
to ever grace the screen is Ava Gardner, who held
her own with the best of them during the heyday of
the 1950s.

AP250   "Picks & Pans - Screen," <u>People Weekly</u>, October 6,
1980

Ava Gardner is the only thing watching in the
ridiculous film <u>The Kidnapping of The President</u>.

See: F58

AP251   Rampling, Matthew, "Ava Gardner," _Paris_, 1981

          International movie actress Ava Gardner is again
          the focus of the entire special issue of _Paris_.

AP252   Crist, Judith, _Saturday Review_, October, 1981

          In _Priest of Love_, Ava is enjoyable in her mature
          beauty and brusque humor as Mabel Dodge Luhan, the
          American patron, would-be mistress, and enduring
          admirer of D. H. Lawrence.

          See: F59

AP253   Kauffmann, Stanley, _New Republic_, October 21, 1981

          Ava Gardner is never more beautiful than in the
          superfluous biographical film on the life of D. H.
          Lawrence, _Priest of Love_.   Ava is good in her role
          as Mabel Dodge Luhan, but the real Luhan was not
          known for her beauty.

          See: F59

AP254   "Picks & Pans - Screen," _People Weekly_, November 16,
             1981

          Ava brings a beauty and pathos to her role in
          Priest of Love, a tender love story of the famous
          writer D. H. Lawrence, his wife, and friend.

          See: F59

AP255   Des Cars, Guy, "Grace Kelly, An American Princess,"
             Paris Match (subsidiary of _Look_), 1982

          This beautiful tribute to Grace Kelly, who died
          after an automobile accident in September, 1982,
          mentions Ava as the only female movie actress to
          remain friends with the Princess throughout her
          film career and private life.

AP256   Hauptfuhrer, Fred, "Ava is Back and Beautiful at 59 -
             but All She Wants is Peace and Quiet," _People
             Weekly_, January 11, 1982

          Handsome, down-to-earth actress Ava Gardner proves
          that her star is still shining. Her health may be
          precarious as of late, but she's not daunted in
          knowing what she wants and needs.

AP257   "Ava Gardner," <u>Hollywood Studio Magazine</u>, November,
        1982

        Ava Gardner now lives in Kensington, England. She
        will be traveling to Rome to film "Regina," for
        Generis Films. Her co-stars are Anthony Quinn,
        Anna Karenina, and Ray Sharkey.

AP258   "Books," <u>Publishers Weekly</u>, November 19, 1982

        The book <u>Ava</u>, by Roland Flamini, is panned. Many
        facts were not researched and presents Ava as being a
        spirited hedonist.

AP259   Noh, David, <u>Coming Attractions</u>, June, 1983

        This issue features a review of <u>Ava</u> by Roland
        Flamini and includes a news "flashback" from 1953
        about the truce between Ava and Frank Sinatra.

AP260   Flamini, Roland, "Ava," <u>Good Housekeeping</u>, January,
        1983

        The magazine featured an excerpt from Roland
        Flamini's biography of Ava Gardner, <u>Ava</u>.

AP261   Hirschhorn, Joel, <u>Video Movies</u>, June, 1984

        Although Ava Gardner's beauty makes it palatable,
        nothing else can make it better in <u>My Forbidden
        Past</u>.

        See: F28

AP262   Weber, Louis, <u>Video Movies</u>, November, 1984

        Ava Gardner looks great, but even her talents
        can't save <u>The Kidnapping of The President</u>.

        See: F58

AP263   Mann, Roderick, "Ave Ava: A Maverick's Homecoming,"
        <u>Life</u>, February 17, 1985

        Ava Gardner is returning to the United States to
        appear in her first television role on night time
        soap opera <u>Knots Landing</u>.

        See: T1

AP264   Zoglin, Richard, "Space," _Time_, April 22, 1985

        The television mini-series _A.D._, in which Ava Gardner
        played Agrippina, only attracted 19.2% of the
        nation's viewers, despite stars James Mason and
        Ava Gardner.

        See: M1

AP265   Coleman, John, _New Statesman_, August 2, 1985

        Beautiful Ava Gardner graced the screen as the
        enigmatic Pandora Reynolds in this review of
        Pandora and The Flying Dutchman, considered to
        be a forgotten film to remember.

        See: F27

AP266   Martin, Peter, "The Life and Times of Sinatra, the
           Real Story Behind the Actor," _Lady's Circle
           Special_, 1986

        Sinatra's marriage to Ava Gardner is highlighted in
        this tribute to the multi-talented singer-actor.

AP267   "Milestones," _Time_, November 10, 1986

        At age 63, the sultry, beautiful movie star Ava
        Gardner is recovering from a bout with pneumonia
        at a Santa Monica hospital.

AP268   Jason, Johnny, "Ava Gardner - The Pin-up Girl Who
           Wasn't," _Hollywood Studio Magazine_, December,
           1988

        Although Ava posed for cheesecake photographs in
        her early career and later for publicity shots from
        several of her movies, she was never really
        considered a pin-up girl. She rarely posed for
        pictures that centered on her shapely legs.

AP269   Speck, Gregory, "Legends: Ava Gardner," _The Cable
           Guide_, December, 1988

        Video viewers got a glimpse of the still-lovely
        actress in this article. She hasn't changed her
        down-home attitude in all her years in the public
        eye.

AP270   "Patsy Kensit's Sultry Beauty Lights The Fire in
         Lethal Weapon 2," People Weekly, July 31, 1989

         At age 8, Patsy Kensit co-starred with Ava in The
         Blue Bird. To Kensit, Ava, Elizabeth Taylor, and
         Jane Fonda were superstars "because they had this
         presence."

         See: F54

AP271   Price, Vincent, Memories, August-September, 1989

         "The real excitement of working in The Bribe with
         Charles Laughton was working with Ava Gardner,
         hands-down, the sexiest and nicest of them all."

         See: F24

AP272   Quine, Judith Balaban, "Grace Becomes a Princess,"
         Vanity Fair, June, 1989

         Quine excerpts her recently-published book of the
         same title, in which she mentions the friendship
         endured by Grace Kelly and Ava Gardner.

AP273   Vincent, Oliver, "Movie Bad Girls," Celebrity Plus,
         August, 1989

         Vincent refers to Ava's "sharecropper" background,
         then ditching her white trash beginnings to hobnob
         with Hollywood royalty, both on and off the screen.
         She stirred up a sexual storm in The Barefoot
         Contessa, but it was on the front pages of the
         tabloids that she really earned her "bad girl"
         reputation.

         See: F36

AP274   Winters, Shelley, "Ava Gardner was Chasing After
         My Hubby - I Threatened to Put Out a Contract on
         Her Life," National Enquirer, September 26, 1989

         This excerpt from Winters' second installment of
         her autobiography relates her dislike of prima donna
         Ava Gardner for trying to steal her then-husband
         Anthony Franciosa during filming of The Naked Maja.

         See: F42

AP275   Brady, James, "In Step With: Ava Gardner," Parade
         Magazine, October 15, 1989

         As a young journalist, Brady had interviewed Ava
         one-on-one at Macy's in New York and never forgot
         the experience. He reports on the autobiography
         that Ava is currently working on at her home in London.

AP276   Peck, Gregory, "Film Festival," Memories, December,
         1989/January, 1990

         Peck reminisces about his favorite roles and co-stars.
         "Ava Gardner was so beautiful she stopped traffic.
         Ava and I were both from small towns, and we struck
         it off like cousins." They stay in touch, and both
         Peck and his wife, Veronique, love Ava. He believes
         Ava gave one of her finest performances in On The
         Beach.

         See: F41

AP277   "Ava Gardner," Variety, January 31, 1990

         Ava's obituary appears in this issue.

AP278   Thomas, Walter, "Amorous Ava," Bazaar, February, 1990

         The author highlights portions of Ava's love life
         at the height of her movie career in this short
         article.

         See: AB235

AP279   "Transition," Newsweek, February 5, 1990

         The seductive Ava had a reputation as a femme fatale
         that carried over from her movies to her private
         life, as noted in her passing.

AP280   "Milestones," Time, February 5, 1990

         Ava's obituary is included, citing that she was the
         box office equal of Rita Hayworth and Marilyn Monroe.

AP281   Green, Michelle, Bacon, Doris, Hoover, Eleanor,
         Nolan, Cathy, Walker, Jane, Kramer, Linda,
         Hutchings, David, and Lemon, Dick, "Many Passions,
         No Regrets," People Weekly, February 12, 1990

         Ava Gardner graces the cover and is featured in a
         respectful article on her life and death.

UNANNOTATED PERIODICALS

UP1   "You Ought to be In Pictures," <u>Lions</u>, April, 1944

UP2   "Beautiful but--Wise," <u>Lions</u>, December, 1944

UP3   "The Killers," <u>Photoplay</u>, November, 1946
       See: F17

UP4   "The Hucksters," <u>Cosmopolitan</u>, September, 1947

UP5   "The Hucksters," <u>Photoplay</u>, September, 1947
       See: F21

UP6   Fulton, M. J., "Sketch," <u>Photoplay</u>, October, 1947

UP7   "One Touch of Venus," <u>Vogue</u>, February 15, 1948
       See: F23

UP8   "Letters from Liza," <u>Silver Screen</u>, May, 1948

UP9   "Hollywood's New Generation," <u>Life</u>, May 24, 1948

UP10   Graham, S., "Sketch," <u>Photoplay</u>, November, 1948

UP11   Graham, S., "Sketch," <u>Photoplay</u>, June, 1949

UP12 "The Great Sinner," <u>Photoplay</u>, September, 1949
       See: F25
UP13 "Movie Review," <u>Holiday</u>, (<u>Pandora and The Flying
       Dutchman</u>, March, 1952
       See: F27
UP14 "New Feature Films," <u>Newsweek</u>, September 29, 1952

UP15 Kass, Robert, <u>Catholic World</u>, November, 1952

UP16 "Film Review," <u>National Parent-Teacher</u>, November, 1952

UP17 "Movie Review," <u>Natural History</u>, November, 1952

UP18 "Film Review," <u>National Parent-Teacher</u>, October, 1953

UP19 "Movie Review," <u>Natural History</u>, November, 1953

UP20 "Portrait," <u>Saturday Evening Post</u>, November 7, 1953

UP21 "Movie Review," <u>Scholastic, Nove</u>mber 11, 1953

UP22 "Film Review," <u>National Parent-Teacher</u>, December,
       1953

UP23 "Knights of The Round Table," <u>Look</u>, December 29, 1953
       See: F35
UP24 "Speaking of Pictures," <u>Life</u>, October 18, 1954

UP25 "Portrait," <u>Vogue</u>, December, 1954

UP26 James, T., F., "Picture Album of Beautiful Woman in
       America," <u>Cosmopolitan</u>, June, 1956

UP27 Kass, Robert, <u>Catholic World</u>, April, 1957

UP28 "Film Review," <u>National Parent-Teacher,</u> September,
       1957

UP29   "Movie review," National Parent-Teacher, November, 1957

UP30   "All Time Great Stars," Showman's Trade Review, 1958

UP31   "Film Review," McCall's, November, 1959

UP32   "Film Review," Science News Letter, December 5, 1959

UP33   "Film Review," Science, December 18, 1959

UP34   "Film Review," Science, April 21, 1961

UP35   McCarten, John, New Yorker, June 1, 1963

UP36   "Movie Review," America, July 6, 1963

UP37   "Movie Review," National Review, July 30, 1963

UP38   "Movie Review," Vogue, February 15, 1964

UP39   "Review," Film Daily, July 1, 1964

UP40   "Review," Motion Picture Herald Production Digest,
         July 8, 1964

UP41   "Review," Box Office, July 13, 1964

UP42   "Review," BFI Monthly Film Bulletin, October, 1964

UP43   "Review," Film Daily, September 28, 1966

UP44   "Review," Motion Picture Herald Production Digest,
       September 28, 1966

UP45   "Movie Review," Vogue, October 1, 1966

UP46   "Movie Review," Christian Science Monitor,
         October 10, 1966

UP47 "Review," Motion Picture Herald Production Digest,
       October 12, 1966

UP48 "Review," BFI Monthly Film Bulletin, November, 1966

UP49 Linet, Beverly, Who's Who in Hollywood, 1967

UP50 Movie Land and TV Time Annual, Fall, 1968

UP51 Movie Screen Yearbook, 1972

UP52 Coughlan, Janice, Who's Who in Movies, 1973

UP53 Pearce, Ruth, TV Movie Star Directory, 1974

UP54 "Film Review," Independent Film Journal, November 27,
       1974

UP55 "Review," Motion Picture Herald Production Digest,
       November 27, 1974

UP56 "Movie Review," Village Voice, December 23, 1974

UP57 Real Life, Special Fall Issue, 1975

UP58 "Review," BFI Monthly Film Bulletin, January, 1975

UP59 In The Know Magazine, May, 1975

UP60 "Review," Independent Film Journal, May 28, 1976

UP61 "Review," Motion Picture Herald Production Digest,
       June 3, 1976

UP62 "The Blue Bird," Vogue, July, 1976
       See: F54

UP63 Kendall, Robert, "Collecting Autographs for Fun and
       Profit," Hollywood Studio Magazine, December,

UP64   Cassa, Anthony, "Robert Walker - The Man Who Lost
        Himself," Hollywood Studio Magazine, February,
        1982

UP65   Shipmann, David, Radio Times, March 27, 1982

UP66   Florio, Allen, "In a Glamorous Fashion - The Glitter
        and Glamour of Hollywood's Golden Age," Hollywood
        Studio Magazine, April, 1982

UP67   Kelly, Bill, "Broderick Crawford, as He Sees It!"
        Hollywood Studio Magazine, April, 1982

UP68   Denny, Dorothy M., "Charlton Heston - Hero Par-Epic
        Excellence," Hollywood Studio Magazine, June, 1982

UP69   "The Book Beat," Hollywood Studio Magazine, October,
        1982

UP70   Michener, Charles, The Movies, 1983

UP71   McCarthy, Mary Arrigan, "A Star is Reborn, Clark
        Gable," Coming Attractions, January-February, 1983

UP72   Luzzatto, Jack, "Hollywood and Vine," Coming
        Attractions, March-April, 1983

UP73   Graham, Lee, "AFI Salute to 'Hellraiser' Huston,"
        Hollywood Studio Magazine, May, 1983

UP74   "Variety-Fortune and Power," Variety's 15th
        International Television Annual, April 18, 1984

UP75   "Cine Revue," Paris, August 26, 1982

UP76   "Cine Revue," Paris, August 30, 1984

UP77   "Classics," Video Magazine, August, 1984

UP78   Jason, Johnny, "Soaps and Stars," Hollywood Studio
        Magazine, June-July, 1985

UP79   "Baby, Look at You Now!" <u>Good Housekeeping</u>, January,
          1986

UP80   Kobal, John, "Heavenly Bodies: Worshipping at The
          Shrine of Hollywood's Goddesses," <u>American Film</u>,
          July-August, 1986

UP81   Kurtis, Bill, "The Trials of Tokyo Rose," <u>Memories</u>,
          December, 1989/January, 1990

REFERENCES IN NEWSPAPERS

AN1   "Mickey Rooney Engaged to Wed Ava Gardner," <u>New York Times</u>, December 10, 1941

Mrs. J. B. Gardner, of Rock Ridge, North Carolina, announces they will be married in Hollywood.

AN2   "Hollywood's No. 1 Box-office Star in New Role," <u>New York Times</u>, January 9, 1942

Mickey Rooney applies for a license to marry Ava Gardner. His license is issued under Joe Yule, Jr.

AN3   "Mickey Rooney Takes Bride on The Coast," <u>New York Times</u>, January 11, 1942

Rooney marries Ava Gardner at a farm in Ballard, California, 40 miles from Santa Barbara. They left for a Del Monte honeymoon.

AN4   "Rooney's Bride Has Operation," <u>New York Times</u>, February 14, 1942

Ava is listed in satisfactory condition following surgery for appendicitis.

AN5   "Mickey Rooneys Part," New York Times, September 8,
          1942

Ava is quoted, "We just didn't seem to hit it off.
Things just weren't happy around home and we
decided to call it quits." She would ask for a
divorce from Mickey Rooney.

AN6   "Mickey Rooney Sued for Divorce," New York Times,
          September 16, 1942

Ava Gardner charged extreme cruelty and asked for
"reasonable alimony," and her share of community
property which amounted to $200,000.

AN7   "Divorces Mickey Rooney," New York Times, May 21,
          1943

Ava received her interlocutory decree of divorce
from Mickey Rooney. She stated they realized they
were too young for marriage.

AN8   Crowther, Bosley, New York Times, May 26, 1944

The movie critic states that Ava's role in Three
Men in White was sympathetic and convincing as a
lady who can suffer and take it on the chin.

See: F15

AN9   Crowther, Bosley, New York Times, March 18, 1946

Ava is miscast in Whistle Stop, a film of sordid
life in a small mid-western town.

See: F19

AN10   "Interview," Los Angeles Times, August 16, 1946

Ava mentions that she wants to finish her education
at U.C.L.A. "What good will money and fame do me
if I have no happy home? And money and fame is
all that the studios and agents who persuade me to
stay in pictures promise me."

AN11   Crowther, Bosley, <u>New York Times</u>, August 29, 1946

         Ava is sultry and sardonic as the lady who crosses
         up Burt Lancaster in <u>The Killers</u>.

         See: F17

AN12   Crowther, Bosley, <u>New York Times</u>, September 1,
              1946

         Crowther says that Ava, Sam Levene, and Edmond
         O'Brien handle their roles capably in <u>The Killers</u>,
         a film that depicts the "vice of the underworld."

         See: F17

AN13   "Ava Gardner Files for Divorce from Artie Shaw,"
              <u>Los Angeles Times</u>, October 25, 1946

         This interview told of Ava's terribly unhappy
         home life with Shaw and his disregard for her
         feelings.

AN14   Crowther, Bosley, <u>New York Times</u>, July 18, 1947

         The author feels Ava was "out too fast" as a
         disappointed thrush because Gable doesn't pay
         attention to her in <u>The Hucksters</u>.

         See: F21

AN15   Cook, Alton, <u>New York World-Telegram</u>, July 17, 1947

         For her role in <u>The Hucksters</u>, Cook feels "she
         fortifies an impression that she is likely to
         become a good actress some day."

         See: F21

AN16   "Stars Not Subpoenaed," <u>New York Times</u>, July 13,
              1947

         Ava Gardner, Lana Turner, and Linda Darnell had
         been rumored to be subpoenaed in the senate
         committee inquiry into investing of Howard
         Hughes' governmental airplane contracts.

AN17   Crowther, Bosley, <u>New York Times</u>, September 17, 1947

Ava Gardner is sultry and empty-headed, as the script calls for in <u>Singapore</u>, a film that was a "poor excuse for entertainment."

See: F22

AN18   Winston, Archer, <u>New York Post</u>, October 29, 1948

For her role in <u>One Touch of Venus</u>, Winston says, "Miss Gardner retains much of the status of her histrionics."

See: F23

AN19   Crowther, Bosley, <u>New York Times</u>, October 29, 1948

Ava's form was lankier than Mary Martin's (who did the original role on Broadway) and she doesn't do much more than flirt. However, she is pretty and endowed, which the camera loves in <u>One Touch of Venus</u>.

See: F23

AN20   Crowther, Bosley, <u>New York Times</u>, January 9, 1949

Mr. Crowther feels Ava holds her own in the splendidly filmed <u>The Great Sinner</u>.

See: F25

AN21   Crowther, Bosley, <u>New York Times</u>, February 4, 1949

<u>The Bribe</u> is a lurid, absurd piece of cition, and Ava "performs the sultry siren with her hips draped in nobility."

See: F24

AN22   Crowther, Bosley, <u>New York Times</u>, June 30, 1949

For her role in the dreary picture <u>The Great Sinner</u>, Ava "plays her role with her emotions and chest well exposed."

See: F25

AN23   Crowther, Bosley, <u>New York Times</u>, December 23,
          1949

        Ava plays the charmer like a hash-slinger in the
        glossy soap opera <u>East Side, West Side</u>.

        See: F26

AN24   "Entertainment," section, <u>Los Angeles Times</u>,
          May 24, 1950

        Frank Sinatra is asked how Ava felt about him and
        their affair: "I never got around to asking her."

AN25   Bredy, Thomas F., <u>New York Times</u>, November 5, 1950

        Ava Gardner is scheduled to play Julie in <u>Show Boat</u>,
        a role originally offered to Judy Garland. Accord-
        ing to director George Sidney, there was hope that
        Ava could do her own singing on "My Bill" and
        "Can't Help Loving That Man," even if she did it
        in a sort of "recitative." But it was the studio's
        opinion that a more accomplished torch singer would
        to the actual dubbing of Ava's voice.

        See: F29

AN26   Schisser, Edward, <u>Houston Press</u>, January 1, 1951

        Ava and Frank Sinatra were having dinner in an
        out-of-the-way Italian restaurant when Sinatra
        caused a fight because he did not want their
        picture taken.

AN27   Pihodua, Joe, <u>New York Herald Tribune</u>, January 10,
          1951

        The critic cites Ava's beauty but blandness in
        <u>My Forbidden Past</u>, co-starring Robert Mitchum.

        See: F28

AN28   Crowther, Bosley, <u>New York Times</u>, April 26, 1951

        As Barbara in <u>My Forbidden Past</u>, Ava is fetching
        in the decollete gowns of the era, although her
        performance does nothing to enhance her career.

        See: F28

AN29   Crowther, Bosley, <u>New York Times</u>, July 20, 1951

Too many close-ups of Ava singing in <u>Show Boat</u>, made Ava's scenes hard to suffer through. "Miss Gardner is much more dramatic than even a show boat soubrette should be."

See: F29

AN30   "Frank and Ava Attempt to Slip Away to Mexico ala Hayworth and Khan," <u>Los Angeles Times</u>, August 1, 1951

Rumors were surfacing that the brash singer and beautiful actress were trying to sneak off to Mexico to be married.

AN31   "Sinatra to Seek Divorce," <u>New York Times</u>, Augsut 10, 1951

Sinatra announced in Reno that he will divorce his wife, Nancy, so that he can marry actress Ava Gardner.

AN32   "Sinatra Announces He and Ava Will be Married," <u>Los Angeles Times</u>, August 19, 1951

Frank Sinatra let the world know that the rumors were true.

AN33   "Ava Gardner Fined as Speeder," <u>New York Times</u>, August 30, 1951

Officer Jerry Greene stopped Ava around 5:00 a.m. as she was traveling 40 MPH in a 25 MPH zone in Carson City, Nevada. She paid an on-the-spot fine of $15. She told him, "I think you're the meanest man I ever met."

AN34   "Wife Sues Sinatra," <u>New York Times</u>, October 16, 1951

On October 15, Mrs. Frank Sinatra filed suit to divorce Sinatra, paving the way for his marriage to actress Ava Gardner.

AN35   "Frank Sinatra Divorced," New York Times, October 31,
        1951

        Nancy Sinatra, Sr., won her interlocutory divorce,
        presumably to give Frank the way to get a Nevada
        divorce to marry Ava Gardner.

AN36   "Frank Sinatra Gets Divorced," New York Times,
        November 2, 1951

        In Las Vegas, Nevada, after being charged with
        mental cruelty from his wife of 12 years, Frank
        Sinatra is granted a divorce to make him free to
        marry Hollywood actress Ava Gardner.

AN37   "Sinatra, Actress Seek License," New York Times,
        November 3, 1951

        On November 2, 1951, in Philadelphia, Sinatra and
        Ava get a marriage license application from Judge
        Charles Klein. Klein told reporters that after
        they left that Sinatra had not received a waiver
        of the three-day waiting period. Ava and Frank
        left for New York.

AN38   "Frank Sinatra is Wed," New York Times,
        November 8, 1951

        Frank and Ava are married in a double-ring ceremony
        officiated by Judge Joseph Sloane. She was given
        away by Emanuel Sacks, vice-president of RCA.
        Attending were June Hutton and her bandleader
        husband, Axel Stordahl. No press was allowed. They
        left in a black Caddy to an undisclosed location.

AN39   Guernsey, Otis L., New York Herald Tribune,
        December 7, 1951

        In her role as Pandora Reynolds in Pandora and
        The Flying Dutchman, "It goes without saying that
        she photographs alluringly, but she is not equal
        to complicated language and deep emotional current
        of her role."

        See: F27

AN40   Wiler, A. H., <u>New York Times</u>, December 7, 1951

Ava never looked lovelier than in <u>Pandora and The
Flying Dutchman</u>, but she never quite seems to
epitomize or project the character of the American
singer who gives her heart and life to the
troubled stranger.

See: F27

AN41   Crowther, Bosley, <u>New York Times</u>, December 9, 1951

The critic feels that Ava Gardner and James Mason
do some "fine philosophizing" in <u>Pandora and The
Flying Dutchman</u>, but the artfully modernized
retelling of the flying Dutchman myth is "a bit on
the precious side."

See: F27

AN42   Wiler, A H., <u>New York Times</u>, February 1, 1952

Ava Gardner stars with Clark Gable in <u>Lone Star</u>, a
king-size western. She plays her part as the
newspaper publisher in a decorative way, torn by
politics and love. She sings "Lovers Were Meant
to Cry."

See: F30

AN43   Waterbury, Ruth, <u>Los Angeles Examiner</u>, March 31,
        1952

Lovely Ava Gardner has the best part of the three
women in <u>The Snows of Kiliminjaro</u>, taking over her
role with warmth and tenderness.

See: F32

AN44   "Movie Review," <u>Variety</u>, March 31, 1952

Several exhibitors' groups complained that people
would not go to see <u>The Snows of Kiliminjaro</u>
because they could not pronounce it. However, Ava
makes the part of Cynthia a warm, appealing, and
alluring standout.

See: F32

AN45   Crowther, Bosley, <u>New York Times</u>, September 19, 1952

        Ava was surprisingly good in <u>The Snows of</u>
        <u>Kiliminjaro</u>. She was pliant and impulsive as
        Cynthia in the film that was taut and eyefilling.
        Footage from <u>King Solomon's Mines</u> was used to
        enhance this Ernest Hemingway story.

        See: F32

AN46   Crowther, Bosley, <u>New York Times</u>, July 16, 1953

        Ava plays her role as the genteel wife of a
        landowner in a "twittering way," in <u>Ride, Vaquero</u>,
        a lusty panorama of a horse opera.

        See: F33

AN47   Crowther, Bosley, <u>New York Times</u>, October 2, 1953

        Gardner easily steals the show from co-stars Clark
        Gable and Grace Kelly in the African adventure
        <u>Mogambo</u>, since she received the advantage of
        shooting position and priority. She is as
        "calculating as a vampire" and goes for the throat.

        See: F34

AN48   Crowther, Bosley, <u>New York Times</u>, October 11, 1953

        Ava is bemusingly bewitching as a high-class Sadie
        Thompson and her dialogue is as tight-fitting as
        the clothes she wears in <u>Mogambo</u>.

        See: F34

AN49   "Sinatras in Divorce Step - Ava Gardner Will File
            Action Against singer Husband," <u>New York Times</u>,
            October 30, 1953

        Ava Gardner announces on October 29 that she is
        seeking to end her marriage to Frank Sinatra.
        He arrived to confer with her. She is quoted,
        "There's no basis to continue the marriage."

AN50   "Sinatra Marriage to Ava Gardner Over," <u>New York</u>
            <u>Times</u>, October 31, 1953

        Sinatra was admitted to the hospital with
        exhaustion following the break-up of his marriage
        to Ava Gardner. Ava did not visit him.

AN51   Hudgins, Morgan, <u>New York Times</u>, November 22, 1953

Ava is lovely but unemotional in <u>Knights of The
Round Table</u>, filmed on the banks of the Liffey
River in Ireland, where the studio built a tent
city for the cast and props.

See: F35

AN52   Crowther, Bosley, <u>New York Times</u>, January 8, 1954

Crowther feels Ava is luxurious and posey as Queen
Guinivere in <u>Knights of The Round Table</u>, a highly
scenic conglomeration of panoply and horse opera.

See: F35

AN53   Crowther, Bosley, <u>New York Times</u>, September 30, 1954

The critic feels that Ava failed to give her role
of Maria Vargas plausibility or appeal in <u>The
Barefoot Contessa</u>. She is "coldly ornamental"
except in two scenes--telling of her childhood
and in the ending scene.

See: F36

AN54   Crowther, Bosley, <u>New York Times</u>, May 25, 1956

As an Anglo-Indian woman whose loyalties are torn,
Ava has moments of staggering power, especially
in the scenes when she expresses the violence
of the women's social sentiments. Otherwise, she
is typically "sorely oppressed" in her role in
<u>Bhowani Junction</u>.

See: F38

AN55   Crowther, Bosley, <u>New York Times</u>, June 3, 1956

Ava plays her role in <u>Bhowani Junction</u> as a symbol
of divided social loyalties that affect many Asian
cultures.

See: F38

AN56   Hawkins, Robert, <u>New York Times</u>, September 9, 1956

Ava and her co-stars in <u>The Little Hut</u> rehearsed
their scenes on a make-shift island.

See: F40

AN57   Crowther, Bosley, <u>New York Times</u>, May 4, 1957

        Although Ava looked very fetching in her Dior
        clothes and grass skirts, there was only vapid
        dialogue for her in the flat farce <u>The Little Hut</u>.

        See: F40

AN58   "Ava Gardner Seeks Divorce," <u>New York Times</u>,
            June 15, 1957

        On June 14, Ava charged Frank Sinatra with desertion
        in her divorce proceedings in Mexico City, Mexico,
        represented by attorney Rigoberto Aranjo Valdivia
        before judge Agustin Espinosa de la Pina.

AN59   Hanna, David, <u>Los Angeles Daily News</u>, July 5, 1957

        Ava's friend and publicist reports of her divorce
        from singer Frank Sinatra after a four-year legal
        separation.

AN60   "Ava Gardner Gets Divorce," <u>New York Times</u>, July 6,
            1957

        Ava and Sinatra had been married almost six years,
        although separated for four. Sinatra did not
        contest the divorce. Neither of them was present
        when the divorce decree was presented in the 13th
        Civil Court in Mexico City.

AN61   Crowther, Bosley, <u>New York Times</u>, August 14, 1957

        Crowther felt that Ava could not convey Lady Brett's
        innate and poignant air of breeding. However, she
        had an occasional look of real anguish on her face
        as she "plays her predatory aspects" on the many
        she has loved in <u>The Sun Also Rises</u>.

        See: F39

AN62   Valder, John H., <u>New York Times</u>, March 8, 1959

        While filming <u>On The Beach</u> in Melbourne, Australia,
        Stanley Kramer became known as a pioneer in making
        films on location so far away from the Hollywood
        studio lots. Ava said, "This film is supposed to
        be at the end of the world. I can't think of a
        better place for it to be made."

        See: F41

AN63   Crowther, Bosley, <u>New York Times</u>, June 11, 1959

The filming of the Spanish painter Goya and his love,
the Duchess of Alba, became an inane fable on screen.
Ava uses little more than her quivering smile and
flaring nostrils.

AN64   Schumach, Murray, <u>New York Times</u>, December 17, 1959

This important and moving film features Ava Gardner
as the worldly woman who craves love in <u>On The Beach</u>.

See: F41

AN65   Crowther, Bosley, <u>New York Times</u>, December 18, 1959

Ava Gardner and Gregory Peck are scheduled to attend
the premier presentation of <u>On The Beach</u> in New York,
Rome, and Moscow.

See: F41

AN66   Crowther, Bosley, <u>New York Times</u>, December 20, 1959

Crowther gives Ava credit for her surprisingly good
performance as the lonely woman who finds serenity
in love after a nuclear destruction of the world
in <u>On The Beach</u>.

See: F41

AN67   Crowther, Bosley, <u>New York Times</u>, January 17, 1960

The cast's performances enhance the impact of this
film as survivors of the planet Earth, without the
necessity to show "real" destruction and dead bodies
in <u>On the Beach</u>.

See: F41

AN68   Archer, Eugene, <u>New York Times</u>, September 29, 1960

In <u>The Angel Wore Red</u>, Ava Gardner remains a fine
figure of a woman as she tries to make something
of her patently unplayable role as the Spanish
prostitute in love with a priest.

See: F43

AN69   Crowther, Bosley, <u>New York Times</u>, December 9, 1962

         Ava co-stars in <u>55 Days at Peking</u>, an epic film
         with a staggering-sized cast, crew, and sets,
         in an "Oriental War on the Plains of Spain" during
         the Chinese Boxer Rebellion.

         See: F44

AN70   Thompson, Howard, <u>New York Times</u>, May 30, 1963

         The critic feels Ava, as an ill-fated, tarnished
         Russian baroness in <u>55 Days at Peking</u>, could have
         used some role clarification.

         See: F44

AN71   Crowther, Bosley, <u>New York Times</u>, February 20, 1964

         Crowther believes Ava gives an excellent performance
         in a secondary role in the film <u>Seven Days in May</u>.

         See: F45

AN72   Crowther, Bosley, <u>New York Times</u>, July 1, 1964

         Ava imbues a raucous/blowzy decadence in her role
         of Maxine Faulk, the owner of a run-down hotel
         in <u>Night of The Iguana</u>. She steams up the screen
         with her free deportment and gibes at her guests.

         See: F46

AN73   "Films in Review," <u>Variety</u>, July 1, 1964

         In <u>Night of The Iguana</u>, Ava gives a gusty performance
         making her play for the deprived ex-minister,
         Richard Burton. She was superlative in a demanding
         role.

         See: F46

AN74   "Ava Gardner in Hospital," <u>New York Times</u>,
            January 12, 1966

         On January 11, 43-year-old American actress Ava
         Gardner was admitted to the Chelsea Hospital for
         Women in London. No other information was given.

AN75   "Film Reviews," <u>Variety</u>, September 28, 1966

Ava is very good in her role as the barren Sarah in
John Huston's <u>The Bible</u>. She wants her handmaiden
to bear a child for her and Abraham. The film was
considered unique and will endure.

See: F47

AN76   Crowther, Bosley, <u>New York Times</u>, September 29, 1966

George C. Scott and Ava Gardner play Abraham and
Sarah in <u>The Bible</u> as though they were posing for
monuments.

See: F47

AN77   "Film Reviews," <u>Variety</u>, December 13, 1972

Ava is a vision and welcome sight to the screen in
her role of Lily Langtry in <u>The Life and Times of
Judge Roy Bean</u>.

See: F49

AN78   Canby, Vincent, <u>New York Times</u>, December 19, 1972

Canby believes Ava looks beautifully worn by life
in her role as the fabulous Jersey Lily, who makes
a whistlestop visit in the epilogue of <u>The Life and
Times and Judge Roy Bean</u>.

See: F49

AN79   Thomas, Kevin, <u>Los Angeles Times</u>, December 22, 1972

Ava graciously portrays Lily Langtry in <u>The Life
and Times of Judge Roy Bean</u>.

See: F49

AN80   Ebert, Roger, <u>Chicago Sun-Times</u>, February 16, 1973

Ava is the ghostly presence as Judge Bean's
vicarious love, Lily Langtry, in <u>The Life and Times
of Judge Roy Bean</u>.

See: F49

AN81   Knickerbocker, Paine, San Francisco Chronicle,
            March 1, 1973

        Ava appears in the Valentine ending of The Life
        and Times of Judge Roy Bean, when she shows up at
        the judge's bar, now converted to a museum.

        See: F49

AN82   Krebs, Albin, New York Times, April 30, 1974

        Sixteen years ago, Richmond, California chemical
        engineer Kent Shelby won a long-term lease on
        Ava Ava, newly named Fiji Island, in a promotional
        contest for the movie, The Little Hut. He now
        refuses to return the lease to the Fiji government,
        stating, "It's everybody's dream to own a South
        Seas island."

        See: F40

AN83   "Film Reviews," Variety, November 13, 1974

        Ava is ravishingly beautiful as the wife of fire
        chief Charlton Heston in the excellent dramatic
        exploitation extravaganza Earthquake.

        See: F52

AN84   Champlin, Charles, Los Angeles Times, November 15,
            1974

        Earthquake is a sobering film with fantastic
        special effects that somehow allow to come
        through Ava's strong performance.

        See: F52

AN85   Sayer, Nora, New York Times, November 16, 1974

        Ava looked magnificent in this epic disaster
        film Earthquake, and she helps convey an
        exhilarating amount of panic.

        See: F52

AN86   "Film Reviews," Variety, May 12, 1976

        Ava was extremely effective in her role as Luxury
        in The Blue Bird, a charming film that seems a little
        past its time.

        See: F54

AN87   Thomas, Kevin, Los Angeles Times, May 19, 1976

The Blue Bird is an exquisite, contemplative film
that has richness and poignant charm. Ava Gardner
and Elizabeth Taylor look particularly ravishing.
Ava is Luxury, who tempts the children who seek
happiness with an opulent world of frivolity and
pleasure.

See: F54

AN88   "Interview," London Times, July 6, 1975

Ava relates her fondness for the British citizens
and the fact that she can live a relatively sedate
and quiet life in her London apartment.

AN89   Canby, Vincent, New York Times, January 2, 1977

Ava in a forgettable role in the forgettable film
The Blue Bird.

See: F54

AN90   Eder, Richard, New York Times, February 10, 1977

The Cassandra Crossing was a film doomed by silly
premise and miscasting. Ava was awful in an awful
role.

See: F55

AN91   Thomas, Kevin, Los Angeles Times, February 11, 1977

The film The Sentinel seems to be a parody of
the earlier cult thriller Rosemary's Baby. The
performances by the cast in this film were florid.

See: F56

AN92   "Film Reviews," Variety, February 16, 1977

Ava is a mysterious real estate agent who is a
formidable adversary in The Sentinel, a grubby,
grotesque excursion into "reliogo psychodrama."

See: F56

AN93   "Actors Accused," <u>New York Times</u>, April 16, 1978

While in Rome filming <u>The Cassandra Crossing</u>, prosecutor Paolino Dell'Anno accuses Ava Gardner and Richard Harris of having illegally exported currency and art work worth $10 million. Later the charges were dropped for insufficient evidence.

See: F55

AN94   "Gardner's Brother, Representative J. M. Gardner, Dies," <u>New York Times</u>, January 16, 1981

State Representative J. M. Gardner, the brother of actress Ava Gardner, died just hours after being sworn in as a Democratic member of the North Carolina General Assembly, at the age of 69. He had previously served two-year terms in the House, had been a town commissioner, and mayor pro tem in Smithfield in the late 1960s.

AN95   "Literati," <u>Variety</u>, February 13, 1983

<u>Ava</u>, by Roland Flamini, rarely brings her close to her readers. Flamini never seems interested in the kind of sultry actress Ava really is. He makes her out to be a female Don Juan, who lived her life like her role in <u>The Sun Also Rises</u>.

See: F39

AN96   Mann, Roderick, "Ave Ava: A Maverick's Homecoming," <u>Los Angeles Times</u>, February 17, 1985

Mann lets Ava's fans know that she is returning to the United States to resume her career. She will make her debut on the small-screen.

AN97   Kaplan, Peter, "From Clark Gable to J. R. with Ava Gardner," <u>New York Times</u>, February 25, 1985

This article discusses the career of actress Ava Gardner, including her roles on TV series <u>Knots Landing</u> and the upcoming mini-series <u>A.D.</u>

See: M1, T1

AN98   "Television Reviews," <u>Variety</u>, April 3, 1985

Ava Gardner intimates with enormous vitality how evil
the near-indestructible Agrippina might have been as
the mother of Nero and niece of Claudius in <u>A.D.</u>, a
lumbering, hard-to-believe mini-series.

See: M1

AN99   "Television Reviews," <u>Variety</u>, October 23, 1985

In her role as long-time mistress of the patriarch
(Jason Robards) of a southern family, Ava Gardner is
a delight and a reminder that a top-class actress is
not being used as much as she should.

AN100 "Television Reviews," <u>Variety</u>, July 23, 1986

Ava was strong in her brief role in this one-hour CBS
pilot movie <u>Maggie</u>. She plays the sister-in-law of
Stephanie Powers, who works for Ava's international
public relations firm. The film was not well-received
because of its inane plot and did not become a series
for Powers.

AN101 "Actress Ava Gardner Hospitalized with Pneumonia,"
       <u>San Francisco Chronicle</u>, August 28, 1986

Legendary beauty Ava Gardner was admitted to a
Los Angeles hospital, supposedly suffering from
pneumonia. It was rumored that she was suffering
from a heart ailment or slight stroke.

AN102 Baltake, Joe, "She was a Smoldering Glamour Queen,"
       <u>Sacramento Bee</u>, January 26, 1990

Baltake relates his appreciation of the beauty and
personality that made Ava a Hollywood glamour queen.

AN103 Barr, Robert, "Ava Gardner Dies," <u>Sacramento Union</u>,
       January 26, 1990

The Associated Press correspondent's article on the
death of actress Ava Gardner mentions that her life
in the fast lane ends at 67.

AN104 "Actress Ava Gardner Dies at 67 in London," Associated
       Press, London, <u>Cincinnati Enquirer</u>, January 26, 1990

Ava's long-time friend Paul Miller was interviewed
after giving the news service information about her
death at her Kensington home. It is mentioned that
Ava would have been happy to have traded her career
for one happy, long-lasting marriage.

AN105   "Spotlight--Gardner: A Frustrated Star," <u>Cincinnati</u>
        <u>Post</u>, January 26, 1990

        Ava is quoted in this obituary that, because she was
        promoted as a screen siren, people made the mistake
        thinking it was true of her real life. "They
        preferred the myths - the roaring lady who smashed
        champagne glasses and seduced bullfighters."

AN106   Champlin, Charles, "Ava Gardner - Image of a Bygone
        Era," <u>Los Angeles Times</u>, January 26, 1990

        Ava's passing was a requiem for a Hollywood that
        no longer exists. Ava Gardner was one of a kind
        in the Hollywood dream factory.

AN107   Flint, Peter B., "Ava Gardner is Dead at 67; Often
        Played Femme Fatale," <u>New York Times</u>, January 26,
        1990

        Actress Ava Gardner died in her sleep at her home
        in London, where her housekeeper found her on the
        morning of January 25, 1990. Her femme fatale
        roles made her a legend. She is to be buried near
        her parents in her home town.

AN108   Folkart, Burt, A., "Ava Gardner, Sultry Film Star,
        Dies at 67 in London," <u>Los Angeles Times</u>,
        January 26, 1990

        Folkart's biography of the life and death of Ava
        Gardner includes quotes from Mickey Rooney ("My
        heart is broken with the loss of my first love.
        The beauty and magic of Ava will forever be in all
        our hearts.") and Frank Sinatra ("Ava was a great
        lady, and her loss is very painful.").

AN109   Teater, Robin P., "Gardner Buried in Her North
        Carolina Hometown," Associated Press, <u>The</u>
        <u>Sacramento Bee</u>, January 30, 1990

        Interviews with friends and relatives relate their
        fondness for the actress, who chose to be buried next
        to her brother, Jack, in the family plot in Smithfield.
        A large flower arrangement featuring white doves and
        a card accompanied the service, indicating "With my
        love, Francis." Whether this was from Sinatra was
        unconfirmed.

ARCHIVAL MATERIALS

A1 "Ava Advocate" is a museum established in North Carolina
    by Thomas M. Banks, address: The Aristocrat, 1608,
    1200 Hibiscus Avenue, Pompano Beach, FL 33062

    Mr. Banks, former publicist for Universal Studios, and
    his wife, Lorraine, are responsible for setting up the
    museum which contains thirty-three years worth of
    memorabilia on actress Ava Gardner.

INDEX

About the Author

KARIN J. FOWLER was born in Berlin, Germany in 1947. After working 25 years as a secretary, her hobby of writing short stories for children evolved into writing for the performing arts series of books for Greenwood Press. She is currently working on a play and hopes to have several other works published in the future.